GINNY
A LOVE REMEMBERED

GINNY

A LOVE REMEMBERED

by Bob Artley

IOWA STATE UNIVERSITY PRESS / AMES

G. Robert (Bob) Artley was born and raised on a farm near Hampton, Iowa. He studied art at Grinnell College and the University of Iowa. Artley's career as an editorial cartoonist began with the *Des Moines Tribune* and continued at the *Worthington* (Minnesota) *Daily Globe*. He has also worked in advertising and published two weekly newspapers. Now retired to the century farm that was his boyhood home, Bob Artley continues to draw for syndication and is the author of several books.

Authorization to photocopy items for internal or personal use, or the internal or personal use of specific clients, is granted by Iowa State University Press, provided that the base fee of $.10 per copy is paid directly to the Copyright Clearance Center, 27 Congress Street, Salem, MA 01970. For those organizations that have been granted a photocopy license by CCC, a separate system of payments has been arranged. The fee code for users of the Transactional Reporting Service is 0-8138-2104-5/93 $.10.

⊗ Printed on acid-free paper in the United States of America

First edition, 1993
Second printing, 1993

Library of Congress Cataloging-in-Publication Data

Artley, Bob.
   Ginny: a love remembered / Bob Artley
         p.   cm.
   ISBN 0-8138-2104-5 (acid-free paper)
   1. Artley, Ginny. 2. Alzheimer's disease—Patients—United States—Biography.
3. Artley, Ginny—Marriage. 4. Artley, Bob—Marriage. I. Title.
RC523.2.A78   1993
362.1'9897'68310092—dc20
[B]   93-1485

This book is especially for Ginny,

and for her family, friends, and acquaintances who were

privileged to be touched by the love, tenderness, and joyful

spirit of that unique lady; and for *all* victims of Alzheimer's

disease and their families.

Victims make acute observers.

SIR ISAIAH BERLIN

There is no death so final as the death of a memory.

PAUL GRUCHOW, *The Necessity of Empty Places*

CONTENTS

FOREWORD

by Princess Yasmin Aga Khan
Vice President, Alzheimer's Association
President, Alzheimer's Disease International

If I had to write my own personal experience of living with and caring for an Alzheimer's patient, I could only hope it would turn out to be as moving and tender as Bob Artley's *Ginny: A Love Remembered.*

Mr. Artley describes the slow deterioration and the emerging symptoms of Alzheimer's disease while sustaining interest and evoking empathy. The reminiscence of his early life with his wife breaks the reader's heart, knowing the inevitable outcome of this sad history. This, however, is a love story, sincerely told, that will leave an indelible memory on those who can remember.

When Mr. Artley mentioned Ginny's inability to comprehend the birth of her latest grandchild, I was deeply touched. My mother, Rita Hayworth, became a grandmother, but I'm not certain that she ever really knew it. Certainly she was not able to enjoy her new role. She missed the pleasures of grandparenting and her grandson missed the love of this caring, beautiful, talented grandmother. Reading those few sentences touched me deeply.

Sadness was just one of the emotions that this book provoked in me. Anger reared its head, too. Alzheimer's makes me mad. It took my mother, Bob Artley's wife, and thousands of victims each year succumb to this devastating disease. The caregiver, like Bob, suffers incredibly also. Financially, emotionally, and physically they are truly the "second victim."

Fortunately today there is the Alzheimer's Association. It is an organization that is dedicated to funding research and offering help to the caregiver in many ways. Its goals are:

- Funding research into the cause, prevention, and cure of A.D. and related disorders.
- Educating the public and providing information to health-care professionals.
- Forming chapters for a nationwide family support network and implementation of programs at the local level.
- Advocating for improved public policy and needed legislation.
- Providing patient and family services to aid present and future victims and caregivers.

I thank Bob Artley for sharing this loving history of his life with his wife. I am hopeful that it will not be long before such stories will have happy endings and Bob will be able to use his obvious writing talent on a fictitious tale.

PROLOGUE

"Bob, I love you."

That was all she said. Just that and nothing more. She said it almost inaudibly in the soft voice I had come to know and love through the years. It was said so quietly that, if there had been any other sound in the room at that moment, I would have missed hearing those words. And once it was said, it was gone, not only from the room, but from her mind—she could not repeat it.

Ginny had told me she loved me many, many times since we had discovered each other, nearly fifty years before, and knew we wanted to spend the rest of our lives together. But hearing that sentence spoken so quietly on that particular day in the fall of 1988 was an experience I shall never forget. I shall not forget, that is, unless I am stricken with the cursed affliction that has befallen my beloved wife . . . Alzheimer's disease.

Most of the time, at this writing, I am not sure she even knows me or knows that I am at her side. But sometimes when I'm feeding her, she will give me a brief, somewhat crippled smile. And the women who regularly take care of her say that when they mention my name to her, she will smile. I like to think that smile is a response given in recognition of the name of one who has meant a lot to her through the years, but I'm more inclined to think that the feeble smile, which passes as quickly as a patch of sunlight through a hole in the clouds on a windy day, is a vestige of a friendly reflex. Ginny has always been a pleasant, responsive person, reaching out to others.

There are many reports of those with Alzheimer's becoming mean and abusive to people around them, of those who become loud and offensive in their speech. Thankfully, this has not been the case with Ginny—she is still easy to love.

While Ginny is certainly not the sharp, vivacious, fun-loving person she used to be, she still displays a quiet dignity and is kindly disposed to those around her, insofar as she is aware of them. In other words, at her core there still seems to be the essence of the quiet, loving, gentle person she has always been.

On one occasion, when Ginny was being assisted into her wheelchair, the attendant bumped her own shin on a sharp corner of the chair. Ginny immediately responded with a heartfelt, "I'm sorry."

Almost from the beginning of the time Ginny came to live at

the Iowa Veterans Home, her verbal communications dwindled, became ever more limited. Thus, our times together, except for my talking to her, are times of silence. They are really not "visits," since we cannot sit beside one another and quietly talk about matters of mutual interest, family matters, or news that I long to share. Our communication is through touch or facial expression. Even these, except for very rare moments, have become less. So in these last years, our visits are mostly just silent times of togetherness, times when simply the warmth of our nearness to one another and the wordless communication of spirit (something we have always had) is all that I can expect. Kahlil Gibran, the Lebanese poet and artist, expressed it beautifully when he wrote, "When love becomes vast, love becomes wordless. Love is a sacred mystery. To those who love, it remains forever wordless."

Our togetherness has become mostly an opportunity to savor through remembrance (on my part) the depth and richness of a life shared through the years, a love and a marriage from which I could ask nothing more . . . except, possibly, an extension of time to enjoy it.

Ginny exhibits no interest nor any sign of recognition when I show her photos of loved ones or tell her about some important family event like the birth of a new grandchild. (We've had four she will never know and who, in turn, will never know their grandmother.)

The closest we have come to communicating in recent years was when I fed her (which I stopped doing when she started having more difficulty swallowing and choked easily)—the basic interaction of my giving and her accepting spoonsful of the pureed food that is her diet. When going to see Ginny, I therefore tried to make a point to be there at her mealtime. For me, at least, this was a way of sharing an experience with her.

Often after she'd been fed and while she was still in her wheelchair waiting for the attendants to put her down for her nap, I massaged her feet. She seemed to enjoy this simple act, which in turn gave me joy.

After her nap we often went for a wheelchair tour around the Veterans Home. It usually led to the canteen, where we each had a small cup of soft chocolate ice cream; I, of course, fed Ginny hers.

As I visited with a young person one day, the subject of love came up. Feeling very ancient, I made the observation that one couldn't really know the full meaning of love until the loving had come full circle—to where just being with one another, even in silence, could produce a quiet inner warmth and contentment. That, I said, is the blessing of mature love. I had in mind, of course, Ginny and me and our "silent visits."

But coming to the place in our lives where we can find a quiet joy in our "silent visits" is the culmination of many years, of experiencing the full range of the husband-and-wife relationship—years of sharing joys, sorrows, anxieties, peaceful moments, dreaded situations, laughter, tears, arguments, feelings of oneness, financial worries, exciting projects, family concerns, expectations, disappointments, sickness, and hope . . . always hope and a faith that God is watching over us—the whole range of what two people in married love experience together.

This, then, is what I have to sustain me as I sit here beside Ginny, holding her hands in our silence. (Not total silence, however, for I'm constantly telling her of my love for her.)

But what about Ginny . . . in her affliction? No memory of our past together and no thoughts of what's ahead. No past to remember and no future to hope for . . . or dread. That is how I perceive my beloved wife's condition at this time and in this place.

It is in my memories, aided by old letters and photographs saved over the years, that I am able to relive my life with this lovely lady. It is largely for this reason that I have written this book—to relive and recreate for myself, our family, and those who knew and loved her, those years when Ginny was vital and loving and full of the qualities that made her a unique and valued person—and to put into perspective the painful years of her affliction. Perhaps this can best be expressed in the words attributed to Camille Pissarro in Irving Stone's biographical novel *Depths of Glory,* when the nineteenth-century French artist was trying to explain to his sweetheart, Julie Vellay, why he wanted to paint her portrait:

> You are what you are. I can only reflect what's in you. Painters
> want to preserve the color, character, vitality of a time or place
> or person, so that they can never be forgotten. The artist is a
> lover who wants the world to see the beauty of his beloved.

I hope that my sharing this very personal experience may offer some measure of help for others whose loved ones are wandering in the shadows of this dark valley of prolonged dying.

My sincere thanks to individuals—family members, nursing staff, friends, and my consultant typist—who have in so many ways helped me in the production of this book.

CHRONOLOGY

1943 Bob and Ginny meet; they marry and make their first home in Richland, Missouri

1944 They room at the Glaubes' home; Ginny's pregnancy and discharge from the service; the move to Possum Lodge; Jeannie born at Hampton, Iowa

1945 Homes in the military in Wilmington and Greensboro, North Carolina; move back to the farm in Iowa

1946 Bob discharged from service; Robbie born; building their house; taking up farming

1950 Move to University of Iowa; home in Stadium Park, Iowa City

1951 Graduation; birth of Steven; move to Solon, Iowa

1952 Move to Des Moines; Bob takes cartoonist job at *Des Moines Tribune*

1953 Purchase home and move to Waukee, Iowa

1955 Joni born

1957 Bob leaves *Des Moines Tribune;* becomes art director at ad agency; then art director at Plain Talk Publishing Company

1966 Start *Waukee Journal*

1967 Move to Adrian, Minnesota, to publish a weekly paper

1969 Establish Print Shop in Adrian

1971 Bob becomes cartoonist at *Worthington Daily Globe*

1979 Ginny not well; close Print Shop

1981 Move to Hampton, Iowa

1982 Ginny diagnosed with Alzheimer's disease

1986 *Worthington Daily Globe* sold; Bob is fired by new management; move to farm

1987 Ginny admitted to Alzheimer's unit of Iowa Veterans Home

1988 Ginny moved to Two East of I.V.H.

1990 Ginny moved to private room at I.V.H.

1991 Ginny put under hospice care at I.V.H.

1993 Ginny died at Iowa Veterans Home, February 25.

GINNY
A LOVE REMEMBERED

THE WAACs ARE COMING

There had been rumors floating around for some time that the Women's Army Auxiliary Corps was coming to Ft. Leonard Wood. As usual, especially around military installations, there were some very creative versions of these rumors. The very fact that *women* were coming to that place, where, except for female nurses, PX personnel, and some office workers, the population was almost totally male, gave rise to all kinds of interesting speculations in barracks bull sessions. Some of them to be sure, were less than complimentary to womankind.

Probably the most prevalent rumor, and the most troubling to those who would be satisfied to spend the duration of the war at Ft. Leonard Wood (married personnel, for instance), was the one that the WAACs would replace the male GIs, thus releasing them for overseas duty. That rumor gave rise to resentment and feelings of hostility.

For me, the idea of the base being invaded by hordes of women soldiers was a fascinating prospect. I didn't feel threatened as far as being replaced was concerned, because I had my application in for duty on a hospital ship. I felt I'd be happy to have a woman take my place in the station hospital lab.

As for the proximity of all that feminine pulchritude, it naturally appealed to me, but only in theory, as I had recently received my "Dear John" in a college romance and was determined to retain independence of the heart "for the duration."

I missed out on the actual invasion of the WAAC contingent as I was on temporary assignment at O'Reilly General Hospital in

Springfield, Missouri, attending a medical laboratory technicians' training school for an intensive short course. Our lifestyle there was quite good, but very "GI." We had to cope with weekly haircuts and "spit and polish" inspections that had us shaking in our GI shoes.

There were pleasant aspects to this life, however, one of them being the availability of the civilizing influences of the Springfield community. Thus, my social life was much more pleasant than was possible in the frontier atmosphere of the Ft. Wood area. These civilizing influences included the Rob Jones family, second cousins of my mother; into their home I was welcomed often for meals and as an overnight guest. Another was the Methodist church that I attended quite regularly. Along with some other servicemen from O'Reilly General, I became an active member in the youth group there.

This bit of church social life resulted in some friendships, one of them being with a young woman whose company I enjoyed during my brief assignment there but to whom I was ready to say good-bye when my classes ended and I was to return to Ft. Wood. I wanted, I reminded myself, no entanglements of the heart.

Thus it was that on the bright spring morning following my graduation, I was getting ready to leave O'Reilly when Russ Wulff, a friend and co-worker in the lab at Ft. Wood and one of a new contingent at O'Reilly for the laboratory short course, greeted me with the news that the WAACs had arrived at Ft. Wood. My interest was piqued, but not much. Then he added that I should get to know one cute little WAAC who had been assigned to the lab. He thought I'd find that she and I had a lot in common.

This, of course, was all very interesting to me, but, I reminded myself again, I didn't want to get involved in anything that might lead to an emotional entanglement. I would certainly check on the "cute little WAAC," but only as a very cool GI who was intent on maintaining his independence.

Pvt. Virginia Elnore Moore came to Ft. Leonard Wood with a detachment of WAACs from basic training at Ft. Des Moines. She had arrived in Ft. Des Moines in early 1943 from Detroit, where she had enlisted in late 1942. She and some of her friends and co-workers at the Parke-Davis Company in that city, in a spirit of patriotism, had decided it was what they should do to help out the war effort.

Pvt. Virginia Elnore Moore, January 1943, shortly after her induction into the Women's Army Auxiliary Corps and shortly before I met her at Ft. Leonard Wood.

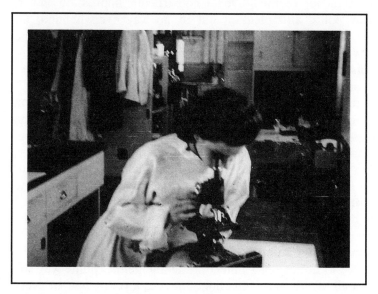

Ginny at her microscope, Ft. Leonard Wood station hospital, 1943.

Ginny, as she was known by her family and friends, had been dating a sailor in Detroit, but the relationship had not progressed, so when she arrived at Ft. Wood, it was with a clean slate romantically. She was firm in her determination to keep it that way for the duration of the war effort. All of this I heard from her own lips when I first showed an interest in getting to know her better.

In the midst of the war years, there was a widespread feeling that wartime marriages could not last because of the instability of the times. Therefore, many felt that romantic involvements should be put on hold. It was in that atmosphere that Ginny and I would feel almost guilty about our feelings for one another. (Obviously, this restrictive theory was not seriously heeded. We have only to note the baby boomers that those times spawned.)

It was good to get back to the station hospital laboratory after being away for several weeks at O'Reilly General. In a way, it was like coming home, seeing some of my old friends and co-workers, but among those greeting me on my return were some new faces—the WAACs. And one of them was the cute one Russ had described.

Pvt. Virginia Moore, as she was formally introduced to me on my first morning back to work, was indeed "a cute little WAAC." Our introduction seemed to make no particular impression on her. She was polite and pleasant but in no way overwhelmed. Of course, I, too, was properly polite and detached—I had the integrity of my independence to maintain.

I discovered, however, that I felt pleased to find out we were both working in the hematology department. Later I also found it pleasant when, in the course of our work, we had to confer on some matter, particularly when that conferring needed to be done in close proximity, such as examining a slide under a microscope.

I also noticed that practically all of the men of the laboratory, whether in her department or not, found it necessary to talk to Private Moore quite often. To my chagrin, I realized that the attention she was getting began to bother me. And the fact that I was bothered by this attention also bothered me. Why should *I* care?

Another thing about Private Moore that caught my notice (why did I have to notice her so much?) was the gentle, polite way she handled all of this male attention. She was a young *lady* in every sense of the word. Her manner was never flirtatious. She had an earnest, direct, almost sisterly relationship with her male laboratory co-workers—including me.

It wasn't long before I began to resent this "sisterly" treatment, for, while I, like the other fellows in the lab, wanted to be protective of her, I realized that my feelings for her weren't entirely fraternal.

Originally, there were four WAAC personnel assigned to our lab, but soon two of them were moved to other positions in the station hospital. This left only Privates Moore and Ida Crawford, a tall, raw-boned young woman from upstate New York. She was capable, practical, and dependable, a good laboratory technician who had the friendship and respect of her co-workers. The two of them, Crawford and Moore, made an unlikely pair as they walked back and forth between their barracks and the lab—both in their WAAC uniforms but each presenting a different picture. Private Moore was of average height, five feet five inches, with a well-formed, petite figure, which she carried erect with an almost prim dignity as she walked alongside Ida, who was tall and angular with a long "country" stride. Yet the two became loyal friends who corresponded up until Ida's death in the late 1960s.

"Ginny," as we soon began to call her, or "Irish," as she was nicknamed by her admiring male co-workers, was "easy on the eyes," as the saying went. Her trim figure did a lot for her WAAC uniform. She was particularly appealing in her white laboratory uniform, which was much like a nurse's. Her black hair and fair, pinkish complexion, together with her warm, gentle, hazel eyes, had us all under her unintentional spell.

In a letter home to my folks, I described Ginny:

> You were asking about Ginny (Virginia) Moore—She is of medium size with an Irish complexion, black hair, grey-green eyes, and a winning smile. She has a pleasant personality, a little on the shy side. She has a mind of her own and has been able to keep these "wolves" here at the lab at their proper distance and still hold their friendship and respect. She has much in her to admire as a person and seems to have good tastes. She is also a lot of fun.

As we all sat or stood around for a Coke break, exchanging

banter, cracking in-house, or rather, in-lab jokes, I found myself interested in what she said and at what she laughed. She neither told nor laughed at off-color jokes in mixed company. I discovered, to my chagrin, that my stock-in-trade one-liners didn't particularly amuse her. But I also learned to delight in her infectious laugh when she *was* amused. Later, Ginny learned to laugh at "funny" things I said—she *was* adaptable.

Not long after my return from O'Reilly, I went home to Hampton, Iowa, on a ten-day furlough. On the way I stopped at Grinnell to see some of my friends from college days. In one conversation, when the subject of getting married in wartime came up, I was quite eloquent, I thought, in my argument against such involvements—how they would be unfair to the wife and would distract the soldier from the job he had to do.

After my short leave, it was good to get back to the post and back to the lab and my associates there, especially to that "distracting little WAAC," as I referred to her in a letter home:

> In fact I'm frankly quite confused in a way that I've never been before in my life. Up until the past couple of months, I have been quite at ease mentally in regards to Genevieve and me and our terminated college romance. Other girls, while being naturally interesting to me, have never caused me any disturbance, and I've been going along with the peaceful idea that *perhaps* someday in the distant future things might change regarding Genevieve and me. I've taken the war and all of its inconveniences as rather a "marking time" process that might change things, and I've felt more or less willing to wait and hope for the best.
>
> Then gradually things began to happen to change or spoil my peace of mind—the idealistic dreams began to appear impractical and too idealistic. What happened was that the *Army went co-ed* and that distracting little WAAC came into the lab. After working with her every day, I began to find myself making needless detours around the lab into her department. This disturbed me and I tried to fight it off. But it was no use.

In other words, this heavenly object was pulling me out of my orbit and causing me to behave in an erratic manner. Furthermore, I became aware that my behavior was being noticed by my co-workers. This bothered me.

On one occasion Captain McCluggage, the lab's bacteriologist, was talking to me as we stood in a passageway of the lab, when Ginny walked by. My attention left him in mid-sentence—much to his knowing amusement. I, of course, did not know this until later, when Ginny, quite embarrassed, told me.

This moonstruck behavior on my part was in spite of the fact that we had not had a single date. Ginny was adamant in her stated commitment to "going it alone" for the duration of the war.

It became obvious to me that, if Ginny, for whatever reason, was absent from the lab, I was painfully conscious of the hole she had left. It also was of interest to me to realize that, even when Ginny and I were not communicating in any audible or visual way, I still felt a warmth in just being at work near her.

Something was happening that was beyond my control—and I was liking it.

Early in the summer of 1943, word came down from the War Department that the Women's Army Auxiliary Corps was to be changed to the Women's Army Corps. This directive provided that those in the former would be given an automatic discharge, and, if they wished to remain in the service, they would have to reenlist. This gave an honorable way out for those who had found that military life was not what they had expected. Ginny was greatly tempted.

When Ginny had enlisted with some of her friends in Detroit, it had been with red, white, and blue surging through her veins and with stars in her eyes. Patriotism, to her, was serious business. Two of her brothers, as well as some of her nephews, were already in the service of their country, and Ginny felt it her duty to enlist in the WAACs so she could do her part. She couldn't have been more sincere.

It was not long, however, before she saw the reality of the military life clashing with her ideals. She found herself with those who did not share either her sense of values or her sensitivity to that which she perceived as good and beautiful. She was disappointed to find herself in an atmosphere of cynicism and blasphemy. She wondered what she was doing there—what possible good she could do for her country by being part of such an organization?

This tainted image, in her view, brought upon the WAACs by a few, was a bitter realization for Ginny—one in whom strong loyalty was an attribute. She felt betrayed. For several years after our marriage, Ginny was still reluctant to let it be known that she had been a WAAC. She never brought it up herself, and some of her close acquaintances in later years were surprised when they found out she had been in the Army.

Ginny and other WAACs who felt as she did had to deal not only with a tainted image; there was antagonism, too. She once told Lab Sergeant Beam how appreciative she was of the fine treatment she and her WAAC co-workers were receiving in the laboratory. Back in her barracks, she had learned that such was not the case in some areas on the post. There were instances of open hostility by men who perceived themselves as being "replaced by a broad."

For several days, during the time of the changeover, Ginny was quite depressed as she argued with herself about whether or not she should reenlist. She kept most of her thoughts to herself on this, but did share her dilemma with some of us in the lab. I, for one, could not advise her. This was before we had acknowledged our friendship, but I hated the thought of her no longer being there. So, as much as I secretly hoped this refreshing young woman would remain with us, I kept my counsel, knowing it must be her decision alone, for I had no claim on her, nor any business telling her my feelings on the matter. And besides, if she did remain in the Army, I reasoned, there was no assurance that she would not be ordered to some other lab on some other post.

Nevertheless, it was a great relief for me the morning that a reenlisted Ginny came to work with her old sparkle, plunging into her work and friendly interchange within the lab community, which was becoming her Army home. And I was glad I had said nothing to influence her. However, I found myself secretly wondering if, maybe, she just possibly could have wanted to not be separated from the people in the lab—even me.

At any rate, I found my heart much lighter at the thought of her remaining among us. This resolved dilemma had also helped Ginny come to terms with her feeling of isolation in barracks life. She and Ida Crawford, the other WAC in the lab who had also reenlisted, were becoming friends.

We arrived at the theater soaked to the skin. (I could feel the rain running down my legs into my shoes.) I felt miserable, especially when I added to my own discomfort what I imagined Ginny's must be. All the moisture had apparently in no way dampened Ginny's spirits. As I took my cue from her, we both laughed at our drenched predicament, even trying to shake ourselves off in the manner of dogs.

I couldn't help but notice, as we stood in the stomping, dripping line of theatergoers (almost everyone else wearing their rain slickers), how pretty my date was with the drops of rain on her Irish complexion. No colors ran, I noticed. They, like the girl, were genuine.

For two hours we two steaming, soggy GIs sat through a bad movie on the wooden-slatted benches that served as theater seats. If Ginny was disgruntled by the situation, she didn't let it be known. However, in spite of her reassuring attitude, I felt responsible and was sure she must be covering up her real disgust at the clumsy ox who had put her in such a situation.

After the show we were still very damp, but the air of the Ozark evening was quite warm. Wanting to somehow salvage what I perceived to be a failed evening, I suggested we get a bite to eat. But when we found a PX that was still open, the grill had been turned off in preparation for closing. The only thing they could offer us was a cheese sandwich. Ginny agreed to have one with me, but when the sandwiches were served, they were on dry bread. Even washing them down with a Coke was difficult. This was, I thought, just another nail in the coffin of my hope to make a favorable impression on this sweet young lady I so desperately wanted to think well of me.

I had failed, however, to allow for the upbeat, adventuresome nature of this dauntless young woman (a trait I saw often in the years to follow). She was treating the whole evening as a delightful adventure—so much so that, when we parted to go to our separate quarters, I was encouraged to the point of suggesting another, drier date in the near future. To this she readily consented . . . and thus ended the adventures of "the *three* musketeers," for, after that memorable evening, Ginny and I found that the *two* of us were quite sufficient . . . thank you.

One day in early September, Ginny's sister Louise came by train from Philadelphia to visit her little WAC sister in Ft. Wood. In fact, Ginny and Louise were not blood sisters, and I would learn more about their close relationship later. I was much impressed by Louise, about ten years older than Ginny, and made a mental note that Ginny must have a nice family. (Little did I know then that about five months later, I would be meeting all of Ginny's large, close-knit family.) After she showed her around some, the two of them left on a short visit to their aunt in Illinois.

Coming out in the open with our feelings for one another had its problems, of course. Ginny and I were now paired off in the collective mind of the WAC detachment, as well as in the medical detachment of the station hospital—and in my barracks. But where the perception of us as a couple had the most impact on Ginny and me was in the lab. Those who were observant had been sending knowing glances our way for some time. I even thought I detected some feelings of jealousy in some of the male co-workers who had shared my interest in "our Irish of the lab." It was almost as if I had sneaked in and stolen something of value on which we had *all* had our eyes.

Of course, Ginny and I were in for our share of schoolyard teasing—all good-natured. When I came back to the lab on the morning after our soaking, I was alarmed to discover that Ginny was absent. I was even more concerned when her friend Ida reported that she had gone on sick call that morning and was in the hospital. I was much relieved to learn that it was nothing serious and apparently had nothing to do with sitting through a show in wet clothing or eating a dry cheese sandwich.

Now that the cat was out of the bag, Ginny and I didn't have to be so secretive about our special friendship. In fact, I was surprised to see how people made allowances for us and, in this way, encouraged our courtship.

The biggest advantage of our acknowledged relationship was that I no longer had to deal with that invisible wall Ginny had kept up around herself since first coming to Ft. Wood. I was especially gratified to realize that, while the wall was still there, as far as the other fellows were concerned, through some good fortune to which I was not accustomed, I was privileged to be within that wall. This perception made me extremely happy. It was the first time I had experienced having my love for another seem to be so fully returned. While I had had the usual past romances, this was the first time I felt that I was not on trial. Ginny seemed to require nothing of me but my love.

With new confidence I was emboldened to be more aggressive in pursuing the recently acknowledged status between us. We had another date, and then another, and tentatively talked of possible day bus trips to the towns of Lebanon, Rolla, or even an overnight trip to Springfield, where we could stay at the home of my cousins. But these bus trips, except to Springfield, never took place. Instead, we opted for picnics for two in the beautiful surrounding Ozark Mountains.

Our first picnic in the Ozarks remains, in my mind, one of the most beautiful experiences of many in our years together. The planning of it, during stolen moments at the lab and on our evening dates at the service club and library, was great fun in itself. It took our combined ingenuity and scheming to procure the food. Because some of the items we would want, such as meat and coffee, were subject to wartime rationing, the task was not easy. But it was enjoyable, and I was discovering even more about this attractive young lady, as I reported in a letter home:

> She seems to be full of pleasant surprises . . . and she's so
> darn modest and self-effacing that one has to discover them
> gradually. We keep finding there is much that we both enjoy.
> And, best of all, we enjoy one another's company.

The Saturday night before our planned Sunday picnic, we had made no date, thinking we would need our rest for the next day's outing, so our time together that evening was spontaneous and totally unplanned. Through some maneuvering (that would be a story in itself), I was successful in getting a steak from the mess sergeant for the next day and went back to the lab to stash it away in the refrigerator until the following morning. I was surprised but pleased to see Ginny and her friend Ida there. The latter had come back to do some extra work and had brought Ginny along. I called Ginny aside to show her what I'd managed to procure.

After Ida had finished her work with Ginny helping her, the three of us walked to their barracks, where Ida left us. Ginny and I went on to the service club library to get a book for our picnic. We checked out *Penrod Jasber,* by Booth Tarkington.

On Sunday morning I was up early, eager for our day together.

Borrowing some clean test tubes and cork stoppers from the lab, I went to the mess hall and surreptitiously filled them with salt, sugar, cream, and mustard from the breakfast table. As I was filling the sugar tube, a fellow sitting next to me asked "what in hell" I was doing. He wondered if I was going to run a test on the sugar. I said that I was. He asked, "Do you think there is something wrong with it?" I answered that I hoped not but would find out.

Making sure that neither he nor anyone else saw me, I wrapped a hunk of butter in a paper napkin and slyly stuffed it into the roomy pockets of my field jacket with the other loot, then left the mess hall, feeling quite guilty.

Back at the barracks, I packed my knapsack with my mess kit, a canteen of water, the book we'd checked out of the library, and the latest *Reader's Digest* magazine. Into it also went my box camera, two rolls of film, some strong cord, Band-Aids, a face towel, some Kleenex tissues for napkins, and two luscious pears taken for the occasion from Saturday morning's breakfast. At the lab I added the steak, French fried potatoes, bread, and pickles I'd stashed there. Then I was on my way.

Ginny was ready and waiting for me in the WAC dayroom, bright-eyed and smiling. She was dressed in her fatigue hat and dress; this was the first time I'd seen her in anything but the WAC uniform or lab whites. I was delighted at my good fortune in having such an attractive picnic companion.

We took a cab as far as the driver said he was allowed to take us, paid the fare, and with the accoutrements of our picnic in tow, struck off up a trail that led along a grassy ridge with scrub oak on either side.

The morning was sunny and bright with ever so slight a breeze, making the temperature just right, a perfect day for two romantic people on an outing. The air was fragrant as only a September day in the Ozarks can be. The birds were singing, and so were our hearts as we stepped lightly along, noting the fall flowers, chipmunks, and other wild things that caught our attention along the way. Yet *I* was mostly aware of the lovely one by my side whose hand I had clasped in mine. We were in love, even though we had not as yet spoken of it to one another.

We walked up hill and down, through forested slopes and across sunny, grassy meadows, until we tired and sat in the shade

Ginny's sister Louise visited Ft. Leonard Wood in September 1943, the first member of Ginny's large close-knit family whom I met.

On our first picnic together in the Ozarks, September 1943, we took a picture of ourselves by means of a string attached to the shutter. Ginny dressed in her WAC fatigues (left), the first time I had seen her in anything but her uniform or lab whites.

of a large oak to rest. It was a wonderful feeling to be away from the restrictive atmosphere of the fort (even though we were still on the reservation) and to have, for at least a little while, left the military, the war, and the world behind, with the better part of a grand day to call our very own. We decided, for that day, we would not talk about the war, which was on everyone's mind most of the time. Every facet of this day was to be ours to cherish.

After resting in the shade for awhile, we took pictures of each other. We also took one with both of us in the picture, accomplished by means of a string attached to the shutter, the same method Dad had used years before, when he was in college, to take a self-portrait to send to Mom.

We then left this place that we forever afterward would feel was special because of our having spent a small bit of our lives there, and we set out to find a suitable spot to camp for the afternoon and build a fire for preparing our meal. Ginny found a place she liked beneath a large, old hickory tree, atop a hill and overlooking a valley below. I agreed that it had the potential to be another special place, and we set about making camp.

Ginny was so jolly and seemed to enjoy the activity so much that her joy and enthusiasm were infectious. I was delighted to just observe her. She said that she had never really "roughed it" before and admitted she was at a loss about how to build a fire, so she set about gathering firewood, spread the blanket, laid out our picnic, and measured out the coffee for boiling. I got the fire going and prepared a green, forked stick on which we cooked our steak.

I doubt that meat cooked outdoors over an open fire ever tasted better. We ate with our fingers, because I'd forgotten utensils, and took turns drinking coffee out of our one canteen cup that had served first as the vessel in which to boil it. It was a festive, joyful meal, short on the amenities but long on the spirit of the occasion. Spending a long time at our simple meal of slightly burned steak, warmed-over French fried potatoes, bread, pickles, and two very ripe pears, we talked and laughed, thoroughly enjoying the food, the day, and each other's company. We were young and, for the time being, life was very good.

Finally we put away for later the food we had not eaten, shook the crumbs out of the blanket, rationed a few swallows of water from the canteen, and settled down to our reading. We took turns reading aloud, first an article from the *Reader's Digest*, and then we started our book, *Penrod Jasber,* which elicited laughter and comments as we read.

Before we were aware and long before we were ready, the afternoon was almost gone. We ate the leftovers we had set aside earlier for supper and read some more. Finally, Ginny, who always had a much better sense of time than I, thought we had best be starting back to the fort.

We had to walk about three miles, and darkness came long before we got back. We talked and sang old, well-known favorite songs all the way, making the distance and the time go all too fast. We were both dismayed at how quickly that very special day had gone and agreed that it had indeed been a most pleasant one. In fact, Ginny suggested we do the same thing the next Sunday, and we started making plans immediately.

That week found us together every night, sometimes at the lab, sometimes in the library or in the WAC dayroom. Here we staked out a claim in a far corner, where I read aloud (but only for Ginny's hearing) from the book we had started on our picnic, while Ginny mended some of her clothing. Later some of her barracks companions told her we two had made quite an appealing domestic scene, especially in that military setting and in those troubled times. One of the WACs told Ginny that her date just wanted to sit and watch *us!*

Over the next few weeks we spent many nights that way until "lights out"—Ginny sewing while I read to her. She even did some sewing for me and put some chevrons on some of my shirts. It wasn't long before another couple began to do as we did in the WAC dayroom. When we spent our evenings at the lab, our roles were often reversed—Ginny reading to me while I worked at my drawing, something I did every chance I got.

One night we left early for a movie so we could stop off at the library. There we returned the Penrod book we had finished reading and selected another one for our upcoming picnic. Spotting a large book of Walt Whitman's poetry, handsomely bound in green burlap, Ginny suggested that would be appropriate for our day in the woods; it was *Leaves of Grass.* Later, as we stood in line at the theater, Ginny, clad in Army green with her little, pointed uniform cap perched on her head, hugged the large green book against herself with both arms and said, "I just *love* books." Then she told of how, when she was a child, she used to read under the covers at night with the aid of a flashlight when she was supposed to be sleeping.

On the Saturday night before our second Sunday picnic in the hills, we met at 6:30 at the WAC dayroom and went first to the library, where we browsed for awhile. Next we went by taxi to the civilian housing area on the post and to the grocery store there. It was fun shopping at a real store, even though most of what we wanted required ration points, and, of course, neither of us, being in the service and eating in mess halls, had ration books. We asked the butcher if there was any kind of meat that was not rationed. He seemed to feel so sorry about our not having ration points that we were embarrassed. After buying some items that were not rationed—apples, two potatoes for baking, and a box of cheese-flavored crackers—we left the store, quite aware that we did not fit into either world—certainly not the military, and without ration books, not in the civilian.

For our meat for the next day, we went to the PX and bought two cube steak sandwiches, which we wrapped in napkins to store overnight in the lab refrigerator. As we left the PX with our "steaks," we laughed over our predicament at having no ration points for meat, but felt triumphant in our method of getting around that technicality.

On Sunday morning, Ginny and I met at 9:30 as prearranged. Neither of us had eaten breakfast, but because we weren't hungry just then, we set out immediately on our excursion into the hills. As on the previous Sunday, we rode by taxi as far as it would take us and then continued on foot. We went in a different direction from the week before, and before long we were on a winding mountain trail that took us down through wooded ravines toward the Big Piney River. Again we were blessed with a beautiful day—cool, clear, sunny, and fragrant with the woodland smells of early autumn.

After some time, the old trail we were following brought us to the river, then turned left and ran along the narrow space between the river and a very steep hill that paralleled the water. We had begun to tire, so we decided to stop for a rest and to eat the ripe cantaloupe Ginny had brought along. Because there was no suitable spot on that stretch of river trail, we began climbing to the top of the steep slope, hoping to escape the nettles, gnats, and other riverside discomforts.

The hill turned out to be a bigger challenge than we had expected. We found it extremely steep, and trying to keep a firm footing on the loose rocks while at the same time lugging the packs containing our picnic supplies was an exhausting struggle. Before we reached the top, I was regretting my poor judgement in bringing Ginny up this hazardous way. One of my greatest concerns was the possibility of encountering copperhead snakes hidden in the foliage and rock ledges along which we had to climb. But Ginny never once complained. It was only after we had safely scrambled to the top that she admitted to being "scared stiff."

After our taxing climb, I think no cantaloupe has ever tasted more delicious than that one did. It, like the person who had brought it, was sweet and refreshing. However, the melon was still cool, while Ginny, after our strenuous climb, was quite warm.

When we had finished our breakfast, we decided to stay in that quiet, peaceful place, which we had all to ourselves and rest and read there above the road and the river. A big hawk circled high above us and we were glad we weren't small creatures that it might find appetizing. We knew it must see us there on the blanket far below, a young man reading aloud from Whitman's *Leaves of Grass* with a young woman now and then putting a cheese cracker into his mouth.

Every now and then a leaf would loosen from a twig above and flutter down upon us. One of them landed in the cracker box from which Ginny was feeding me, and when I paused in my reading with my mouth open for the next morsel from her hand, I found myself chomping down upon a dry leaf. At this Ginny exploded into the hearty, fun-filled laugh that I came to know and love through the years. Later on, after I'd resumed reading, I became conscious of her shaking all over. It was a deep silent laugh at first, but soon burst into bubbling merriment. She had spotted a big black ant walking across the page I was reading.

By that time the mood definitely did not fit Walt Whitman, and the spell was broken, so we reluctantly left our cozy resting place in search of a spot where we could build a campfire without the danger of starting a forest fire.

After walking from woods into open glades, still in the uplands, we came upon a place that Ginny liked. I was not particularly impressed at first, but as Ginny set about making it *our* place, I began to see its merits. It was airy and shaded by a large oak. The lush grass invited us to spread our blanket. There was a bare spot for making a fire ring of stones, and it was secluded . . . away from the bothersome world. We were in a happy place.

In no time Ginny had our blanket spread, the knapsack unpacked, the coffee ready to put on the crackling fire I had going, and we were "at home." She prepared the apples and potatoes for baking, then disassembled the steak sandwiches in readiness to heat the meat and to toast the bread on forked sticks over the fire.

We ate heartily of our simple meal. (Snacking on crackers—and leaves—had not spoiled our appetites.) We had forgotten the butter for the baked potatoes and the test tube of cream for the baked apples, but we made up for their absence by finishing with a candy bar each. No doubt, this fare would not have tasted very elegant in a dining room, but out there, in that place with one another, we wanted nothing better.

After putting away our picnic and shaking crumbs from the blanket, we settled down to read from our book again. While Ginny was reading aloud, lying on her back and holding the book upright on her chest, I propped my chin, leaning on my elbows, and feasted my gaze upon the delicate features of that lovely face before me—the well-formed nose, natural eyebrows (exquisitely drawn by nature), sweet lips ever so slightly colored with lipstick, and beautiful hazel eyes from which shone the light of a loving, sparkling, and mischievous soul. I was enjoying the sound of her low, well-modulated voice and not paying much attention to Walt Whitman's words as she read. Presently I saw her eyes assume a playful glint, and I became aware that she was inserting her own words into Whitman's poem. At first I wasn't sure, until "Ginny" and "Bob" were inserted, and she exploded into laughter.

At this point, we realized that Walt Whitman, like our friend Russ Wulff, had served his purpose. While one was a great poet, and the other a good, desirable friend, they were no longer needed in our becoming a twosome. Those sweet lips I'd been watching as they formed a soft, modulated voice into words, were suddenly desirable to me for another purpose, and I leaned down and kissed them.

Ginny's eyes momentarily showed surprise; then they were instantly warm. Letting the book slide from her hands onto the blanket, she reached up and drew my face to hers for a repeat performance. It was a long, sweet embrace, one for which I think we had both been yearning for a long time (about three months on my part). This was no casual kind of kiss given freely and without feeling. In that sanctified moment we both became acutely aware that we were really and truly, deeply in love.

As I had been yearning for our first embrace, I also had longed to express my love to her in words, and to do so felt good and right. Likewise, I had been hungering to hear Ginny tell me explicitly that I was important to her, and she did. "Bob, I love you." It was simple, direct, and thoroughly convincing.

Forty-some years later, as I sat beside her in her final illness, that very same sentence with those same words was the last coherent thing she ever said to me. I'm not sure which time those words meant the most to me, the first time or the last . . . or during all those sustaining years between.

However, I am sure that on that special day in that lovely spot in the Ozarks, hearing from Ginny's own sweet lips such words of love for *me* was life itself. With the exception of my parents, no one had ever before made me feel so genuinely loved as Ginny had just done. I knew then that I wanted to spend my life with this lovely woman and in my reckless joy blurted out, "Would you like to be the wife of an artist-farmer?"

Her eyes, expressing something I could not discern, first looked off into the distance, as if she were trying to see into the future. Then she turned and, with tenderness in her lovely eyes, looked deeply into mine and said, "Bob, dear, can I think about it?"

Well! *I* didn't need to think about it any more than I had already for the past week or so! Never in my twenty-six years had I wanted so passionately to spend my life with someone. Almost everything I'd come to know about Ginny was what I wanted for a wife and the mother of my children. There were a few things on which we differed, but they were minor. I knew we had discussed in depth, earlier in the summer, the wisdom of making no commitments of the heart in times such as these—no marriages in wartime. But, thunderation! that was before things had changed and developed between us, before we had come to *want* to be with one another. Hadn't we just moments before expressed our great love for each other? Didn't that change the very basis of all that for-the-duration rhetoric?

Apparently, Ginny, with her discerning nature, saw the hurt and bewilderment in my eyes; leaning forward, she ever so gently kissed me on the lips and assured me with, "Just remember, Bob, I love you."

This beautiful day had come to an end all too quickly. Ginny, assuming a practicality I was to see in her many times in the years that followed, noted the lateness of the hour and set about gathering up our things. Soon we were heading back to civilization (if one can use that term in connection with an Army post).

In spite of what I felt to be something of a rejection, Ginny, with her vivacious spirit, in what I am sure was partly an attempt to ameliorate my feelings, did manage to bring a jovial, loving ambiance into our return walk. She carried the conversation and, as the darkness began to overtake us on the winding trail along the top of a ridge, pointed out the first star to appear. Clasping my hand, she recited,

> Star light, star bright,
> First star we've seen tonight,
> I wish I may, I wish I might
> Have this wish I wish tonight.

I knew what *my* wish was, and I asked Ginny about hers. She said that our wishes, in order to be granted, must be kept secret.

Her little-girl-like enthusiasm and her obvious concern for my feelings were effective. We soon were swinging along, hand in hand, on that Ozark trail with the faint glow of the fading sunset, the sliver of a new moon, and a clear, star-studded autumn sky. The air was sweet with dew-enhanced fragrances from the hills and woods about us. To the quiet night-sound accompaniment of crickets, katydids, a lone owl, and a distant baying hound, Ginny led out with some of our favorite old songs. Then we sang some of the popular songs of the day, "Don't Sit Under the Apple Tree," "White Cliffs of Dover," "Don't Fence Me In," "I've Got Spurs That Jingle Jangle Jingle," and "Always." This last we claimed as *our* song, and on this particular night it had special meaning. (At least I hoped it did to Ginny as much as to me.) We even sang Christmas carols, including Ginny's favorite, "Silent Night."

We stopped our starlight concert before we were within hearing of the outlying barracks of the fort. But Ginny had managed, by her vivaciousness and warmth, to assure me of her love, giving my sagging hope a genuine boost. When we parted at the door of the WAC dayroom, after our first-ever good-night kiss, I returned to my own barracks, marveling at the extraordinary occurrences that had taken place on that beautiful, memorable day. As I went to sleep that night, my thoughts were on that most remarkable young lady whom I had asked to marry me. And, though she had asked for time "to think about it," she *had* assured me of her love. I had hope that her answer would be, "Yes, let's."

THE PLANNING

During the week following the picnic and
my proposal, we saw one another every day in the lab, as usual.
Ginny was especially warm toward me, and when our eyes would
meet, hers had a soft look and conveyed an intimacy that seemed
to say, "It's all right, I love you." Every evening that week found
us together, sometimes, if we were tired, only briefly for coffee or
a milk shake at the PX.

One night Ginny suggested that we go to a movie, and, when
I called for her, she pressed the money for the evening—car fare
and the price of the theater tickets—into my hand. When I
protested, she said that that way, she felt she could suggest some
of the things we did together.

We also took walks, strolling along the streets of the fort, hand
in hand, while we talked quietly of many things, just as we had
been doing over the weeks. Not once did Ginny, nor I, mention
the question I had so impulsively put to her during our memorable
picnic in the hills.

I didn't intend to bring up the subject again—not yet, at least,
as I had the feeling I had rushed Ginny too much. In spite of her
well-known stand of "no romantic involvements during wartime,"
I had forced her into reestablishing her thinking and reordering
her priorities on short notice. I felt remorseful.

Some of our evenings were spent as before, in sewing/reading
sessions at the WAC dayroom or in drawing/reading sessions back
at the lab after supper. All in all, the week following my ill-timed
proposal was spent with each of us trying to reassure the other

that, in spite of my recklessness, no damage had been done to our love. And at least once each evening, we managed to seal that love with a discreet kiss.

A *discreet* kiss was not easily achieved, however, on a heavily populated Army post where the word *private* had nothing in the least to do with privacy. One night when we managed to be alone on a darkened street, we thought we could express our love with a kiss and embrace—if we hurried. But we weren't fast enough. A jeepload of GIs came screeching around a corner, and headlights momentarily spotlighted our precious moment. There was an immediate shout of "We saw all of that!" accompanied by hoots and whistles.

Ginny was mortified, not for herself, she explained, because those soldiers didn't know her, but for the cheap image it cast upon the uniform she wore. Ginny was all too painfully aware of the tarnished name the WACs were being given. I, for my part, was furious at those anonymous GIs.

When Friday night came and I stopped to pick her up at the dayroom, she was even more appealing and loving than usual, in her circumspect way. But she seemed preoccupied. We hadn't walked very far when she said, "You know what we were talking about Sunday on our picnic?"

"Yes," I certainly did.

"Well, I've been thinking about it. . . . If you still want us to get married . . . ?"

If there was anyone around to see our smothering embrace, *this* time we didn't care. Such a voyeur would have had to have been grossly insensitive not to have recognized this as something more than a casual encounter of passion. Every cell in my body had suddenly come alive, and I wanted to shout, sing, run, jump, and dance for joy. Ginny's lovely eyes, seen in the glow of the dimly lit street, sparkled more than usual as tears of happiness spilled out and ran down her cheeks. I kissed them away.

For reasons I cannot remember, we decided to not yet broadcast this great good news, but to share it first with a select few. A letter home, written the following morning, tells it.

Sta. Hosp. Lab.
Ft. L. Wood, Mo.
Oct. 9, 1943

Dear folks,
　　Ginny and I officially decided, as of last night, that there
should be two chins like Dad's in the same family. Nothing
definite as to plans as yet because of various things—only
tentative plans—They'll be worked out later.
　　We were going to phone the good news last night but
discovered it was too late. We aren't announcing it in the lab
yet for various reasons, but are letting only a restricted few
here in on it—Sugi and Russ from the lab.
　　Gosh! It's great.
　　Will write more later.

Love,
BOB

　　But Ginny did want to tell some of her family that very night,
and not realizing the lateness of the hour, we decided to make a
long-distance call to Laura, her sister in Detroit. We found a
phone booth and both squeezed into it, closing the folding glass-
paneled door. Carefully counting out the required coins from both
of our resources, Ginny fed them into the slot and we listened to
the bell that tallied each one. Ginny gave the operator the number.
We positioned the receiver so that we could both hear and then
waited for the call to go through to Detroit.
　　After several rings, during which time we realized how late it
was, we heard a sleepy voice say, "Hello. . . . What's wrong?"
　　"Hello, Laura, this is Ginny. Nothing's wrong. Everything is
fine. I just called to let you know I'm getting married."
　　There was silence at the other end, then, "What?!"
　　"Bob and I are getting married; you know, I've been writing
about him."
　　There was another pause, and then a voice that was fully
awake by now, "Well, you've made your bed. Now lie in it!"
　　I drew my ear back from the receiver, feeling I'd heard too
much and realizing that Laura didn't know I was there. They
exchanged a few more words. (In those days one didn't waste
words in the three-minute limit of a long-distance phone call.)
Then Ginny said good-bye.
　　The joyful mood we'd had when entering that booth was
suddenly dampened, and Ginny was both embarrassed and

crestfallen. I tried to shrug it off, saying that we'd gotten Laura out of bed and she probably wasn't quite awake. Also, the more I thought about it, I could imagine how she must feel.

Laura, Ginny's next-to-oldest sister, with whom Ginny had been making her home for several years, actually thought of Ginny as a daughter. Now her Ginny was in a far-away Army camp where some GI, about whom no one knew anything, had talked her into a wartime *marriage.*

Subsequently, Laura, like the rest of Ginny's family, was very supportive of our marriage and made me feel totally accepted. Laura and I became friends and laughed over that late-night phone announcement and her reaction to it.

There was so very much to discuss and plan, once we had made the commitment to each other and made it known. We spent our nightly dates talking about all aspects of our future together. We tried not to use time in the lab for those in-depth, personal planning sessions, however.

The fact that we were both in the Army, with no idea when we would be free to order our own lives, made it difficult to do any concrete planning other than for the wedding itself. We thought it would be nice to have a wedding in the spring when the fragrant blooms of the Ozarks were abundant. But it wasn't long before we began to think that, because we knew without a doubt that we wanted to be together, the sooner the wedding could be, the better. This line of thinking was given impetus by persistent rumors that personnel from our lab were to be sent out as replacements to field hospitals and other station hospitals. In fact, I had applied months ago for duty on a hospital ship, thinking it would combine my interest in life at sea with my desire to serve in the medical field. Once, that had been something I had wanted quite intensely; however, lately my ardor for that adventurous assignment had cooled considerably. Now I wanted desperately to not be separated from Ginny.

Making our situation even more immediate was the fact that, in our case, we both were pawns in the military chess game. Each of us could be sent in a different direction. That constant concern caused us to realize even more that all we really had was the moment at hand. Thus, it seemed that an earlier date for our wedding was vitally important. Our married friends in the lab encouraged that view.

But first things first. We had just become engaged and I

wanted Ginny to have a diamond and be able to wear it for awhile. I contacted the Rob Jones family, our cousins in Springfield, and asked if I might bring Ginny and stay overnight with them. They promptly and graciously consented, and the date was set for that Saturday, October 16.

Early that Saturday morning we took the post bus, a school bus painted Army green, with straight, uncomfortable seats, to Waynesville, the unhappy little Ozark town that was a short way from the front gate of Ft. Leonard Wood. That formerly peaceful little mountain village was now overcrowded and corrupted by the worst elements that are often on the fringe of military installations. There we were let off at the bus depot to catch the cross-country bus to Springfield.

The bus depot was crowded that particular Saturday morning with many GIs trying to get away from Army life for the weekend, and a long line had formed at the ticket counter. I left Ginny standing by herself in the center of the room as I joined the line for tickets. As the line moved slowly forward, I turned to establish eye contact with Ginny and was alarmed to see that a group of soldiers had swarmed around her like flies around a sweet morsel of food, all but burying her from my view.

A flash of rage surged through me, and, leaving my place in line, I waded into that cluster of olive-drab–clad GIs, who were very interested in the cute little WAC they had found unattended. They reeked of beer, and the most offensive one of the lot was quite drunk. As I forced my way, in no gentle manner, to Ginny's side, I found her wide-eyed and embarrassed at the commotion that centered around her, trying valiantly to cope with the situation.

I am by no means the hero type and am prone to go to great lengths to avoid a confrontation. But there was my Ginny, whom I prized above all others and whom I perceived to be, if not in physical danger, at least threatened with the possibility of having her sweet sensibilities sullied. In my reckless rage I was ready to take them all apart, if necessary.

My mood must have impressed them for they all immediately backed away, and the drunk was effusive in his slurred apology. From then on, I kept Ginny at my side, and we were happy to be out of that place and on the next bus to Springfield.

Upon arriving, we went directly to the jeweler's. The choice of diamond engagement rings the jeweler showed us was overwhelming—and so were the prices. Seeing our disappointment, he pulled out another tray with smaller and less expensive diamonds and settings. We finally narrowed them down to two. The one I wanted was considerably larger and more expensive than the one with which Ginny claimed to have "fallen in love." Her choice was, I thought, almost a microscopic stone. The setting, I supposed, was designed to make the stone seem bigger. But, Ginny, sensing my financial status, insisted on the smaller one.

How much fun that was—picking out the ring. Ginny found the occasion to be especially enjoyable, and her eyes outsparkled the trays of diamonds before us.

We also picked out the wedding band. Because of our slim resources, we decided to get only the one for Ginny at that time and to get the matching one for me later. (And we did just that after a few years.) I gave the jeweler a down payment on the rings and arranged to pick them up in three weeks, after the next payday.

I felt bad that it would be so long before Ginny would have her diamond to wear. In the movies, the man always slipped the ring onto his intended's finger at the time she accepted his proposal. What a difference, I thought, between the make-believe and real worlds.

Ginny had made a trip to Springfield in the spring with some of her WAC friends, and she remembered an eating place called the Town House. It was an elegant old home made over into a very pleasant restaurant. There, we had our own little engagement party. We were ushered to a room on the second floor where several tables were set in style. Because we were early for the supper hour, for some time we had the entire place to ourselves, except for the employees, of whom we saw little. A waiter took our order and, while waiting to be served, we went to an adjoining room, where we played the nickelodeon and danced—all by ourselves.

Finally, the waiter came to tell us the soup was served. We pretended that we were in our own palatial home and that the waiter was our butler. Ginny asked the blessing, as we planned to do in our own home, and we began to leisurely enjoy our engagement supper. Next our "butler" cleared away the dishes from the first course and served chicken as the main course. There were two of each choice piece on the platter served family style, plus all the delicious trimmings that went with it.

This memorable meal was one of which we spoke often in later years. Both of us were happy, and it was such an elegant setting.

After we had eaten all we could and had each tucked an extra piece of napkin-wrapped chicken into our pockets, we ate our dessert of maple nut ice cream. Having finished our meal, we danced some more. The tune we played the most on the nickelodeon was "Wait for Me, Mary, 'Til the Skies Are Blue Again." We sang along quietly because we were alone, and I changed the "Mary" to "Ginny."

When we left the Town House, we noted it to be another place made special by one of our happy occasions. Then we went to the Joneses' house. Ginny, being more socially mature than I, suggested we stop to buy them a box of candy.

Predictably, the Joneses were quite taken with Ginny, and they made us both feel very welcome. It was Ginny's first visit with some of my family, and it felt good being with her in a real home.

After visiting for awhile, Ginny and I excused ourselves and went back downtown to see a movie. When we returned after the show, our hosts had gone to bed so we sat for a long time on the sofa, talking and smooching. It was the first time we had ever had the use of such a piece of traditional courting furniture (except for the WAC dayroom, which was too public).

We retrieved the leftover chicken from our pockets and ate that as a bedtime snack. Then bidding one another goodnight, we went our separate ways—Ginny upstairs to the guest room and I to a bedroom off the kitchen.

The following morning, after a pleasant breakfast at our hosts' table, Ginny and I went to services at the Methodist church I had attended during my time at O'Reilly. We had Sunday dinner with the Joneses, and afterwards they drove us to the bus station, where we bid them good-bye. In a letter home the next day, I wrote:

> The Joneses were so grand to us. I shall always love them
> for taking us in that way and accepting Ginny, making her feel
> so much one of the family.

It was near midnight when we arrived back at Ft. Wood, and we were two very tired but happy people as I took her to her barracks and then made my way to my own.

We were extremely happy in one another's love, but troubled as to just what we should do about our wedding date. Should it be soon, as many were urging, because of the uncertain times, or should it be put off for the same reason? We kept searching for answers from sources outside ourselves, for we knew we wanted to be together as soon and as much as possible. Some of that dilemma is noted in Ginny's first letter to my folks, written the night after our return from Springfield:

> Ft. Wood,
> Mon. eve.
> Oct. 18, 1943

Dear Mrs. Artley and family,
We decided that I would write to you tonight. Bob is beside me signing lab slips while I write.
I am anxious to meet all of you and am looking forward to the time when I can. I suppose he told you that we picked out the rings Saturday. I didn't want him to buy me an engagement ring, but he insisted. But it certainly will mean everything in the world to me for I know that I have the prize package of Ft. Leonard Wood. I surely will be proud to be Mrs. Robert Artley. (I wouldn't let Bob read the last two sentences.)
What do you think of our getting married before the end of the war? I want to make Bob happy, but I don't want to place a worry on his shoulders. I would surely appreciate any advice that you may give.
We had the most wonderful time last weekend. It was swell to be in a home again, and your cousins gave us such a lovely time.
Well, I must close now. I never was a long letter writer. My folks are so anxious to meet Bob.
> Love,
> Your future daughter,
> VIRGINIA (GINNY)

The same concern is reflected in a letter from her sister Louise, to whom Ginny had put the same request for advice:

Philadelphia,
Monday

Ginny dear,
    I just read your note. How strange that I should have
written my letter to you *before* learning of your engagement!
I'm so happy. He's the one for you, honey. If you decide to be
married right away, I'll think it is wonderful. I've certainly
done an about-face on war marriages, but where you are
concerned, it is different.
    Every night I pray especially for you and Bob. Don't be
confused, dear. Everything will work out all right. I have so
much faith in you, and know that only good can come to
anyone as sweet and *good* as you.
    Even when you're Bob's wife, you'll always be my baby sis-
ter, whom I've worshipped since you were a tiny tot and were
so jealous of me that you didn't want anyone else to take my
hand. How will I ever be able to keep my mind on my work
tomorrow?

Love and best wishes
from WEES

P.S. Give this note to Bob.

    I also received my own letter from Louise, whom I had met
briefly back in September:

    Just a note to my future brother-in-law to tell him how
happy I am to learn of his engagement to the sweetest girl in
all the world.
    I'm sorry, Bob, that I didn't have a chance to spend more
time in your company, but truthfully, of all the fellows I've
ever met, you're the only one who has ever had my approval
for Ginny. There is nothing as important to me as her happiness, and I feel so confident that everything will work out for
you two and that you will be happy always (regardless of the
war).
    I'd like to write pages, telling you why I know Ginny is the
sweetest girl there is. You see, I've known her since she was
eight months old. She'll explain to you, and then, you'll know I
don't love her because it's the usual thing to love one's sister—but because she's the dear, sweet girl she is.

And so, Bob, all my best wishes for your happiness *together*. I do hope we will meet again soon.
Good luck,
LOUISE

As one might guess, this letter from a member of Ginny's family was a great encouragement to me.

A reply came from my mother to my question regarding a wartime marriage:

You asked me to put myself in Ginny's place, Bob I'm trying to—in a way, it's hard for she's in the Army, too, and subject to call if Uncle Sam wants her somewhere else, isn't she? I don't want to tell you what to do—whatever you two decide upon, we'll hope it's the best way. . . .

. . . It must be heaps of fun, being able to see each other every day—better than if you were in college, isn't it, 'cause you don't have to study nights. . . .

And a rare note from Dad, penned at the end of Mom's letter:

. . . Suppose you feel great and happy. It's hard to advise you, but you will enjoy being engaged for awhile at least. We can talk better when you both are here. Come soon.
Love to both,
DAD

On our long walks, Ginny and I sorted through all the possibilities, probabilities, and eventualities we could imagine as we struggled with our decision. More and more, we were concerned about the possibility of being separated because of the exigencies of war. And there were constant rumors to aggravate that concern. No matter how we reasoned or how "wise" we tried to be, each time we came to the same conclusion: we loved one another deeply.

We were sure of our love for each other; we knew that, more than anything, we wanted to be together. If the war should separate us, we told ourselves, we would not be the first of those who loved but were separated by war. We personally knew many couples in such circumstances. But, we agreed, if that fate should befall us, we would at least have our love to sustain us. It would be better, we reasoned, to have known the fullness of complete married love, with the commitment it carried, and then be taken from one another than be separated without the memory of that completeness.

With all these thoughts, and with the general support of family and friends, Ginny and I decided our wedding would be soon. We knew we were right and felt secure in our decision. As to a specific date or just *how* soon, we had yet to decide.

Neither of us was in line for a Christmas furlough. We did not relish the thought of spending that special family time (Ginny's first away from home) in an Army camp apart from one another. Therefore, we decided the wedding should be soon enough so that we could be together in our own home over Christmas.

Probably some of the greatest enjoyment of any undertaking is in the planning of it. That was certainly true in our case as we planned, not so much for the wedding itself (for we felt that to be only a necessary procedure, required by society, to get us to where we wanted to be, and we hoped others could take care of those bothersome details), but rather for the life we wanted to live together.

We talked of the family we wanted to start (Ginny wanted "lots of kids") as soon as it seemed prudent in the crazy, mixed-up world in which we were presently living—when there was peace and we could be settled. A girl, Ginny thought, should have the name of Elsie, Jean, Louise, Laura, or Meriam—all names of family members. When my mother learned of this, she wrote:

> Planning about your children is right and natural but not an "Elsie." I have never liked my name and I'd not like to wish it on a grandchild of mine. But it was sweet of Ginny to want to. (Better plan on boys' names.)

We also talked of our home and what it would be like—its spiritual quality and atmosphere. We wanted it to be blessed by the spirit of God.

We both thought our home should be, if at all possible, in the country—if not on a farm, then at least a small acreage. We both loved the out-of-doors and wanted our children to have the benefit of such living.

Ginny had spent many of her grown years in the city atmosphere of Detroit, but when a little girl, she had lived in the small western Pennsylvania coal mining town of South Fork. It was not a pretty place, gritty with cinders and covered with coal dust and soot. But Ginny, the little girl, had looked up from those drab surroundings to the beautiful hills around the town; those hills were lush with vegetation and fragrant with woodland wildflowers, brushed by white fluffy clouds against a bright blue sky. And she had dreamed childhood dreams. She carried the beauty of those hills and those dreams into adulthood. It was this that she brought, as an offering, to our marriage and wanted to make a part of our home—a most wonderful dowry.

Thanks to the advent of Ginny in my life, the letters to and from the farm and to my brother Dean in Texas took on a new dimension. Dean seemed almost as caught up in the excitement as I was:

> I suppose you and Ginny are planning on going home soon. I surely hope it works out okay and that you can. [Dean, too, was well acquainted with the uncertainties of Army life.] Wish I could get there, too. Mom wrote that she's getting the house clean, and they all seem to look forward to you two coming. She also sent a copy of the letter Ginny's father and sister wrote to you—they surely sound like nice people. I'm anxious to meet them all.
> It's all very exciting to me—going to have a sister-in-law. . . . Won't it be fun to all be home and have one added member to our family? Gosh! Life can be beautiful. . . .
> Everything sounds nice and fall-like at home. The longer I'm away from the farm, the more I want to go back. I think there's a great fortune in it—not in the money but in living—one that we have already enjoyed but probably never realized like we do now. . . . How does Ginny like the farm? I hope you and Ginny get to go home and know you'll have a good time.

As Dean had surmised, Ginny and I were planning a trip home for her to meet my family, but everything was happening so fast and furiously that there was little time to savor the fun.

On Sunday, November 7, just one week before our planned trip home, Ginny and I took a bus to Springfield to get the rings we had ordered three weeks earlier on the weekend of our engagement party. Because Ginny had had KP duty in the WAC mess hall, we had not been able to go on Saturday, and we had arranged for my cousin, Rob Jones, to pick them up at the jeweler's. It was a hurried, exhausting trip, but we were buoyed by the excitement of our mission. After a brief but pleasant visit over Sunday dinner with Rob and his wife, I reimbursed them for their payment to the jeweler, and we took an early bus back to Ft. Wood.

Ginny's eyes far outshone the tiny diamond she proudly displayed on her ring finger. One would have thought it was the famous Hope Diamond, judging from Ginny's pride in it. But, of course, it *did* embody a great deal of hope for the two of us, and our friends back at Ft. Wood seemed to share the joy that this sparkling gem symbolized in our lives.

I can't imagine that Ginny and I were of much use around the lab those days in November of 1943. The affairs of our hearts had complicated our existence tremendously, it seemed—at least they did for me.

Before we could go home, Ginny and I each had to apply for our own three-day passes. Because getting those passports to the outside world seemed so fragile a process in the hands of the orderly room bureaucracy, I marveled every time one came through. There was always the lurking doubt whether or not one could make any definite plans. And we had *two* requests to sweat out in *two* separate orderly rooms.

A letter from home written on November 8 (Monday) shows that our hectic life also had repercussions on the home front. Mom wrote:

> Did you get the bonds before you went to Springfield? Dad took the letter up to the mail as soon as he got home from Walter's. I'm hoping you got it in time, that you both had a grand time, and that Ginny is now wearing your ring, which I know thrills you both. Bless you both with all the happiness in the world.
>
> . . . About the wedding—it would be fine if you could be married at Laura's. We'd feel much better if it could be a home wedding.
>
> Dad fixed that little oil heater of Grandma Crow's, so we can heat the spare room for Ginny. And we got a new wool blanket to keep her warm. . . . Don't forget to let us know what train or bus you'll come on.
>
> We're both anxiously eager to see you both. . . . I'm not

planning anything—will just let you and Ginny do what you want when you get here . . . if you want to take her around to see the family, to see what she's getting into, or stay here.

Before we could go home, Ginny and I had many things to do to prepare for the wedding. We had already subjected ourselves to the blood tests required before applying for the marriage license, going by bus to the Pulaski County courthouse to apply for that important document. We also had to apply for ration books, one of the necessities for living "on the outside." It was strange for Ginny but also thrilling for both of us when she signed her name as "Virginia *Artley*" for the first time. The clerk seemed to enjoy our about-to-be-newlyweds behavior.

Among the new adventures we experienced during those hectic days of preparation for our wedding was searching for a place to live. That was no easy task in that "frontier" Ozark area where all available (decent) housing seemed already taken by civilian workers at the fort or by married military personnel lucky enough to have found something.

Besides the basic requirements of affordability, cleanliness, reasonable comfort, and privacy (meaning a bathroom we didn't have to share with others), there was the necessity of being within commuting distance to the post—and there must be transportation available, because a car of our own was out of the question.

Our search did not produce immediate results. With only days until our wedding, we began to have visions of being married only in name, each having to live in our own barracks. Then we heard of a place in the small Missouri town of Richland, about twenty-five miles from Ft. Wood and served by a commuter bus. Ginny and I received permission to take time off from work for a quick trip to check out the place. It was a second-floor, one-room (bedroom/living room) apartment with a private bath (tub and everything) and a closet-sized kitchenette furnished with a small gas stove, a refrigerator, and a small table with two chairs, dishes, pots, and pans.

Ginny thought it was perfect for us so we agreed to take it, paying the deposit and picking up the key at the home of the landlord just two doors up the street. Dr. Hudson and his wife, both elderly, seemed to take a liking to us, especially to Ginny, and I felt it was because of her that they agreed to rent the apartment to two GIs, for they informed us that they were quite particular about to whom they rented. So we had our first home.

What a relief it was to actually have our three-day passes in our hands; each of them had been approved and signed by our respective commander. We were on our way to Iowa for Ginny to meet my family. However, the official blessings in the form of three-day passes were not the only concerns we had in making the trip. There was the transportation. In searching for it, I was to discover yet another side of Ginny's personality—to my chagrin.

I had asked around the station hospital for word of someone with whom we could catch a ride to Kansas City, where we could board the Rock Island train for Hampton. Unsuccessful in that search, I had decided, without saying anything to Ginny about my plans, to make a small cartoon notice to put on the bulletin board. I had drawn a sketch of a soldier and a WAC standing by the side of a highway as hitchhikers trying to get a ride. Under the drawing (which I thought was quite clever) I had penned the pertinent information requesting a ride for the two of us. In this bit of advertising, however, I had failed to take into account two entities—the Army and Ginny. While my effort did produce results, they were not the kind for which I had hoped.

My first mistake was in posting a personal notice on an official bulletin board. The hospital commandant called me to his office and asked in a stern, unsmiling manner, who had given me permission to post my sketch there. (The officer seemed not to appreciate the humor in my work.) I, of course, had not asked for permission.

Thankfully, he forewent the firing squad, and I was given a reprimand instead. After I was dismissed, with the incriminating piece of evidence in my hand and with my tail between my legs, I went to Ginny, hoping for some succor. Ginny, to my surprise, was no more amused than the commandant had been. In fact, she was quite upset at my including her in the ridiculous presentation, and she felt I had somehow cheapened our togetherness in my public display. At *that* reprimand, I destroyed the evidence and all but swore off ever drawing another cartoon.

I have brought ire down upon my head many times since, through my cartooning, but this, I felt, was undeserved. After her initial reaction, however, Ginny in her loving and gentle way explained her feelings to me, the most important message being that she still loved me and was looking forward to our trip home.

As a result of that episode, I spent the money for two round-trip tickets to Kansas City, in addition to the train fare, and I came to understand that Ginny was a very private person, not wanting to be exposed to public view.

Ginny wanted to present herself to my family in the best possible light, so she had made an appointment to have her beautiful black hair "done" the morning of our departure, just before boarding the bus. The timing was close so, as Ginny came out of the hairdresser's, I was waiting for her with our luggage.

When she emerged, there was a distraught expression on her lovely face. The person who had done her hair had goofed, and my Ginny's beautiful hair was frizzled. Poor Ginny. She was already nervous about making a good impression on my folks, and now this! My arguing, however, that her loveliness could not be hidden by a poor hairdo, plus the excitement of the trip ahead of us, seemed to revive her spirits, making for a pleasant trip home.

The Rocket pulled into the Rock Island station in Hampton at about 9:30 that night. It was dark and cold, and Ginny's apprehension had reemerged. However, as we descended the steps of the train coach and she looked down to see Dad and my brother Dan standing on the brick-paved platform, smiling up at us, she knew she was in friendly territory.

After our luggage was loaded into the folks' 1934 Plymouth and during the five-mile drive to the farm, there was much chatter and laughter. I leaned back in my seat, basking in the warmth of acceptance all around. As we approached the farm from the south, coming down Freie's hill and then ascending the gradual slope of the road to where we turned into our lane, I saw the familiar light in the dining room window of our old farmhouse . . . home.

Coming home to this familiar scene always evoked a feeling of excitement and warmth. But this time the feeling was further enhanced by the fact that I was bringing to this place my *chosen one* . . . to join our family.

Ginny, as we drove into the farmyard, tightened her grip on my hand. She already felt accepted by Dad and Dan, her soon-to-be father-in-law and brother-in-law, but she knew she had the biggest hurdle yet to clear—gaining acceptance, love, and respect from her husband's mother. Wasn't it common folk knowledge that the mother of a son was always jealous of the woman who had stolen her son's heart? And wasn't there expected to be a rivalry between mother-in-law and daughter-in-law? These nagging bits of old wives' wisdom were baggage with which the two most important women in my life were burdened as they were about to meet for the first time.

The greeting between Ginny and Mom was a trifle guarded at first, but very soon there was a rapport established between them that continued through the years. The next couple of hours after our arrival were joyful. As Mom wrote some time later:

> At first, Bob, we loved her because you did. But almost immediately, we loved her because she was Ginny.

The five of us visited excitedly. Dan, being a high school junior, was very appreciative of the pretty young woman who was soon to become his brother's wife. The two of them bantered back and forth, establishing a lasting brother-sister relationship.

As for my parents, they both seemed pleased and comfortable with the woman I had brought home to be their first daughter-in-law—the daughter they had never had. Dad and Ginny developed a special understanding and appreciation of one another that we laughingly said must have some connection with the fact that they both had "determined" chins. Each seemed to be able to perceive what was on the other's mind, and they carried on a continuing good-natured battle that provided much fun for all of us for years to come.

A three-day pass was quite short when it was used to travel to Iowa from Ft. Wood, because travel each way consumed almost an entire day. This time, however, considering the travel companion and the purpose of the trip, the whole three days were richly satisfying for everyone concerned.

Although we both were tired, we slept very little on our return trip. Instead, we delighted in recounting to one another the good time we had experienced at home. We basked in the memory of the warmth that had enveloped us as a result of the mutual love and acceptance expressed between Ginny and my family.

Ginny was especially pleased that Mom had kissed her when we had arrived and that they all, including Dad and Dan, had kissed her when we were leaving. As Ginny explained, she, too, was from a "kissing family." She was also moved by the special effort, the little extras the folks had provided for the occasion of her visit—the portable oil heater for her room and the new blanket.

For my part, I felt my family had acted beautifully, just by being themselves and by taking my chosen one so completely into their hearts. I was sure of my love for Ginny, regardless of how my family felt, but I felt especially happy—and lucky, too—that the introduction had met a response of mutual love and acceptance.

Not only had my immediate family and Ginny taken one another to heart, but the same had happened with the other relatives we had been able to see during our brief stay. We had made a special point of seeing Grandma. She and Ginny had taken an instant liking to each other that was maintained up to the time of Grandma's death in 1949.

In the zeal of our love for each other, reinforced by our happy reception at home, only the presence of the other passengers in the crowded bus and train restrained us from melding into a continuing embrace all the way back to Ft. Wood. We settled, instead, for just holding hands. We took turns leaning our heads on one another's willing shoulders during our intermittent naps in those less than comfortable coach seats. As a letter home, written after our return, expressed it:

> We had several good visits on the way back—the results
> of which made me . . . realize why I love her so much. We
> slept very little. . . . We enjoyed the lunch you sent, Mom.
> . . . We shared a sandwich with a little boy we overheard
> telling his dad how good it smelled when we opened the box.

Ginny's eyes sparkled with mischievous amusement and then melted quickly into a show of sympathy as we remembered how Mom had nearly dropped the bowl of potatoes she was bringing to us, all gathered at the round oak table, when she had asked if we'd set a date for our wedding. She was, no doubt, expecting it to be sometime in the distant future, but Ginny, in her eager, straightforward manner, replied, "Next Saturday."

After we returned from our visit home, we were tired but happy. Our wedding was only four days away, and there was much to be done. I had asked Russ Wulff to be my best man, and Ginny had chosen Ida Crawford as her bridesmaid. We met in the WAC dayroom Tuesday night for a planning session.

I couldn't have picked a better person than Russ to assist me. He had served in the same capacity three times previously so was well experienced in such matters. He took charge of arranging details I had never considered.

In spite of our preference for a quiet, private wedding to simply meet the minimum requirements of society, the people in both of our barracks and our co-workers in the lab had other ideas. Before long, an elaborate affair was being planned, to be held in the post chapel. It was to include music, flowers, an official photographer (from the signal corps), and even some rice, a rare commodity during those times.

Ginny had asked Captain Foster of the lab to walk down the aisle with her. Two or three days before the big day, he called me into his office for a private briefing on wedding night protocol from a physician's perspective. I was a little uncomfortable as he instructed me in the intimate details. However, I did appreciate his thoughtfulness . . . and the helpful information that he provided.

Ida, Ginny's maid of honor, took her responsibilities seriously and was a real help. She also saw to the finer points of traditional behavior concerning those about to be married. On Saturday, the day of our wedding, when I inadvertently encountered the two of them while I was running about attending to last-minute details, Ida became quite upset, saying that it was bad luck for the betrothed to see each other on their wedding day before the ceremony. But Ginny and I were happy for this unscheduled, if brief, chance to see one another. When Ida, flustered by this unexpected meeting, tried to hurry us apart, Ginny called back over her shoulder, "Bob, *please* don't be late." That plea was one I was to hear from Ginny many times during the forty-plus years of our marriage.

It had been generally understood that, because of the distance and the restrictions of wartime travel, none of our family members would be able to attend the wedding. However, Laura, Ginny's sister from Detroit, had held out the hope that she might be present—up until two days before the wedding, when she wrote to Ginny, saying that it would be impossible for her to come. In her letter Laura wrote:

I'm so glad, Ginny, that you have found someone like Bob, because you know I've always been afraid that you'd find someone who would take advantage of that unusual loyalty and love of which you have so much.

If Bob understands you at all, you will surely get along, but remember all the things I've told you about playing square in married life. Never let a little quarrel drag into a big one. There's no harm in making up first, whether you are right or wrong.

I am enclosing twenty-five dollars, and I only hope that it gets there okay and by Saturday. I will get fifteen from your account at the bank tomorrow night. But ten dollars is a partial wedding gift from Bo and me. It will help take care of your expenses on Saturday, as I can't imagine you are too flush with money. It goes so darn fast.

I'll expect a call on Sunday around noon, if you have time. I'll sure be thinking of you both at six o'clock and wishing I could see you being married. Write me all about it next week.

Kiss Bob for me and I'm sure that he'll kiss you for me, too. With my best love to you both.

(I've never felt more like your mother than I do right now.)

LAURA

Ginny was disappointed, of course, but was well aware of the complications in traveling so far for so short a stay. Also, Ginny and I consoled one another that because I, at least, had to work most of Saturday until shortly before the six o'clock ceremony and then we would be leaving on our one-day honeymoon immediately afterward, there'd be very little time to be with family.

How much I longed for Ginny's reassuring presence during the hour or two before the wedding. Russ, of course, was indispensable, but Ginny was the one I needed most (even as I do now, while writing this, with her mute form beside me in her bed, in her final illness). Somehow or other, Russ managed to get me to the chapel on time and in a reasonably calm condition for one who had never before even attended a wedding.

As Russ and I waited with Chaplain Renz in the little anteroom at the front of the chapel, I peeked through the crack of the door to see the guests taking their places. Someone, as prearranged, was singing the three songs Ginny and I had requested,

"Oh Promise Me," "I Love You Truly," and "Always." The beauty with which they were sung was moving to the point that I wished it were proper for a man to shed tears at a wedding. (Later I was amazed and reassured, as we walked down the aisle after the ceremony, to see some of the "he-men" of the lab with tears streaming down their cheeks.)

As the strains of Mendelssohn's "Bridal March" began to fill the chapel, it was a great relief to look out over the sea of faces and see Ginny, on the arm of Captain Foster, appear in the doorway at the back of the chapel. She looked happy and beautiful in her WAC uniform and carrying her bridal bouquet. As our eyes met, hers bright with happiness, she smiled and I somehow felt calmed; my quivering knees became more firm. In many more instances, over the ensuing years, Ginny has been my strength, as she was that night.

The rest of the people in the room became one big blur. Only Ginny seemed real, and I eagerly reached out and received her from the arm of Captain Foster.

While I was experiencing all of this with near traumatic feelings, Ginny was taking it all in stride, and even with humor. As she told me later, she almost giggled as she and Captain Foster made their way slowly down the aisle, each step measured to the solemn music of the "Bridal March," when some lines from Walt Whitman came to her mind: "Oh, Captain, my Captain, our fearful trip is done." *This* was the woman I was taking as my wife! How fortunate I was!

The ceremony progressed smoothly, and I managed to say the right words at the proper times, even though Ginny told my folks in a letter describing the wedding that she thought I paused much too long when it was my turn to say "I do." With the staunch support and timely prompting of Russ, I even managed to get the wedding band on Ginny's ring finger. And when the chaplain said I could kiss the bride, I felt as if he thought he was giving me permission to do that which I had not done before. We gave our guests a performance that reflected much practice, however—and we managed it without our noses colliding.

It was a great relief to hear the chaplain pronouncing us "husband and wife" and to know we had somehow made it over this hurdle. Now we could get down to the business of *being* husband and wife—a business in which we intended to be engaged for many years to come.

*We were a serious couple at our wedding, November 20,
1943, at Ft. Leonard Wood. Left to right: Chaplain
Renz, Russ Wulff, me and Ginny, and Ida Crawford.*

*After our wedding, we were driven to our first home in
Richland, Missouri, near Ft. Leonard Wood. Note the
rice in Ginny's hair—a rare commodity during the rationing years of the war.*

RICHLAND

A few days before the wedding, when we discovered that we had been successful in finding a furnished apartment, we decided that, instead of making the long trip to Springfield, where Russ had reserved a room for us, we'd spend the two nights and one day of our honeymoon in our own home. (We could not help but wonder what the people at the hotel thought when the reservation was canceled on such short notice. No doubt, they shrugged it off as "another wartime romance.") So after the ceremony was over, the congratulations given, and the bride kissed by the guys in the lab (who for some time had been referring to me as "lucky"), Ginny and I hurried through a shower of rice to the car that was to take us to our "bridal suite" in Richland.

Willoughby, a civilian worker in the lab, with his wife had generously offered to drive us and our few pieces of luggage there. With wartime rationing of gasoline and tires, this was a considerable offering on their part, and it bothered Ginny that she had nothing more than a hastily concocted pot of coffee to offer them in thanks.

While we did appreciate their generosity in transporting us and our luggage to our apartment, we weren't quite prepared to entertain them for the rest of the evening. After the coffee cups had been refilled two or three times and we had long since run out of things of common interest to talk about, our guests, seated on our only two chairs (the straight-back kitchen variety), gave no indication of leaving. Instead, in the awkward silences that made up a good share of our visit, these two self-described "hillbillies" would look at one another and grin as if they had a private joke. They made remarks to the effect that they *should* probably go because we probably wanted to go to bed. Then they would laugh, and Ginny and I would try to be good hosts and laugh along with them.

After what seemed like a long time in this social exchange, with Ginny and I sitting on the edge of the bed in our one-room apartment, facing our two guests on the straight-back chairs, Ginny offered them the last dribbles from the coffee pot. They declined the offer and this time *did* stand and move toward the door. After they had actually left and we had heard their steps down the stairs and out the front door, I turned the night lock on the door and pulled Ginny to me for the *real* embrace and kiss I had been longing for ever since we had performed the proper one for our guests at the wedding ceremony. After a long moment in that sweet encounter, we drew back, and I feasted my eyes upon the face of the lovely woman who had just become my wife. Her eyes had a dreamy, far-away look, and I said, "A penny for your thoughts." I expected her to have been envisioning our future together, or some similar sentiment, but when she replied, it was with, "I hope we didn't seem too eager to see them leave."

We still had some groceries we needed to get for the next day, so Ginny sent me out with a shopping list, the first of hundreds she would give me in the years ahead. I felt a warm glow near my heart as I hurried down the main street of "our" town while Ginny was getting our few things unpacked and arranged around our apartment, making it our home—the first of fifteen.

As I emerged from the store with a large paper bag of groceries in each arm, I noticed a clothing store across the street and hurried there to make one more purchase—a pair of pajamas. It simply wouldn't do, I thought, to present myself to my bride on our wedding night in the khaki GI shorts and T-shirt that was my usual nightwear.

In spite of the heavy load in both arms, I fairly ran up the darkened streets, as if being drawn by a magnet to my brand new wife. "My wife." I repeated the phrase over and over to myself. Events of the past several hours had been so hectic and so crowded with people that I had not had a chance to fully savor this new phase of our togetherness.

As I rounded the corner, my heart nearly burst with joy when I saw the light from the window of our second-floor apartment in the remodeled old frame house. I knew that my Ginny was there waiting for me to return and that no authority on earth could keep us apart—no man-made rules could keep us from melding body and spirit into the oneness that was a true marriage. We had met the requirements of our society by observing the decorum and restraint that had kept us apart until now, and now we were free to come together in the passionate expression of our love, as God, through nature, had provided from the beginning of the human race. If anyone, man or beast, had attempted to stand between me and my bride that night on that dark street, there would have been a terrific battle, such was my love for her.

As I maneuvered myself and my load through the front entrance and hurried up the stairs to where Ginny was standing at the open door of our apartment, smiling and with her arms outstretched, I thought of the pajamas I'd purchased and of how utterly silly and irrelevant they were to this night.

It was a dark, frosty Monday morning in Richland, and we were chilly from our long wait for the bus. We had made a point of being there well ahead of time to be sure not to miss it on our first day back to work after our wedding on Saturday night. Because Richland was one of its early stops, the bus was not yet crowded, and we were able to sit together. By the time we would get off in front of the station hospital an hour later, there would be standing room only, and the air within the bus would be blue with cigarette smoke.

I slipped my cold right hand into the ample pocket of Ginny's coat and clasped her warm hand, my fingers searching for the diamond ring and wedding band on her ring finger. She squeezed my hand and smiled, and we each snuggled down within our wool GI overcoats and closed our eyes for the long ride ahead—each with our own thoughts.

After we had settled into our Richland apartment (which was much like settling into a hotel room because we had few personal things and the place was furnished), we could hardly wait for the Richland-bound bus after work each night to take us to our secluded "nest" away from everyone. It was a place where we could pretend, at least for the next twelve hours or so, that we were living in a normal world without war.

We soon made connections with a private ride to and from work; this gave us more time at home. One evening on our way home, one of the riders in the car asked me if I would like to go coon hunting with a group of fellows that night. I had never taken part in such an adventure, which they assured me it was, and under ordinary circumstances might have welcomed such an experience. But the thought of spending most of the night with a bunch of men and a pack of baying hounds chasing a hapless coon while Ginny sat at home alone just didn't appeal to me. I begged off "this time." (I was never asked again.) That was *one* time that I made the right decision in such a situation, for Ginny, who had been very quiet, later expressed her thankfulness that I had declined the invitation.

We were barely settled in our home when we were reminded of the uncertainties of military life. Ginny alluded to this in her letter to the folks just a few days after our wedding, writing, "I had to submit a letter to the post commandant, requesting permission to live off the post. I still haven't received an answer. But we surely are enjoying it while we can." In another letter, Ginny wrote to Dan:

> I still don't know whether or not I'll be permitted to live off the post. However, we went ahead and bought a little Xmas tree and trimmings. If we can't be here for Xmas, we'll spend it either in the lab, dayroom or at the Red Cross. I hope the war won't be going on next Xmas.

A few days later I wrote:

> We still don't know about living off the post. But in the meantime are doing so and enjoying it. We have our Christmas tree up and decorated. It's not very grand, or very big, but looks nice and smells good—scents up the whole room with its fragrance.
> . . . We had Sugi (Hiroshi Sugiyama) and Olander, two of our lab friends, out for Sunday dinner today—our first guests. Ginny made a very good meal—steak, fried "taters," corn, lettuce and tomato salad, raw carrots and celery, and ice cream and fruitcake. Our guests ate heartily and seemed to enjoy themselves. . . . Ginny was happy to think her first meal for company was such a success.

This morning I was awakened to find breakfast waiting beside the bed and Ginny all smiles with a wash cloth and towel for me, too. I thought for a moment I must be sick in bed.

Ginny said she would have written tonight but to tell you she had to get *my* cards out so people would get them *before* Christmas. She'll write soon.

In another letter written to the folks shortly after the one Ginny had sent to Dan, I wrote:

Ginny is taking her bath and singing "Silent Night" softly to herself. . . . While I'm waiting for my turn in the tub, I'll start this.

Gosh, how grand it is living like this! It's *too* good and we realize that more now than ever. Ginny was told yesterday that she cannot live off the post! It's all because of that damned Col. Duval. He's caused more trouble and dissension since he's been in charge of the post than anyone I've ever known. . . . He's doing his best to cause all married personnel to move back onto the post and play soldier. . . . Last night we wrapped packages for mailing and had a laughing, jolly time doing so. Ginny said she'd never laughed so much until marrying me. I'm not sure if that's a compliment or otherwise. . . .

Two days before Christmas, Ginny wrote:

We received your packages . . . Thank you. We opened the smaller box and had a delightful time crunching the delicious popcorn while we read to one another in bed.

We take great pride in our little dressed up Christmas tree. We decorated it with red paper, tinsel icicles and angel's hair. The angel's hair caused us a lot of trouble. It is made of spun glass. We had it all over us and the floor. We itched all through the night and we're still itching a little. (Moral—never get angel's hair.)

As it turned out, neither Ginny nor I had to work on Christmas. We were to spend our very first Christmas Eve and Day together in our home—something many loved ones could not do that year nor the next two.

As Ginny's first Christmas away from home (my third), it was a sad time for her; even though we were thankful to be together,

I sketched Ginny, reflected in the mirror, as she snapped this photo, winter 1944.

Ginny wrote in a 1944 letter: "Last night I was reading to Bob but fell asleep in the midst of the article. I awoke now and then, but not completely, seeing him standing at different angles, sketching me."

GINNY 1944

it was so very different from any she had ever known. As we sat on the floor before our little tree with its tinsel reflecting the light of candles Ginny had placed on the window sill, the Christmas music that played softly on the radio evoked memories of past Christmases spent with all her family and dear ones. In spite of herself, Ginny could not stifle the sobs that welled up within; soon the tears were spilling down her cheeks. I took her in my arms to comfort her as best I could, and before long, the emotional overload turned into smiles and quiet laughter as we talked about opening "just one present each" and saving the rest for morning. This arrangement was a compromise between our two families' traditions. Ginny's family had always opened their gifts on Christmas Eve, while mine had saved that exciting time for Christmas morning.

As I remember, we ended up opening more than one each that night, but a balance was met—one that became the tradition in our home as our family developed. The only two presents I recall from that evening were the ones we gave to each other. I gave Ginny a silver name bracelet. On its front was engraved *Virginia M. Artley,* and on the reverse side it said *To Ginny from her Husband.* (Little did I know that some forty years later I would have a jeweller add the words "Alzheimer's victim.") She gave me a briar pipe and a can of Prince Albert tobacco. I did not smoke, but Ginny had heard me say that I might like to smoke a pipe. So that first Christmas, our apartment smelled of tobacco smoke as I tried out my new toy. I smoked that pipe and one other off and on for a few years, mainly for the nostalgia of our first Christmas, but eventually I put them aside as something that I enjoyed but found unnecessary.

As thankful as we were to be together, we were painfully aware that Christmas, for both of us, was a lonely time if it could not be shared, preferably with lots of family—something we had in common from our past Christmases. We could only hope and pray that next Christmas would find us with our families again. But that was not to be.

The next few days after Christmas, we spent our evenings enjoying our life in our home while we could . . . and preparing to obey the commandant's order to move back to the post, each to our own barracks.

FAMILIES

With heavy hearts made keenly aware of the power of the military over our lives, Ginny and I divided our few personal belongings and moved from our Richland home of only a little more than a month back to our respective barracks.

Our friends at the lab and at each of our quarters were sympathetic and supportive. Sergeant Beam, the administrative noncommissioned officer of the lab, in his own way, indignantly expressed the general feeling of everyone there as he bellowed, "It isn't as if you two were a couple just shacking up somewhere! You're trying to start *a home!*" Ginny and I even considered sharing the cot that was in the lab storage room for the use of the person on emergency duty. One night, soon after our return, when Ginny was on all-night emergency, we *did* share that cot—and felt deliciously guilty in pulling something over on the Army.

Only a few days after our forced return to barracks life, however, Andy Glaube, civilian bookkeeper at the lab, told us that he and his wife, who lived in the civilian housing area on the post, had an extra room that they would be glad to rent to us. Ginny and I thought this a great idea—we could live together husband and wife and yet be legally on the post. We gladly accepted their kind offer and were soon settled into Maud and Andy's guest room, sharing with them a bath and the kitchen for breakfasts. As far as officialdom was aware, we were being obedient GIs, each living in our own barracks, where we kept our cots made up. We also took our noon and evening meals in our respective mess halls and closely watched the bulletin boards for special formations we were expected to attend.

We continued with that living arrangement until June, when we would again move off the post, after Colonel Duval's zeal for a strict Army life cooled some and the rules were relaxed. Until then, we rode the post shuttle bus each morning and evening and observed the lengthening of the days as winter gave way to spring. We enjoyed just being together and spent our evenings reading to one another, or Ginny was my model while I sketched her. Sometimes on weekends in the early spring, we spent lazy afternoons in the hilly, wooded area behind the row of houses, or at night we lay in one another's arms, talking quietly of our hopes or fears, of the uncertain road ahead.

In January of 1944, after we had more or less settled into the routine of living on the post again in our unofficial housing arrangements with the Glaubes, we were able to each get a three-day pass to make a trip to Detroit, to the home of Ginny's sister, Laura, and family. On the train, as Ginny briefed me on the family members I would be meeting, I knew how Ginny must have felt when I took her home to the farm to meet *my* relatives for the first time.

Laura and her husband, Leonard (Bo) Halleran, had an unpretentious but attractive, comfortable home. With them lived their two daughters, Jean, about two years younger than Ginny, and Ruth (Chickie), ten years Ginny's junior.

Ginny had come to live with Laura and Bo in Detroit when she was sixteen. Before that, although she grew up in Pennsylvania, she had spent a lot of time at Laura and Bo's home during summers and school vacations. There she and her niece, Jean, became more like sisters than aunt and niece. They spent many hours together, playing, reading, and otherwise sharing their girlhood, thus forming a bond for life.

Because Jean was crippled from an injury at birth that had affected the upper part of her body, making it difficult for her to speak and use her arms and hands, she became the target for playground cruelty. This vulnerability of Jean's became Ginny's personal concern. On at least one occasion, Ginny tore into a playground bully, took him down, beat him up, and sent him home blubbering with a bloody nose—he had unwisely made some cruel remarks to Jean in Ginny's presence.

As our train clicked over the rails on its way from Newburg, Missouri, near Ft. Wood, to Chicago, where we would change to one bound for Detroit, Ginny told me these things and filled me in on what to expect from each of her family members. So, at nine o'clock on Saturday morning, when we were met at the station by Laura and Chickie, I felt I had a running start on our acquaintance.

The feeling that I had a handle on the situation was short-lived, however, when that same night, as a surprise for Ginny, her brothers Art, Bill, and George arrived from South Fork, Pennsylvania. (Thankfully, I thought, brother Bob was in the South Pacific, and brother Ed was somewhere else in a GI uniform.) They had apparently come to check out the Iowa farm boy who had talked their little sister into a wartime marriage. Each of Ginny's five brothers was special to her, and it was obvious that they all considered their baby sister *extra* special; they were protective of her and her interests.

The Moores, as I came to know them later, were a warm, fun-loving family with innate integrity, courage, loyalty, and good humor—traits I was glad to have in the gene pool our children would inherit. However, they came on strong and were quite overwhelming to a shy outsider who'd had the presumption to become a part of their close-knit family.

I was glad, therefore, when Ginny rescued me long before the party was over, saying that we were exhausted from our long trip (which was true), and led me to the quiet seclusion of our bedroom where we could assure one another that *we* were the ones who mattered most to one another, where we could reestablish our togetherness, "forsaking all others." This was the same assurance of oneness Ginny asked of me in later years when we were living near *my* overwhelming family.

In late February, we each managed to get a ten-day furlough, during which we planned to go to Pennsylvania, first to South Fork and then on to Philadelphia, to meet the rest of Ginny's family.

Ginny's father, with his extensive family and declining energies due to advancing years, wrote few letters, so Ginny cherished those she *did* receive from him. Anticipating our visit, he wrote on Croyle Township School District letterhead, welcoming us and telling how he was looking forward to our visit.

Ginny (left) with her best friend, Betty Wirick.

Ginny as a fifteen-year-old schoolgirl, just before she left Pennsylvania for Detroit.

South Fork, Pa.
Feb. 12, '44

CPL-T G.R. Artley
Dear Son and Daughter,
    I am writing this, as you see by the date, on Honest Abe's birthday. I have been confined to the house all week. A cold on the bronchial tubes. But I am some better at present. Your welcome letter was duly received. I hope you and Virginia will be able to come and see us. You will be very welcome. Just here, let me say my advice would be to try to get a through train that will stop at Johnstown and then get a bus to South Fork. It is only about eight miles, and there is a bus stop just about seventy-five feet from our door. Tell Virginia to pull the signal when she is opposite J. Hifflert's. Try to get to Johnstown no later than 10:30 p.m. as the last bus leaves at 11:15. The first bus is at 5:30 a.m. We are looking forward to seeing you.
    This is a very stormy day here. George, Jr., is in the Army now. This morning's paper gives the names of 102 from this area who have passed their medical tests. The gasoline rationing is getting stiffer all the time. William cannot get tires for his car, but we must win, regardless.
    Paul Hillegat is home. He was on a fortress at Guadalcanal and sports four medals. He seems quite nervous.
    I have not heard from Robert for some time. I have not seen Meriam for six weeks. Renna was to see me recently. She is putting all her salary in war bonds. Her son, Earl, expects to be called about May. I feel sure Art will be called soon.
    Verda Jensen has been home on furlough. She looks fine. She is stationed at Fort Sill, Oklahoma. This is of no interest to Robert but Virginia will be interested. Quite a few boys from here are in England, and some in Italy. Art's wife was here to see me two evenings this week. William is working quite a lot of overtime.
    Well, I will close this rambling epistle. Looking forward to seeing you both soon.
    With much love and good wishes, I remain,

Your old dad,
W. H. MOORE, SR.

Once again, as on our trip to Detroit, Ginny used part of our time on the train to acquaint me with the rest of her family. Our first stop would be in South Fork to visit the Moores—brothers George and Margaret and family; Bill and Mary and family; Art and Laura and family; and Ed and his wife and their small daughter, Renna. Also, we would be seeing Ginny's aged father in the family home that he now shared with Bill and Mary. At the family gathering, scheduled for soon after our arrival, we would also be seeing Ginny's older sisters, Renna and Meriam, and their families.

If I had thought the Detroit encounter was overwhelming, it was small compared with this, where the numbers had increased impressively. But this time I was more prepared. (I was battle hardened, so to speak, from the Detroit campaign.) Also, I sensed that Ginny's brothers had returned from Detroit with friendly reports concerning the new son-in-law/brother-in-law/uncle. So while the happy hubbub was more intense, mostly because of the increase in numbers, I felt I was not being subjected to an acid test, but that, for better or for worse, they considered me a part of the family . . . or perhaps that they were stuck with me and had better just make the best of it.

Ginny's father, unlike many of his boisterous offspring, was a quiet man. He had a dignified, almost formal demeanor and held his near six-feet-height ramrod straight. (This same posture is evident in his son Bob, in Ginny, and in our older son Rob and our youngest child Joan.) He and I got on well, and I soon felt that he had accepted me as one with whom he was willing to trust the welfare of his youngest child.

During the few days we spent in South Fork, we visited at each of the families' homes and were given a whirlwind tour to points of interest in the area. Here in the town of Ginny's birth, she tried to imbue me with some feel for her family and roots in Pennsylvania, where she had been born, about twenty-five years earlier, on August 19, 1918. She was born in a drab, narrow three-story house, built by her father's own hands and perched precariously on the edge of the southbound road out of town, almost overhanging a steep, cindery hill on the other side that descended to the railroad tracks and the river and valley below.

Virginia (Ginny) was the eighth and last child born to William H. Moore and Renna George. Renna was his second wife; his first had been her sister, Viola, who had died, leaving him with *their* three children, Renna, George, and Laura. He had married Viola's sister, Renna, a year later. Before having Ginny, they had become the parents of William, Meriam, Edwin, Robert, and Arthur. Two more had died as toddlers, and their gravestones in the cemetery atop the mountain would soon be joined by their mother's.

The summer that Ginny was born, the First World War was in its final agonizing months. Just eight months after Ginny's birth, her mother, Renna, fell victim to the flu epidemic of that time and died. The tragic event left Ginny's father, widowed for the second time, with a baby and a houseful of grieving children for whom to care and provide.

Just a few doors down the street from the Moore family lived Luna and Sam Ritchey, good friends of the family. After the funeral, when they had returned from the cemetery, Ginny's father approached Mrs. Ritchey and asked if she and Sam would please take the baby home with them for a couple of days, until he could "figure out" what he was going to do. Being compassionate friends, the Ritcheys agreed to help their neighbor in his predicament and took the baby into their home . . . for sixteen years.

The Ritcheys did not *adopt* the baby and take her away. She was only a few doors down the street from the Moore house, always available for the family to hold and play with and cuddle and love any time they wished.

So Ginny became a part of the household of Luna and Sam Ritchey, taking her place as the youngest child in their home, along with Leslie, Rupert, and Louise, who was ten at the time. The Ritcheys could not have loved this motherless child any more if she had been of their own flesh. In later years, her eyes softening, Ginny would speak lovingly of Daddy Sam and Mother Ritchey, Leslie and Rupert. Blood sisters could not have been closer all through the years than were Ginny and her Wees. As time would have it, years later, Louise would be Ginny's last surviving sister.

As the years passed, I became familiar with the little incidents in both homes that gave evidence of a child who felt loved and secure. She told of how, when she was a little girl awakened by a bad dream or a crashing thunderstorm, she would run into Sam and Luna's room and crawl into bed with them and feel warm and safe; of how patiently Daddy Sam would sit with her on his lap as she tore off little strips from the newspaper he was reading and, wetting them with saliva, stick them onto his bald head, making "hair" for him.

Ginny's father, old enough at the time of her birth to have been her grandfather, worked for many years as a carpenter in the coal mines of South Fork and vicinity. Later he worked in and then took over a grocery store owned by his father, William R. Moore, a Civil War veteran. Her father was a highly respected man in the community and took an active part in its affairs, serving for several years on the school board. Ginny spoke lovingly and respectfully of Dad, as did the rest of the family.

Ginny often spoke wistfully of the mother she could not remember. She never tired of having older family members and friends tell about the lovely woman who had been her mother. Old photos and family accounts indicate that mother and daughter Ginny were very much alike, in looks as well as personalities. They both were gentle, loving, and full of fun.

She *did* know her grandfather, who had a great influence on her life. Ginny told me and our children about William R. Moore, "a good Christian man," who at the age of sixteen had enlisted in the Sixth Army of the Potomac, was wounded in the Battle of the Wilderness, and was later discharged in 1865 at Washington, D.C., at the close of the war, after serving three years.

The children were taught to respect their grandfather's privacy and entered his room only on invitation. There he would assemble his grandchildren when his small Civil War pension came each month and give to each of them a coin or two with which to buy a small special treat: candy, ice cream, or soda. But he admonished them never to spend it on anything that had to do with the devil, such as playing cards or moving pictures.

In spite of the strict guidelines their grandfather laid down for them in his attempt to keep them on the straight and narrow, his family seemed not in the least to bear him ill feelings. They knew he loved them and had their best interests at heart, and that he would stand up for each of them if and when needed. Besides, in spite of his "narrow" views on having fun, he was also one with whom they knew they could laugh and joke and have rollicking good times. He died in late September of 1929, at the age of eighty-three, and was buried in the mountaintop cemetery in South Fork.

Ginny (front row, far right) with her classmates at South Fork public school, circa 1924.

After the hectic days in South Fork passed all too rapidly, we resumed our train ride to Philadelphia, to meet Ginny's sister Louise and her husband, Webster Jones, and Mother Ritchey, who made her home with them.

My first meeting with Web was like my first meeting with Louise had been several months earlier, when she had come for a short visit at Ft. Wood—I immediately liked that jovial, warm-hearted, intelligent professor. The meeting was the beginning of a long, warm relationship between us two couples that added much to the richness of our lives.

They took us directly to their home, a comfortable second-floor apartment across a busy street from a fire station that provided almost daily entertainment. Mother Ritchey was waiting there to greet us. Having heard so many good things about that warm, jolly, grandmotherly person from Ginny, I found her easy to love instantly.

Our days in Philadelphia, like those spent in South Fork, were emotionally warm and fulfilling. In addition, we were introduced to some of the cultural features of that fascinating city—the historical and art museums. And, of course, we visited the national shrines there, such as Constitution Hall and the home of Betsy Ross. At the end of our furlough, we had much to talk about on our long train ride back to Ft. Wood.

Just as we, as a newly married couple, had worked at being assimilated into Ginny's families in Detroit, South Fork, and Philadelphia in the months of January and February, the next three months were used for doing the same with my family in Iowa.

This, as always, involved working within the perimeter of Army regulations—three-day passes and furloughs. Furloughs, of course, being longer, were hard to come by and were parceled out sparingly, as any earned vacation might be. Thus, because the farm at Hampton was within range (but barely) of a three-day pass, we relied on that as a way for Ginny and my family to become acquainted. We took one pass in March and another in May.

In late March another pass was used, this time by my brother Dean, a civilian flight instructor at Jones Field in Bonham, Texas, training fighter pilots for the U.S. Army Air Corps. He came to visit us the weekend of March nineteenth, just a week before our trip to the farm.

Ginny's niece Jean was only two years younger than Ginny, and they grew up together more as sisters than aunt and niece. Detroit, circa 1942.

Ginny teaching her niece Chickie a dance step in the alley behind Laura's home in Detroit, circa 1937.

That weekend was a meaningful time for all three of us, because it was the first Ginny and Dean had met. For Dean, having a sister was a new, pleasant experience. And Ginny warmly accepted Dean into her already large collection of brothers. They immediately liked one another, and we soon had a three-way exchange of banter just as we had had with Russ Wulff back in our three musketeers days. In a letter to the folks at home, I told of his visit:

> He arrived Sunday morning to find us still in bed. Ginny flew around like you do, Mom, trying to get the room in order and herself dressed so Dean could come in. They were ill-at-ease with one another for only a very short time and then were both acting natural and as if they had always been brother and sister.
>
> Sunday night Ginny's original company had a party celebrating one year here at Ft. Wood. She went with the women out to where the party was held, and Dean and I took a taxi out later and brought her back to our room and talked until a late hour. Dean slept in my sleeping bag on the davenport in the living room. . . .
>
> This morning Dean came in with us. We ate breakfast in the service club cafeteria and then came to work where Dean visited and became acquainted with about everyone in the lab. Sugi was especially glad to visit with him again, remembering his trip to the farm with me last year.
>
> After dinner he hung around the lab until time for him to leave, when Ginny and I, in our white lab gowns, walked with him to the hospital entrance to bid him farewell. We hated to see him go, but are so glad he could come.

Later I added to the letter:

> We are looking forward to being home with you this weekend. We have turned in our pass requests and shall call for them and start on our way Friday P.M. We'll probably be in Hampton around 11:00 Saturday morning. But again I say don't count on it too much—one never knows for sure in the Army.

By means of those three-day passes and by letters in between, Ginny and my folks worked to cement a growing, loving, and lasting relationship, as the following letter attests, written two days after returning from our trip to the farm.

Mar. 27, 1944

Dear Mom, Dad, and Dan,

Here we are, back at Ft. Wood. It is just like spring down here—the grass is green, the weather is warm, and Bob and I are in love.

Despite the time going too fast and the visit being too short, every minute of our time there was richly filled and enjoyable. Just like the analogy used by one of the characters in *The Robe,* "Our life is like a long journey. We have steep hills to climb and descend, and rich plains to rest upon and enjoy. But we can never tarry. We must always keep going."

A few nights later Ginny wrote:

Dear Mom, Dad, and Dan,

Bob and I are in the housing area. We will stay here tonight until 11:15 and then back to the barracks. While Bob has been drawing, I have been reading to him.

We received your letters today. Bob and I have read them over a couple times already. I appreciate so much how you feel towards me. I could never express the feeling I had within me when I read the letters. Thank you very much.

Bob and I are always planning for after the war. Whenever we have a certain kind of pie in the mess hall, he tells me to write it down in the little black book, to make for him after the war. I told him I would have chocolate pie one day, lemon pie the next day, etc.

Last night I was reading to Bob but fell asleep in the midst of the article. I awoke now and then, but not completely, seeing him standing at different angles, sketching me. I was so sleepy that I didn't realize what he was doing. Tonight he showed me the sketches.

EXPECTATIONS

Over the years, each of Ginny's four pregnancies was precious, culminating in each one of our beloved children. However, her first pregnancy was *extra* special.

When we first hopefully suspected that Ginny might be with child, the then common "rabbit test" was performed in the laboratory. The lab personnel, of course, were very interested in the test that would mean so much to their Ginny, their "Irish." So when it turned out to be positive, there was an air of celebration, and we received many congratulations.

Not only were we anticipating the first child of our love, but, because of military rules then in force, Pvt. First Class, Virginia Artley would be given an honorable discharge from the WAC, "for the convenience of the Army."

It would certainly be for *our* convenience—now we would have only to be concerned with how the military was to have direct power over *me*. Now we wouldn't have the constant concern of possibly being separated by individual orders. Ginny would, of course, be affected by the seemingly capricious orders of the brass, but indirectly as my dependent and not as a hapless GI on her own.

Soon after the pregnancy had been confirmed, Ginny, on lab emergency, wrote a letter to Dean in Texas:

Hi, Brother,
We're looking forward to the day that you will be Uncle Dean, My papers have gone through for my release from the Army. Now if Bob does go to another camp, I can trail along with him. Our little one will arrive either the latter part of

November or first part of December. We're tickled about it! Bob and I are with each other constantly. We have so much fun together. I only hope he's around to get the pleasure of raising the baby that I will have. Golly, but I will be glad when this old war is over.

With love,
your sister,
GINNY

Then in a letter home she wrote of receiving my baby pictures that Mom had sent, saying, "Probably our baby will look like that." She also wrote of her coming discharge from the WAC:

If I'm out of the Army by next weekend, Dad, I won't be able to wear my uniform home. However, it really would save money if we both traveled as GIs.

Bye now,
Love,
GINNY

P.S. I received my first Mother's Day present. Bob and "it" gave me a box of candy.

We *were* able to get home on pass that weekend and had a renewing family time—short but satisfying. On our return trip, our bus from Kansas City was late into Jefferson City so we missed our connections. Because there was no later bus that night, we were stranded. Taking our bags, we went to a small, family hotel. As the two of us, both in uniform, approached the desk and requested a room for the night, the clerk looked from one to the other of us and then asked to see our marriage certificate.

It had been a long, tiring trip and, through no fault of ours, we had missed our connection to Ft. Wood; now this question with its implications! I exploded in anger, saying something to the effect that we didn't make a habit of carrying our marriage certificate around to show to suspicious hotel clerks.

My burst of indignation must have convinced the clerk and his wife, for after a short whispered conference between the two, they gave us a key and showed us to our room. So the situation passed, and we did get a reasonable night's rest. However, Ginny's self-esteem had been somewhat sullied by being even briefly perceived as one who would be "shacking up"—making her even more anxious to be rid of her uniform.

As if to make up for their initial appraisal of us the night before, the hotel owner and his wife provided us with a morning cup of coffee and helped us get a ride with a Star Route man hauling mail between towns. He would get us to Waynesville, where we could get a shuttle bus to the fort in time to turn in our passes on schedule.

Even though we were on the best of terms with our kind hosts, the Glaubes, Ginny and I were constantly tuned in to any possible opportunities to find a home of our own to rent. Perry Stucker, a fellow GI and lab technician, knowing of our constant quest, invited Ginny and me to be house guests at the place where he and his wife were temporarily living a few miles away from the fort, down by the Big Piney River.

The Big Piney was quite familiar to me, first from basic training days and later when I had been in the 89th Engineers, building pontoon bridges across it (before my transfer to the medical detachment). It was also along this stream I had sometimes wandered in exploratory walks, alone or with GI friends, first with Stewart Mace until he was shipped out, and then with Sugi, my friend and fellow technician in the laboratory. Then, of course, the Big Piney had a romantic link for Ginny and me from our memorable picnics the previous late summer and fall. Thus, we accepted Perry's invitation and enjoyed a very special weekend.

Ginny's discharge finally became a fact, and I had a civilian wife on my hands. Her separation from the Army was not without poignancy, however, for, after all, this had been her life for over a year. And while she no longer would be expected to do extra duties, neither would she be eligible for special privileges those in the military enjoyed. However, the predominant feeling Ginny experienced was that of elation at being "set free."

A few weeks later, Captain Foster arranged for her to resume working as a lab technician as a civilian. She no longer had to take part in military formations nor stand special duties, such as KP, CQ, or lab emergency.

As the month of May slipped into June, we were more eager than ever to get to the out-of-doors and enjoy the beautiful Ozark spring. Perry Stucker acted as our unofficial agent and arranged for us to move from our room in the civilian housing area on the post to a cabin by the Big Piney where we had earlier enjoyed our weekend at his invitation. Russ Wulff and his wife Penny were also living there. As Ginny's letters tell it:

Glaubes'
Housing Area
Ft. Leonard Wood, Mo.
June 9, 1944

Dear Dean,

I have the dinner all ready to put on. Yes, I am now the housekeeper and *cook* (ahem). Mrs. Glaube has gone to St. Louis for two weeks so, hence, the job.

Bob and I are moving in a week and a half. We are renting a little cabin at Possum Lodge—Away out in the Ozarks. Then you can call us "Ozark mountaineers." We'll have two large rooms and a screened-in porch. We'll have two beds, so, Dean, how about a visit?

We won't have running water or electricity. When we want to go from one room to another, we'll carry oil lamps with us to light our way. We have a river running alongside where there is supposed to be good fishing. It will be a nice place for Bob to paint. I told him that he could have his pictures laid out all over the rooms.

With love,
your sister,
GINNY

Wednesday evening
June 14, 1944

Dear Mom, Dad and Dan,

I am in the back yard reclining in a large lawn chair, with a big glass of milk in my hand. Bob and the rest of the Ft. Wood Army must stand retreat this afternoon in this hot sun while "Herr" Duval stands beaming maliciously in the shady sidelines. So Bob will probably be a little late this evening.

We're going to move Saturday. We're anxious to get the moving over with and settle down with corn cob pipes and a jug of corn liquor. Just drop around any time and see us. Seriously, we certainly wish you could.

POSSUM LODGE

The five months we lived at Possum Lodge, during the spring, summer, and autumn of 1944, was probably the most idyllic period of our marriage. We viewed it as our delayed honeymoon. During seemingly endless days and nights, we could devote ourselves to one another, getting to know each other more completely, in that rustic setting. It was as if we had taken a long lease on some of the picnic settings of our courtship. It was a continuation of that beautiful period of our lives when we became ever more deeply in love.

Of course, there was always the ominous military presence of Ft. Wood, only twelve miles away, to which I commuted daily for my duties at the lab. But when I came home after work, I would shed GI khaki down to the civilian me, and Ginny and I would don our bathing gear and recline on a blanket on the grassy riverbank, in the shade or in the sun, whichever our moods dictated, and drink iced tea and talk or read.

Sometimes we would take the boat and row out into the middle of the stream and swim. We didn't enter the water from the shore because of the water moccasins prevalent along the streams and in the swamps of that region. Yes, there were snakes in our Eden. But, unlike Eve, Ginny did not strike up a conversation with the first one she encountered.

The very day after moving to our "cabin in the wilds," I could hardly wait for my ride after work to take me home to my Ginny and our rustic retreat. Running from where I had been let out of the car, up the stone steps to our cabin, I pulled off my tie and stripped off my shirt as I went, anticipating about fourteen hours of living and breathing in the beauty of that Ozark place. As I approached, Ginny opened the door, big-eyed and with a broomstick in her hand. I entered, somewhat perplexed at this greeting, and she wilted into my arms, almost whimpering, "Let's move back to the fort." Then I heard the story of her stressful day.

Soon after I had left for work, Ginny, always a morning person, had cleared up and washed our breakfast dishes, made our bed, bathed, and dressed in something light for the warm June day ahead. The morning was such a beautiful one that she decided, before unpacking some more of our belongings, she would step out for an early stroll along the trail by the river. As she opened the door to step down onto the limestone slab that served as the first of the steps that led around the cabin to the crushed rock roadway at the front, she paused. In an instant she saw it, before it slithered into a small opening under the cabin—an enormous (they grow to be as long as forty inches), fat copperhead snake. Like its cousin, the water moccasin, the copperhead was poisonous.

Her first reaction had been to slam the door shut and retreat into the kitchen. Knowing the snake had disappeared under the house, she climbed onto a chair and from there surveyed the kitchen—its board floor, mostly covered with Congoleum and a worn rug—wondering if there were any holes in the corners or where the wall and floor met that were big enough for a snake to enter. After all, she recalled ruefully, this was a crudely built, rustic cabin. Ginny felt this type of construction left us terribly exposed to all kinds of wild, creepy things that might choose to move in with us.

Cautiously, she moved, with broom in hand, throughout the cabin and searched out its corners, overhead rafters, and under the furniture, choosing not to look into the drawers just then.

After searching the two rooms and the screened porch and finding no intruders, she picked her way hurriedly down the steps to the crushed rock drive and made her determined way to the main lodge and the landlord of the place. Her terror had turned to indignation.

As a result of Ginny's complaint to the landlord, he had come back with her and spent a good share of the day removing stored lumber from the sheltered slope beneath the cabin, cleaning up brush and other potential hiding places for nearby snakes, and was even persuaded to check the soundness of the cabin itself against the invasion of unwanted reptiles.

Supper, as I recall, was late that night, and, as we prepared it together, I tried lamely to point out the advantages of living like this. Little by little (with a setback now and then, like when I pointed out that, with snakes in the house, we wouldn't have mice—and Ginny assured me that we wouldn't have her either), we began to recapture the peaceful ambiance of the place we had first experienced earlier that spring.

Our introduction to that place in the Ozarks known as Possum Lodge had taken place on a rainy, late afternoon early in that spring of 1944 after Perry Stucker had invited us to visit him and his wife, Alma, who were acting as caretakers of the place while the owners were gone for the winter. He warned us that it was not modern, meaning it had no indoor plumbing. This, of course, was familiar to me, having grown up on a farm with the same conditions, but for Ginny, it was something new.

Possum Lodge consisted of a main house called the Lodge, a cluster of three or four one-room cabins, some outbuildings used as bunkhouses, and a roofed but open-air shelter known as the Pavilion. This group of rustic buildings was at the end of a long country lane that wound and undulated its way for about a mile along a portion of the Big Piney River before ending at the Lodge. This lane, parallel to the river, was at the base of a long limestone bluff or escarpment that was also parallel to the river. About a quarter mile from the Lodge, the lane ran past a group of three more cabins; their fronts were supported by posts and faced the lane and the river. The back of each of the cabins rested against the steep slope of the limestone bluff that rose up behind them. To reach the entrance of any of these, it was necessary to walk up the slope on stone steps. The largest of the three, the one farthest from the Lodge but the first one encountered on the lane from the main road, had its entrance door on the high or bluff side. These three cabins shared a rowboat, a pump, and a "modern" WPA (Works Progress Administration) privy.

Beyond this group of cabins farthest from Possum Lodge, the lane left the river, ran along a hayfield, past the farmstead of people by the name of Fields, and wound up a steep climb to the graveled main road at the top of the ridge behind the limestone bluff.

Perry Stucker was a romantic with a theatrical sense. When he drove Ginny and me out that Friday afternoon, he let us out on the high gravel road and pointed out a footpath through the dripping foliage of that rainy evening, instructing us to wind our way down a steep wooded ravine toward Possum Lodge, which was not visible from our starting point. Perry explained that this was the only way to be properly introduced to this magical, rustic place. He said that his wife would be coming up the path from the other direction to meet us.

Ginny and I entered into the spirit of the adventure for which Perry was priming us, and as his car sped off down the wet gravel road so that he would be at the Lodge to greet us on our arrival, Ginny and I struck off, picking our way down the footpath he had indicated.

Perry was right. This *was* the way to get our first impression of Possum Lodge. Because the season was early spring, the foliage was not yet full blown but was lacy and green against the wet, black branches and trunks of the trees and shrubs. As we followed the path down toward the river, the green slopes of the ravine were dotted with cloudlike patches of white—the dogwood blossoms. Here and there among the layer of last year's leaves and patches of emerging green grass along the footpath were early spring flowers; the ones I recognized were violets. The moist air was fragrant with the freshness of new growth and the nutty smell of decaying leaves and twigs especially peculiar to oak forests.

Ginny's eyes sparkled with the excitement and wonder of our adventure; she had a childlike joy at the anticipation of surprises, which I found infectious. After about five minutes of our descent on the winding, sometimes slippery, path, brushing through the dripping foliage in our army slickers, we heard a "yoohoo" and, looking across the wooded ravine to the spot from which the call had come, we spotted Perry's wife, Alma, beckoning us.

With Alma's guidance, we made our way to her side of the ravine and, before long, had descended through more dripping trees to Possum Lodge. Darkness was fast falling in that tree-shaded place beside the river on that gray, rainy evening. Perry had a wood fire going in the stone fireplace in the Pavilion. Penny and Russ Wulff, who lived in one of the small, one-room cabins, were also there to greet us.

We had a joyous supper around the fire that evening, talking and singing until our eyelids grew heavy. Ginny and I were shown to our bed, a mattress made up with fresh sheets and blankets under the attic eaves. It was pleasant going to sleep in one another's arms that night with the sound of a steady spring rain on the sloping shingled roof over our heads and the gurgle of the Big Piney River over the rapids nearby.

The following letters tell something of our new home in the Ozarks. On June 20, I wrote to Dean a description of our place at Possum Lodge, to which we had just moved on the 17th:

> We like our new home very much. It definitely is not on the fancy side. The furniture is ill-matched and anything but modern. The cabin itself is build of hard wood and rough boards at that. There is a wallboard lining on the walls; however, one can see the bare rafters or the underside of the roof overhead. It has two large rooms and a large screened-in porch running the full length of the cabin. We have one oil lamp and two large candles at present for our illumination. We asked the folks if they would send us the old mantel lamp. So far, we have only four folding chairs, but we bought an arm chair from Glaubes for $1.00, and our landlord said he'd try to get us a rocking chair. Then perhaps with a little ambition, scrap lumber, and time, I could build a stool or two and Ginny could cover them. Our home is rather rough and unimproved, but it has great possibilities.
>
> The river is only a few feet in front of the cabin and separated from us by a narrow lane and a grassy bank shaded by great trees—elm, sycamore, and maple. . . . We get our eggs and milk fresh daily from a farmer, Mr. Fields, just up the road about three quarters of a mile from us. They are nice people. So are the Perkins, our landlords. We like them, we like our cabin, I like Ginny, and Ginny likes me, so in our own limited little sphere, all is right with the world.
>
> The next chance you get, you must come see us—we have a real bed for you to sleep in now.

Following is a post card Ginny wrote to Dean, in Bonham, Texas, from our Possum Lodge cabin soon after moving there. It shows how she entered into the spirit of our new lifestyle.

Sat. night
June 24, 1944

Dear Dean,
Bob and I are both writing by candle light. We are sitting across from each other at the table on our screened-in porch. The bugs are really enjoying themselves around the light and us. We're really pioneers. I do the "writin." Pappy sends his mark.

Here a large X was scrawled in the middle of the card, and beside it she wrote:

He's kind of sloppy with the pen. But he's larnin' fast. Ah reckon it's a gittin' kinda late. Pappy had his shootin' arn down t'day ahuntin' skunks. We're thinkin' of takin' a bath tomorry. We sure hate thet. I'll sure have some time hog-tyin' Pappy down. Write soon.
Love,
GINNY

In spite of its near primitiveness, we found that rough-board cabin to be a cozy home. Besides our kerosene cookstove, we had an ice chest, a cake of ice needing replacement every two or three days, an old-fashioned kitchen cabinet, and a once tall chest of drawers, the drawers now replaced with shelves for dish storage. There were two double beds—one in the bedroom, along with a dresser, and the other on the porch. Also on the porch was a long table, in addition to a smaller one in the kitchen.

While in that cabin, our third home thus far, we bought two round five-gallon tinned canisters with tight-fitting lids, in which we stored our flour, sugar, and other cooking ingredients we wished to keep dry and free from invading bugs. Those tin canisters moved with us through the rest of our years of keeping house, and one of them ended up finally in the attic on the farm.

A few nights after we had settled into our cabin at Possum Lodge, we experienced another initiation to that unique world.
The June day had been unbearably hot and humid. As evening came on, not a breath of air was stirring in our sheltered place between the tree-lined river and the limestone bluffs rising behind us. The leaves of the great sycamores, maples, and elms along the

river bank hung motionless, and our breath seemed to remain close around our faces in suffocating clouds to be drawn back in with the next inhalation.

After the supper dishes had been washed and put away, and our living room had been "rid up," as Ginny termed it, we prepared to enjoy our evening as best we could. The still, sultry air made our usual place of relaxation along the river, or even a quiet boat ride, unthinkable because of the biting insects that thrived in such weather conditions. Instead, we elected to try finding comfort within our screened cabin. We sat at the table, Ginny sewing on some dish towels while I read aloud from the library book we were currently enjoying, all the while mopping our brows and drinking iced tea.

Eventually, the encroaching darkness made it necessary to light the kerosene lamp. As the shades of night enveloped our cabin more completely, tiny gnats wriggled their way through the wire mesh of the screens on the open windows and zinged around the hot glass chimney of the lamp in maddening, suicidal spirals, getting into our faces, eyes, ears, and nostrils, before finally succumbing to the heat of the lamp and falling into a growing heap at its base.

Leaving the sewing and reading for another, more comfortable time, we retreated to the darkness of the screened porch. In the stagnant night air, we could mop our brows in relative comfort and engage in quiet talk. We soon became aware of the concert being performed by the chorus of summer night creatures: frogs, katydids, crickets, tree-toads, and the deep base "c'thump" of the bullfrogs. High overhead in the darkness was the occasional cry of the night hawk, feasting in its aerial acrobatics on the myriad flying night insects in the hot June night.

Competing with the great numbers of fireflies flashing their little starlike lights back and forth over the lowland meadows, along the river to the north of us, we noticed, over and beyond the trees to the south, lightning flashes in a cloud bank.

A thunderstorm, on such a night as this, was a hopeful prospect for cooling relief, so we promptly removed ourselves from our concert seats around the long table at the north end of the porch and went to the guest bed at the south end, where, lying propped on our elbows, we could watch with fascination the spectacle of an approaching storm.

The lightning played almost continuously throughout that magnificent cloud mass, boiling up thousands of feet into the sky. The flashes, buried deep within, revealed first one and then another facet of that massive cloud, displaying different shapes, colors, and intensities of light. But so deep within that turbulent mass of vapors were the electrical discharges that we could not see the jagged lightning bolts of the frightful storm.

The electrical show entertained us for a long time. Eventually, we were able to hear faint rumblings. This was an indication that, however slowly, the great summer storm was moving our way. There was a childlike thrill in this knowledge, and, in spite of the oppressive heat, we snuggled closer together.

The storm now seemed to be stalled and not coming our way after all, so we decided to go to bed and let it carry on by itself. We made our bedtime trip to the privy, locked the door, put out the light, and got into our night clothes. With the needless sheet and blanket draped over the footboard, we spread out as much as two people can on a standard-sized bed and were both sound asleep in moments.

A tremendous explosion of sound jolted us both awake, and we went scrambling for the covers, pulling them up around us. Immediately following was another bright flash and loud booming thunder that echoed off the limestone cliffs above us in long, drawn-out reverberations. Then came another and another until it seemed that perhaps the cliffs above us were knocked loose and were tumbling down to crush us in our bed. We lay there, locked in one another's arms, feeling helpless and vulnerable. That distant storm we had found so beautiful, so mysterious and enjoyable an hour or so before had finally arrived, and we were now in the depths of one of the most violent thunderstorms I have ever experienced. The rain pouring down upon our roof was a torrent, as if we were under a waterfall, and evoked visions of our being washed away in a flash flood. It certainly was not the friendly patter of rain on the roof of our attic room that we had been treated to as guests at Possum Lodge several weeks earlier.

At Possum Lodge there also were beautiful summer days, especially after a storm, when the air was fresh and dry, fluffy white clouds floated quietly in a deep blue sky, and the sunlight was hot, but the shadows sharp-edged and cool.

On such days, or evenings after work, it was a wonderful place to be. Sometimes Ginny and I would walk up the graveled lane to the Fields', at whose place we bought our eggs and milk and spent some time in neighborly chatter. Or we would walk the quarter mile or so in the other direction to the main lodge. The couple living in the lodge or main house, our landlords, Mr. Perkins and his wife, kept goats and ducks that had free rein and were almost like pets to all of us. The goats, true to their nature, loved to climb the precipitous escarpment behind the cabins and were often seen standing on the roofs of some of the sheds that fitted up against it.

Ginny and I especially enjoyed the commonly shared boat, often in the company of our fellow tenants, but most often by ourselves. When we went bathing or fishing in the river, it was from the boat out in the middle of the stream. Sometimes we took the boat the quarter mile or so to the little store that sat, just a few rods from the river, alongside the paved highway—U.S. Route 66.

> Day Room
> Med. Det. Sta. Hosp.
> Ft. Leonard Wood, Mo.
> July 2, 1944

Dear Folks,

First, I want to thank you all for the birthday present. You couldn't have sent a more welcome gift than that blanket—even in this weather, for down where we are the nights get quite cool, even chilly. And it's so soft and nice. I asked Ginny if she didn't wish she had one, too. But I told her that if she'd be good, I'd share it with her.

Yesterday was a very happy birthday. I told Ginny I felt like a kid again. I think it was the most outstanding one I've had since we were little at home and you always made such a fuss over it.

Ginny forgot about it until after we got to work, and then she came back to my department and sneaked me a birthday kiss with her apologies.

All the things you sent came yesterday, including the blanket. So when 4:30 came, we gathered our packages together and went home—stopping on the way at the store,

Ginny relaxing beside the Big Piney River at Possum Lodge, summer 1944, the most idyllic period of our marriage.

Ginny and Bob (in lab gowns) with Dean at Ft. Leonard Wood, 1944.

where Ginny bought some groceries, including a cake. (We have no oven as yet.)

Ginny suggested we not open any of the packages until we sat down to supper so, while I was getting the water from the well, emptying the swill pail, and doing a few other chores (putting a partition in the knife-and-fork drawer), Ginny was flying around getting supper and busy in the bedroom, rattling paper and being mysterious.

We sat down to a supper that is one of my favorites: raw-fried potatoes; fried eggs; spaghetti with tomato sauce; raw, sliced tomatoes; bread and butter with jelly; and raspberry-flavored Kool-Aid.

In the center of the table was the birthday cake in which there were seven candles (for 27) which Ginny had painstakingly made by hand Friday evening out of the melted remains of an old candle. She had all the packages piled on the floor beside me. Between mouthfuls of supper, I opened them. We saved for last the two packages containing our things from home we had asked you to send. I had Ginny open them. It was like Christmas and a lot of fun.

Ginny had sent for an art book on lettering (one I'd once expressed a desire for), but it had not arrived, so what did she do but sneak off to the PX to do some last minute shopping. The result was that, as I ate and unwrapped packages, there were two pair of socks, two t-shirts, and swimming trunks that can also be worn as leisure shorts.

Ginny, bless her heart, has the ability to make any occasion special by her wholehearted involvement and infectious enthusiasm. She's all I ever dreamed of in a wife. I can see our home will be filled with fun family celebrations. We noted that this was the first birthday in our new family. Hers will be the next on August nineteenth, and our little one's will be the third that we'll celebrate.

Ginny lit the seven candles and we made a wish that was more of a prayer. Ginny sang "Happy Birthday" to me, and then I blew them out with one huff.

The cake was very good, for a bought one. We finished it this morning for breakfast.

Thank you very much for sending the mantel lamp, but I didn't intend for you to send the *good one*—I meant the metal one. However, now that you did, I'm glad for it certainly looks nice, and it's the pride of Possum Lodge. And what a difference it makes in light. Ginny is very pleased with it. And the rug you sent added to my birthday festivity. Ginny put it right

down by our bed for us to step onto when we get up—the
floor gets pretty cool for bare feet.

Are those really feed sacks you sent? They look more like
muslin one buys in a store. Ginny is anxious to get to work on
them, making curtains for our dish cabinet and wash stand.
We heard yesterday that the Perkins (our landlords) were
finally able to get some material and are making curtains for
the windows. But if they aren't, we'll have enough material
from the feed sacks, from the looks of it, to make them ourselves. You sent so much we feel maybe you could have used
it for yourselves.

You had everything packed so carefully and complete with
penciled instructions for the lamp.

Later in the evening we had Perry and Mrs. Stucker over
for coffee and some of our cake. They brought a big pitcher of
iced Kool Aid.

I'd like to take Ginny to someplace nice in St. Louis or
someplace soon where we could go places and do things
before she gets "weighted down" and won't want to be out in
public much.

This is our schedule for now: The alarm goes off at 5:00
A.M. We aim to get up shortly after and put on the coffee and
heat water for washing and shaving; crawl back into bed again
to take off the chill; then up again. I shave while Ginny gets
breakfast. I also do the morning chores like getting water from
the well and taking our "old white cow out to pasture."
(That's what we call a certain useful article that is needed
when modern indoor plumbing is lacking.)

Then we eat breakfast, "rid" the table and straighten
things up in general before leaving about 6:40 with Perry
Stucker.

Ginny packs our lunch, which we eat together at F-8,
Fliegel's studio, where I'm doing the blood cell paintings. We
usually eat our suppers at the medical detachment mess hall;
she eats where the other civilians eat, and I, of course, with
the other GIs in our usual place.

We meet at 5:00 and go home to spend the evening in
various ways and then take our sponge baths and to bed by
10:00, if possible.

                              Love,
                              BOB

Then a week later I wrote:

Sunday night
At home in the Ozarks

Dear Folks,

This has been a very rushed and hectic week—not enough
time for anything.

Dean sent two enormous bath towels for my birthday—
one for each of us. We're writing him tonight to thank him.

We had lots of things planned for today but hardly managed any of them—letter writing being one. About 2:00 P.M.
Harry Evans, a fellow lab technician, and his wife and another
soldier couple drove out to go swimming with us. They were
here over two hours. After they left, Ginny was just starting
to prepare supper when the newlyweds, Mr. and Mrs. T-5
Springer (he's a co-worker in the lab), came in, bringing the
supper with them—spaghetti with chopped meat, potato salad,
bread and butter sandwiches, cookies frosted with cherries on
them. Ginny had fried potatoes and chocolate cake and Kool
Aid, chilled with ice cubes Springers had brought along.

After they left, Ginny and I took a boat ride to cool off.
Later, Russ and Penny and Russ's mother, who had ridden
down with Penny when she brought the car Saturday, came in
for a chat and some coffee.

Up until about noon, Ginny and I had spent the time
variously, sleeping late, eating breakfast, watering and weeding
our tomatoes and napping.

Last night Ginny and I stood up for Springers at their
wedding. It was in the same chapel and at the same time as
ours was last fall. It brought back pleasant memories for
Ginny and me. Perry brought them and us home (them to
their cabin) and then Penny and Russ and Springers and
Ginny and I went to a place up the road a way for supper.

Ginny has been hearing unpleasant tales about the hospitals around here in the way they treat soldiers' wives. She
thinks she'd like to go to Hampton to have our baby. What do
you think of that idea? The facilities there are pretty good,
aren't they? She thought, with Aunt Lavina working as lab
technician in the hospital there, that would make it nicer, too.
Perhaps she'd go up there in October and then after the birth,
when they're both O.K. to travel, they could come back.

Ginny would like to go to Detroit, but thinks maybe the
hospitals there might be like around here, with so many service people around there. She thinks Hampton would be more
friendly. This was entirely Ginny's idea, but, needless to say, I

liked the thought a lot. I would like having her nearby, but wouldn't want to risk her getting wrong treatment or neglect when the baby came.

There is only one thing, though, that Ginny is hesitant about—She's afraid she'll be a bother there at home. We'll pay for the board and trouble—we'd want to do that.

Mom wrote right back, *"The idea!!! 'Pay for board and trouble'!!"* And then went on to say how happy they would be to have Ginny come there to have the baby. Of course, I wasn't surprised at their reaction, and plans proceeded along those lines.

Laboratory
July 16, 1944

Dear Mom,

This will be a late birthday greeting, and I'm sorry. It's the same old story—a combination of putting off and being busy.

I was on lab emergency last night so Ginny stayed in with me all night.

At ten this morning we will be relieved and go home by way of thumb. (Ginny never hitchhiked until she married me.)

I'm on temporary duty, helping letter a big batch of signs for a conference of generals that is to be here the latter part of July. Fliegel and I are working on them in his studio in F-8. It's rather fun for a change, from lab work.

Ginny picked out a gift for you at the PX yesterday while I was busy.

I'm afraid this isn't much of a birthday letter, but it will have to do for now. May you have many, many happy returns.

With lots of love from
both of us,
BOB

An added note from Ginny:

Happy birthday, Mom. Will be thinking of you on July 17.
Your present, as well as the greeting, will be late. I guess I'm starting to take after Bob!

Love,
GINNY

Ginny felt inadequate in her culinary abilities. When she had lived with Laura's family in Detroit, she had not been encouraged to do any cooking or baking. As Laura explained to me in later years, because Jean's severe handicap made it impossible for her to take part in any such activity, Laura had not wanted to make her feel any more excluded from life than she already did. Laura felt that to pass on to Ginny her cooking and baking skills (which were legendary in the family) while Jean, close to Ginny's age, was not able to participate, would cause just that much more hurt to one as sensitive as Jean. Thus, Ginny brought to our marriage a wealth of recipes and cookbooks, but no practical kitchen experience.

During her brief stint at homemaking in our Richland apartment, I thought Ginny had done very well in preparing tasty meals. But she was unconvinced. So when we set up housekeeping in the rustic cabin at Possum Lodge, she renewed her endeavors into the world of cookery with a vengeance. Her cookstove, furnished with the cabin, was a four-burner kerosene stove without an oven. Ginny, who had already dealt with our landlord in the snake episode, succeeded in having him provide an oven for the stove. It was a portable one set on top of the stove over two of the burners. She immediately studied the instruction booklet that came with the new oven, and when I came home the first night, she had it mastered. Our supper included a chocolate pie, complete with a beautiful meringue topping. Ginny thought it a failure—too much chocolate—but with my taste for strong chocolate, I thought it the best chocolate pie I'd ever eaten.

Ginny produced many good meals on that kerosene stove and from that oven. Especially pleasing to me was being greeted upon my return from work by the homelike aroma of fresh baked bread (along with Ginny's loving arms and welcoming kiss).

We had cooperative meals with Penny and Russ, pooling our ration stamps and using Ginny's new oven, after they had moved from their small cabin near the main lodge at the end of the trail and had taken the cabin next to ours. So the four of us neighbored often, as we also did with Perry and Alma Stucker, who had moved to the third cabin in our cluster after the landlord and his wife had returned from their winter home and reclaimed the lodge.

Later in the summer, Perry got his shipping orders to another post, as was always happening in the military, and we said our good-byes to the Stuckers. That particular farewell was especially poignant for us, because Perry and Alma had been instrumental in helping us discover that special bit of the Ozarks.

More letters describe our days at Possum Lodge and Ginny's disdain for the Army brass's way of doing things:

Ft. Leonard Wood, Mo.
July 25, 1944

Dear folks,
    Bob just left for his workshop (Fliegel's studio at F-8). He likes working on something like that, but if only he could get down to business and do something worthwhile instead of making a lot of foolish signs for a bunch of "star gazers" (generals very conscious of one another's rank), he would feel better. And now these "star gazers" are making the guys to stay on the post Wed., Thur., and Fri. nights. I would like to thank you for sending our dishes. We're so proud of them. The Wulffs and we went together on our Sunday meal. I set the table with our new dishes. They made our table look very ritzy.
    We had a surprise Sunday afternoon. Bob was visiting with the neighbors, and I was in the kitchen fixing dinner. All at once, I had the funniest feeling. (I suppose you can guess.) I called Bob to come quickly. We watched my tummy with great fascination as our wee one fluttered from within. It certainly was an experience!

Evening
    I'm lying on the bed. I'm trying to get Bob to do a cartoon of his GI shoes, entitled, "The Original GIs."
    We were watching "it" moving around again. It certainly gives us a funny feeling.
    This is our last night together until Saturday night—all for no reason at all. Just a selfish desire of a few "star gazers."
    Well, I must close now. Bob wants to add a few lines. By the way, the salt and pepper shakers landed safely. Thanks. It surely meant a lot to us to receive all those things of ours.

Love,
GINNY

The very next night, after the above letter, Ginny wrote the

following, showing just how uncertain our existence was during
those times:

> Possum Lodge, Mo.
> Wed. night
> July 26, 1944

Dear folks,

Just a brief note. Our stuff will be coming back again. Bob
is being transferred to Camp Barkley, Texas, the first of next
week. I probably will go to Detroit until after he makes arrangements for me to be with him.

The way things are now, I have a feeling this is the last
we'll be together for some time. He doesn't know a thing
about the camp there.

Well, I must close now. I'll probably see you in the fall.

> Love,
> GINNY

P.S. There's a small chance I may go with him. I have my
fingers crossed.

> Possum Lodge, Mo.
> Sunday, July 30, 1944

Dear folks,

We've been busy all day packing. We have so much to do
that this will just be a note. Will you please deposit this money
in the bank for us? I'll write when I get to Detroit.

> Love,
> GINNY

> Ft. Leonard Wood, Mo.
> Monday morning
> July 31, 1944

Dear folks,

I'm at the lab, all set to leave for Detroit, *if we go.* I'll tell
you the story from the beginning:

Wednesday Bob was on the shipping list to go the following Monday (which is today). A large group of generals were
here inspecting the fort. It seemed that post headquarters had
overestimated the strength of the hospital; consequently, a
large load of non-coms were being sent out to bring the quota
down. General Kirk, the head surgeon from Washington,
didn't realize the actual strength of the hospital. When he

found out that so many technicians were being sent out, he
blew up and immediately wired Omaha.

In the meantime, we had packed everything. Friday we
were told that everything was suspended for a while.

So we unpacked. The following evening we were told that
they *would* have to go after all and *would* have to leave on
Monday unless the orders came back from Omaha to rescind
the first. They might have to go all the way to Texas and then
have to come back, if the orders *were* rescinded. So Sunday we
spent all day packing again. This morning we came to the fort
all ready to leave—both of us.

But now the orders have been held up until Wednesday.
So in the meantime we'll be living out of boxes. We told
everyone at Possum Lodge to help themselves to our groceries. But as long as we have to wait, there is hope. We could
never find a place as nice as Possum Lodge.

For two days, Friday and Saturday, we honeymooned—
just swimming, boating, fishing and taking it easy. But yesterday (Sunday) we *really* worked.

We have our fingers crossed. Will write later.

Love,
GINNY

A few days later, the disruption of the Army orders, counter
orders, and general fouled-up mess had apparently subsided and
we'd settled back into the routine of extracting the most we could
out of each day—one day at a time.

Regional Station Hosp.
Ft. Leonard Wood, Mo
Aug. 4, 1944
Morning, on CQ

Dear Mom, Dad, and Dan,

I'm still on duty as CQ, will go off duty in about an hour
and won't have to worry about this detail again for a few
weeks. I'm getting so I don't mind holding reveille any
more—there's really nothing much to it anyway. The officer of
the day didn't even show up today so I didn't waste much time
with formalities.

We would like having you come visit us very much. Now
that Ginny is home all day (not working at the lab) it would
be extra nice having you. I'm sure you'd like it here.

The other evening I went home (the first Ginny had been

home all day since we heard we were probably going to stay
here) to find Ginny all prettied up (sweet as honey) and the
house tidy and cozy looking and a good supper waiting.

We both had lots to talk about. She had finished making
the curtains for the washstand and dish cabinet out of the
muslin you had sent.

Since I was on CQ last night, Ginny came in with me
yesterday and spent the day with me at F-8 where I'm doing
some more art work for the lab. Last night she stayed with
Glaubes again. I'm glad there is some place she can stay when
I'm on emergency so that she won't have to stay out there
alone at night.

The work I'm doing is in line with what I've been wanting
to do ever since coming to the lab. I have already painted (in
oils) two panels showing normal white blood cells. The captain
liked them and now wants me to paint six more panels showing blood cells in disease. At Ginny's suggestion he is going to
loan us his personal microscope so that Ginny can spend some
time during the day at home looking over blood slides and
picking out typical cells for me to paint. That will help me a
lot and save a lot of time for me to do straight painting. She
knows the cells better than I do—in fact, she's really sharp at
them.

Ken Nishi, the artist, came over to see us at F-8 yesterday
and brought some more art supplies. He's assigned to special
services and has charge of all kinds of interesting things like
that. He talked of bringing some more for the cartoons I'm to
do. I told you, didn't I, or perhaps Ginny did, about the cartoons I am doing for the orientation centers here on the post.
That, too, is through Nishi.

They have centers at the different service clubs on the
post, where displays are set up and changed every two weeks.
The displays consist of maps, photos, and charts and posters.
Maybe one time it will be on China and another time on
another country—current events and war news. Well, they
thought it would be nice to have some cartoons along with the
other stuff. I made one (Private Paddlefoot) and submitted it.
Ken liked it and so did the officers he works with. I'm doing
another one this weekend. Ginny is very interested in my work
and is always making suggestions and helping out in one way
or another.

We, especially Ginny, liked sharing our country life with
others. One weekend Ken Nishi and his wife Suki were our

weekend guests. Their visit was a particularly pleasant time, as they, like we, enjoyed the wildness of the place and found pleasure in simple things, especially boating and swimming.

Another happy weekend, Dean stopped off on his way home to Iowa from Texas. It was a pleasant family time for us, an opportunity for Dean and Ginny to further a brother-and-sister relationship that they maintained over the years. Dean especially enjoyed the homey atmosphere Ginny created in our Ozark cabin (something that was wistfully appreciated by those people displaced by the war during those years).

Years later, when Dean visited Ginny in her final infirmity, he greeted her in his usual jovial way, and just for an instant, there was a flicker in her expression that suggested the way she used to respond to him.

The following letters reflect something of our life at Possum Lodge as the summer wore on. Ginny had exercised her prerogative as a civilian and had quit her job at the lab, and our thoughts became more occupied with what lay ahead. .

Possum Lodge, Mo.
Aug. 26, 1944

Dear folks,
    We've certainly been having plenty of rain. The river is so muddy that it is impossible to use our "bathtub" anymore. Consequently, we are planning to bathe in a little round tub (wash tub) every Saturday night. The Wulffs also use the tub.
    Am I an early bird! I ordered the bulk of our Christmas presents from Spiegels yesterday. Bob thought it was too early. But we're going to have to get all that done as soon as possible. I had put some money away from the pay I had received last month, so we used that.

At the bottom of the second page of Ginny's letter, I penned a few lines, starting out with a remark about her growing pregnant condition:

Dear folks,
    Ginny left me about as much room here as she does on the bed.

One night after my regular shift at the lab had ended, I sent word home with those going to Possum Lodge, letting Ginny know that I had to work late and that she was not to worry for I would catch a ride with someone later in the evening.

When I was free to leave the lab, my available ride turned out to be going, not along the gravel road on our side of the river, but rather on the paved highway that ran along the other side toward St. Louis. As a result, I was let out at the country store across and down the river from Possum Lodge. Even though it was summer, the hour was late enough that darkness had already settled in. As the taillights of the car that had given me the ride disappeared down the highway, I walked past the little country store, where Ginny and I sometimes shopped, and started on the trail that led under the dusky canopy of trees to the edge of the river.

At the ford, the spot where the trail entered the river, I slipped off my shoes and socks and rolled up the legs of my khakis to wade across. I had gone only a few steps, however, when I realized that the water was so deep that I could not roll my pant legs high enough to keep them dry. So I retreated to the packed gravel shore and removed my trousers, careful not to spill out my wallet and loose change, then waded back into the river and crossed to the other side.

Because there was no traffic along this seldom-used trail and no one was likely to see me in my semi-dressed condition, I continued on my way, carrying my pants, socks, and shoes, thus allowing my feet and legs to air dry.

It was a warm summer night. With only the stars for light, I was barely able to see in the darkness. The only sounds that accompanied the scuffing of my bare feet on the dusty trail were an occasional car on the highway I had just left, the quiet murmur of the river I had just crossed, the chorus of night insects, and the distant baying of a hound. Now and then the rhythmic beat of my footsteps on the road was broken when I stepped on a sharp pebble. I chuckled to myself at the spectacle I made going home in this manner, dressed only in shirt, tie, cap, and underwear. By simply slipping on my shoes, I could have easily met the criteria set forth at the doors of restaurants nowadays, warning: "No shirt, no shoes, no service." Soon I was able to see the dim, yellow glow of a kerosene lamp flickering from the distant, shadowy area at the base of the limestone bluffs that rose against the western star-lit sky. There stood the three furthest out cabins of Possum Lodge. I knew that the light I saw was from the one on the end—our home—where Ginny was waiting for me. As it had always been, the closer I got to home and to Ginny, the faster I was impelled along, as if by the magnetic pull of her warm love.

When Ginny opened the door in response to our coded knock and saw me standing there with my shoes, socks, and pants in my hands, she gave a momentary look of "You were *working* late?" At my explanation she burst into her merry laugh and threw her arms around my neck. I was home safe.

As the summer season began to blend into autumn, bringing about inevitable change, just as surely, the time moved closer to our having to leave that place of our halcyon days. Knowing that, we tried to extract all we could from the bittersweet time that was left to us there. We were about to enter another phase of our marriage—a time of being apart.

We, in our naiveté, thought that we could have *another* Possum Lodge some day in the far distant future—when there would be again just the two of us to live simply in the warmth and fullness of our love. But that was not to be.

Of course, we didn't realize it then, but after leaving that place in the Ozarks (which, despite our good intentions, we would not revisit), never again would our beautiful relationship be quite the same. For as our family of two became three, then four, five, and six, and all the pressures of making a living and dealing with the concerns of family and community mounted, never again would Ginny and I be able to enjoy the closeness we had there in that first year, in the freshness and sweetness of our love—never again, that is, except in brief, stolen moments, such as when our eyes met in a silent signal across a crowded room; or a surreptitious hand squeeze; or an intimate word of assurance whispered in an ear; or our private times, in one another's arms.

Thus, after a brief moment of tenderness and beauty, the petals of the blossom of our love fell from the branch to be replaced by the growing fruit from that blossom. As the years were to pass, exposing our love to storms, as well as sunshine, it was to deepen and mature. Ginny and I were truly fortunate to have a marriage sustained by a love able to withstand the exigencies of life and become richer in it.

On Friday, September 29, 1944, in late afternoon, with the sun about to descend behind the wooded escarpment of Possum Lodge, Dad, Mom, and Grandma Artley, in Grandma's 1934 Airflow Chrysler, pulled up in front of our cabin. Following the map and instructions we had sent them, they had come to take Ginny home to have our baby.

After knocking, peering through the screen door, and calling out, "Anybody home?" with no reply, they went back to sit in the car to wait, the open door suggesting that those absent would soon be back.

Presently, as they sat quietly commenting on the surroundings, there came into view, rising up over the small hill in the lane, first a large straw hat, then a face, then a very pregnant barefoot woman beneath that face and straw hat. Trailing along behind her, as she approached the car in the lane, were four or five goats and behind them a string of ducks in single file, waddling as if mimicking their human leader.

Later that evening, and for years thereafter, Dad delighted in telling, to Ginny's feigned disgust, about their arrival in the Ozarks to be met by "this hillbilly" and her entourage.

The following night our friends at Possum Lodge and the lab had arranged a farewell party for Ginny. Ration points were pooled for steaks that were grilled over an open fire and eaten with all the other picnic goodies and drinks furnished by those throwing the party.

It was a bittersweet occasion for all of us, but especially for Ginny, who realized that this would be the last time she would see most of those people who had been so much a part of our lives for the past year and more. The beams of a full moon reflected off the quiet surface of the Big Piney, and the limestone bluffs, towering above us, echoed our voices as we sang familiar old songs and talked and laughed around the campfire, trying to smother the sadness that lurked among us.

My folks enjoyed the occasion very much, meeting and visiting with those whose names they had come to know through our letters.

The next morning, with the car loaded down and a big wooden shipping crate left in the middle of our kitchen for our friend, Russ, to haul to the freight depot for us, we headed north toward Iowa and home.

I had been given a seven-day furlough so that I might accompany Ginny and help her get settled. Mom, Ginny, and I were in the back seat of Grandma's car. Ginny and I, side by side, were choked with sadness at the thought of being apart and leaving this place and all it had meant to us. But we had *hope* for the future, and we talked about that.

How different it was forty-some years later, when, accompanied by our two grown sons, Rob and Steve, in Rob's van, Ginny and I again sat side by side, holding hands, on our way to get her settled into the Alzheimer's unit at Iowa Veterans Home in Marshalltown. This time there was *no hope* for the future to assuage our grief at being apart.

A LIFE APART

It was a great comfort to know that, though Ginny and I could not be together, she would be living at the farm with my family. It would make the uncertain times ahead much easier to bear, knowing that my loved ones were concentrated there at the center of my universe. And knowing that it was Ginny's idea, originated without any prompting from me, made it all the better. In retrospect, I suspect she most probably read my heart. For she, throughout our years together, has continually demonstrated her generous concern for me and perceived my needs, many times before I was aware of them myself. She could, as she said, "read me like a book"—which was a rather disturbing thought at times.

It was heartwarming, also, to know that my folks had welcomed Ginny so completely with open, loving hearts, not only into the family but also into their home. Dad had arranged to have a new furnace installed so that the upstairs might be warm for their new daughter and her expected baby. And Ginny, by her very nature, was to inject a whole new life into the old farm that until then had been predominantly a male world. As Dad expressed it, the clothesline had taken on a different look on wash day—with so many female garments flapping in the breeze.

Having grown up in western Pennsylvania and Detroit, where streets and roads are not laid out on a grid as they are in north central Iowa, Ginny was completely mystified by the natives' constant reference to the points of the compass when giving directions. Soon after settling into her new life on the farm, Mom asked her to get something out of the east drawer of the kitchen cupboard. Not wanting to appear dumb, Ginny did not ask which drawer was the east one; instead, she went into the kitchen and looked around. There was only one built-in cupboard. And there were only three drawers in it. She reasoned, to herself, that the east drawer would have to be one of the two end ones. As she faced the cupboard, she knew that the drawer on her right was the utensil drawer, so it must be the one on the other end near the window. Then she remembered that the sun's morning rays shone through that window, and because the sun came up in the east (even here in Iowa, she presumed) . . . she pulled out the drawer and, eureka! There was the item Mom had asked for.

From then on, that east cupboard drawer became the reference point from which Ginny oriented herself as she became acquainted with her new surroundings.

The few days of my furlough sped by all too quickly. Besides getting her settled into her room at the head of the stairs, Ginny and I spent our time together those fine October days, walking about the farm, where I pointed out "historic" points of interest that had to do with my growing up years. She took it all in, eager to become all the more a part of my world.

Dean, having finished his stint as civilian flight instructor in Texas, had enlisted as a cadet in the U.S. Army Air Corps. He was at home for the time being, awaiting orders for his new assignment. Thus, we were all at home together for those few days.

While waiting for word as to where he would be going next, Dean helped Dad build a new cattle shed, replacing the one our Grandfather Artley had built many years before. As we all, including Mom, Dan, just home from school, and Grandma Artley, looked on as sidewalk superintendents, Dad inscribed with pencil all our names on a timber that was to be covered by siding boards. When it came to the name of the baby Ginny was carrying, he carefully printed, Jean or David, and then added the date to the "time capsule" that would be uncovered years later when the shed was dismantled.

Besides that time capsule in the new cattle shed, there was another effort to preserve something for posterity. Grandma Artley, who had taken a special liking to Ginny, made an appointment for Ginny and me to have our portrait taken at the photographer's in Hampton. She thought it was "high time" we had a

In November 1944, Grandma Artley thought it was "high time" for a "proper" wedding portrait. And indeed it was; Ginny was eight months pregnant.

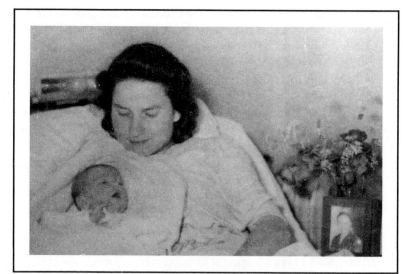

When our first child, Jeannie, was born, Ginny was in Hampton, Iowa, with my family, while I was preparing for a rainy march at Camp Barkley, Texas, December 1944.

"proper" wedding portrait. (It was high time, indeed, with Ginny being eight months pregnant.) Grandma didn't consider the shots taken at our wedding the year before by the post photographer "proper." How thankful we have been, especially I, in recent years, that Grandma did this for us, as it turned out to be our only photo of the two of us until a couple we had taken in our home, years later, at the onset of Ginny's final illness, when I became acutely aware of how quickly life was passing by.

As the hour came on Sunday, October 8, for me to leave, we were all choked with emotion. Not just at my leaving—I'd done that many times before. But the whole family was sensitive to the pain of separation for Ginny and me—a separation that was to be . . . for how long? I was returning to Ft. Wood to await orders and prepare to be shipped out to Camp Barkley, Texas (this time for real). These orders were to mark the first step of being shipped to somewhere overseas, where my medical lab training could be put to use in one of the theaters of war. Two years earlier I would have welcomed the prospects for adventure, but now I wanted to be close to Ginny.

Ginny wrote to me after I left on Sunday, the first of many letters in the next several months that were our attempts to reach out and hold each other close—if only by words on paper. How important to us was the U.S. mail during that time!

Hampton,
Monday Morn.
October 9, 1944

Hi, my darling husband,
      I must get this off at noon so that you will get it Wednesday. Tell me if you get it Wednesday, Sweetheart.
      Well, the unpleasant part is over. Naturally, we all felt badly last night, but think of what we have to look forward to from now on, Darling. Won't it be wonderful?!
      In the middle of the night I was awakened (as usual). So I reached up and turned on the little lamp which you fixed for me (I'm so glad you put the string on it.) I got out of my warm, comfortable bed, got a *Reader's Digest,* and read "Pied Piper." I haven't finished it yet. Right in a most interesting spot, it put me to sleep. Did you ever see the picture, "Pied Piper," or read the story? Monte Wooley played the part in

the movie. It was very good. It was a story of France when the Germans were taking over. Monte Wooley was an Englishman vacationing in France, trying to get back to England, while the Germans were on his heels. He was also taking a few French children with him—some of them orphans and some those whose parents wanted them safely away from the Nazis.

After reading stories like this, I feel as though we are about the most fortunate people in the world.

I just stopped to dry the dishes for Mom. We talked as women do. We talked about you. We said a lot of nice things about you, too, my darling. (Imagine our doing that!) We talked about how slow you and Dad are. But we did agree that you two were very thorough and dependable—Ahem. We said that we had more confidence in our husbands than in anyone else in the world.

Dean came in to change. He's going to help Dad fill silo at Mahncke's. I was kidding him about putting on clean pants just to meet some pretty girl there.

I do hope you got a seat on the train last night. I hope you slept. You know, dear, it will do us both good to be parted a little. Now we'll understand about others. But we are so much more fortunate than most.

The folks are so nice to me, dear. You don't have to worry about me a bit. Mom and I are going to look at baby clothes in the catalog today. The little dickens seems to know I'm talking about "it." "It" is moving about inside me. I wish you were here to tend to this baby of yours. (Of course, the baby is *yours* when it is bad.)

Mom has been cleaning the shelves on the cellar way this morning. We saw a piece of chocolate pie there and felt badly that you didn't eat it. But I'm going to eat it after I finish this letter—Then maybe your stomach will feel better.

Last night I pretended that you were lying beside me. I kissed you goodnight. I could almost feel your lips on mine. I said my prayers and prayed for guidance. I thanked God for what He gave me—especially the wonderful husband and also the baby that I am carrying. I also said a morning prayer when I awakened. When I got up, Dad had me put on a jacket because it was so chilly. (However, now it is a sunshiny day.) We ate in the kitchen. I had my "eye open" egg that Mom always fixes especially for me.

Last night Dad thought I should take a hot water bottle to bed with me to keep me warm. But I didn't need it. I didn't need an extra blanket either. I was nice and warm. I wrapped the blanket around me and made myself a warm little nest.

The railroad express called. They said my packages were there. Darn it, why couldn't they have come when you were here!

I don't know whether we'll get our portrait proofs and express boxes today or not. More than likely, we'll do it to-morrow—we may not have a chance to get into town today.

I do hope you get this Wednesday, dearest. I must close now and get this out to the mailbox.

Be sure to take your vitamins. And, darling, take good care of yourself. I love you more than anyone or anything else in the world. All my love, respect, admiration, faith, and confidence are placed in you.

Until tonight when I write,

Your loving wife,
GINNY

P.S. XXXXXOOOOOO (Kisses and Hugs)

Hampton,
Tues. noon
Oct, 10, 1944

Dearest,

It is a beautiful sunshiny day. I am writing this on the front porch. I can look out over the wide, vast, cultivated land which you love so well. I see the beauty of it through your eyes, my darling. This is Iowa—our future home. Oh, what we have to look forward to!

Sweetheart, I received your letter this morning. (You must have written it on the train and mailed it enroute.) It is a beautiful letter. I read it while I was still outside. I took it with me—walking down in the south field. I felt so close to you. Darling, you have a wonderful philosophy. As I walked, I held my head high and thanked God for my wonderful husband. Darling, you are always in my thoughts and prayers. I love you.

I cleaned my room this morning. It is a lovely room. I placed your painting where I could see it all the time. I put your hat away and also your working pants and shirts. I plan to wash your Army shirts and send them soon.

Later:

Good afternoon, darling. Mom took the kerosene heater up to my room so that I can take a sponge bath. Afterwards, we're going to town. . . .

We picked out the birth announcement folders. This is what they look like:

Here Ginny made a sketch showing its front and back and indicated size and color.

I did the dishes for Mom this afternoon while she cleaned the house. She went flying around like I used to do (before you and I decided to have babies). She showed me old letters and books. She also showed me your baptismal book and a letter from Sugi. How beautifully he writes. I must go now and take my bath. . . .

The following morning Ginny wrote of going to town with Dad and Mom and Dean, when they picked up the freight that had arrived for us (including some presents for the family) and the proofs of our portraits taken while I was at home. She told of the delicious supper Mom had made that evening and then how "after supper I went up to my room and promptly lost all I'd eaten." Then she told of how Mom had come up to help her and "tuck me into bed." She guessed it was nothing serious, just a "little stomach upset," and she expressed her appreciation of and affection for my family.

Isn't it wonderful that we can write long letters to one another? I am looking forward so much to yours. Writing you is the next best thing to having you with me. We are fortunate, Darling. Ours is a great love. Our belief in God is so great I'm sure everything will come out right. We have such a wonderful married life. I think back to the beautiful moments that you and I have had, and think of the beautiful moments that you and I are yet to have. We have so much to look forward to.

I must close now, sweetheart. Until this afternoon.

I love you,
Your devoted wife,
GINNY

Oct. 12, 1944
Thurs. p.m.

Dearest Husband,
Mom and I are both sitting here at the table writing letters. I just finished my regular afternoon siesta.

It's another beautiful sunshiny day. They are filling silo
here today. When I took some letters to the mailbox this
morning I walked out by the barn to see what they were
doing. Dad hollered down to me from the top of the silo. Dan
came from the field with a load of corn and asked me to
watch how they put it up into the silo. It surely is astonishing
the way it is done. (Darling, I'll be glad when we have our
farm.)

When it was time to go for the mail, I took Ted with me.
(Good, old faithful Ted, such a lovable dog.) The mailman
hadn't come yet so Ted and I walked down the road for quite
a way, and then we walked slowly back. I waited by the mailbox while Ted started back toward the house. He would sit
down every now and then and look back to see if I was coming. So I walked down to the gate with him. I walked over
near the pigpen, fascinated by how the pigs ate and acted.
(Some people do eat and act like pigs, don't they?)

The mailman finally came, and I walked down to the box
and was there when he arrived. We said "hello" and he said
he was sorry to be late. I said, "I hope you have a letter from
my husband." He smiled and handed me the mail and there
was your letter, darling.

The first letter from you in Ft. Wood to your wife in
Iowa. It was a wonderful feeling. I didn't read it right away. I
just held it in my hand and walked back up the lane. I held it
high for Dad to see from his perch up in the silo. Mom came
outside and I showed it to her. I still didn't read it. I was like
a child with money, seeing so many things to buy and yet
being afraid to buy anything because that feeling of wistfulness
and anticipation would be gone.

I opened and read it on the front porch. It was sunny and
nice and warm there. It was such a nice letter, dearest. I'm so
glad you didn't have any trouble getting back. It made me feel
good to read of your reaction to the stack of socks and clean
underwear I'd packed for you—and the vitamin pills.

I just said to Mom, "Aren't we lucky to have such wonderful men? I don't envy anyone." Mom said that she didn't
envy anyone either. It's too bad there aren't more like you.

After I read your letters, I cleaned up for the silo-fill-
ers—Ahem. I then read your letter to Mom. I had just finished when Ed Mahncke came in. He kidded me about getting
a letter from you. Mom and I ate in the kitchen while the men
ate at the big table in the dining room.

Later Mom and I did the dishes. She washed them while I

sat down and then I dried them while she sat down. We visited about many things—each told about our old romances and
how silly they seem now. She told me about when you were
born. I asked her a few personal questions—just between
women, you know—Ahem.

Dan thinks I write to you twice a day. Imagine my writing
to you *that* often!

I read a couple pages of *A Tree Grows in Brooklyn* this
afternoon. It's getting a little better. I do think the author
could leave out a bit of the smut. So many of the modern
authors seem to think a book can't "go over" without a tinge
of that anymore. However, it is interesting and does express
good thoughts and ideas. Also, the characters have high ideals.

I'm anxious to hear from Penny concerning her place.

Tomorrow's Dad's birthday. Gee, I surely hope the cake
turns out okay. We're giving the wallet to Dad, as you know,
so I put the picture of us in it—the one of you and me on our
picnic in the Ozarks last year. I also put in pics of Mom, Dean
and Dan. The one I put in of Dan was the one he had taken
in a dress for the freshman initiation. You know how curious
he is. When he looks through the wallet and sees that one—
oh, boy! But no one can hurt me nowadays, in my condition,
and they know it. They're saving their retributions until after
the baby comes. I think I'll do a disappearing act after the
baby is born.

Dan worked on the farm this morning but went to school
this afternoon. He's a little devil. I told him I'd put him across
my lap and spank him, but he retorted, "How can you, when
you don't have any lap?" Bob, how can you have such a terrible brother?! (I wrote this last because he knew I was writing
to you about him and was looking over my shoulder.)

We are going to the movies tonight to see "Going My
Way." All the family is going, except the animals. I wish you
were here so you could go, too, darling. I don't like to think of
you being lonesome. But when I think of poor Les, we can't
complain. I do hope things work out ok between him and
Teddy. She sounds pretty selfish to me.

How is everyone in the laboratory? Please tell them all I
said "hello." As soon as I answer my family letters, I'll start
writing to them.

Dear, tell me everything you do. I can hardly wait until
tomorrow when I hear from you. But just because I write long
letters to you, don't feel as though you have to do the same.

For I have more free time than you do. As long as I hear
something from you, it is all right. It will even be all right if
you just send me penny postcards, for I know how busy you
are. After all, dearest, I have all day and all evening, and it
means everything to me to just write to you.

I wrote to my nephew, Crickie, George's boy, who's in a
bomber crew in Europe, and started one to Pat Wilson (I've
owed her for so long). I have so many letters to write.

Dad and Dean just came in. I bet they are tired. They've
been helping fill silo at Muhlenbruck's this afternoon, after
finishing here.

Well, dearest, I must close now.

Love,

your wife,

GINNY

With letters coming almost daily, my days apart from Ginny
were made more bearable.

About two weeks after leaving Ginny at the farm, I was again
with her. This time for only a couple days, on my way to Camp
Barkley at Abilene, Texas. Needless to say, this farewell was
harder than the previous one, due to the fact that I was shipping
out.

Several of us from the station hospital went by train to Ft.
Worth and then across the rolling cattle range country of west
Texas. I thought of how Dad would enjoy seeing this landscape,
the kind so often described in the Western stories he liked to read.

Camp Barkley was a temporary Army camp—a vast collection
of tarpaper barracks spread out on the dusty plain south of
Abilene. We thought we were to prepare for an overseas assignment but, typically, it was as if the Army didn't know what to do
with us once they had us there. So we were given basic training all
over again (I had been through it all in the autumn of 1941 back
at Ft. Wood). There were some in our group of basic trainees who
had not only been through that ordeal but who were veterans of
the North African campaign against Germany's "Desert Fox"
Rommel. Some were non-coms with medals and with an impressive
string of hashmarks on their sleeves. This made for an awkward
situation, to say the least, when a cadre of smooth-faced "shave-
tails" and boyish drill corporals attempted to put us through close
order drill and other GI maneuvers meant for raw recruits. In spite

of myself, I felt sorry for the staff put in such a predicament.

Our training included setting up laboratories in field stations under simulated battle conditions, preparing us for what possibly lay ahead. This period of intensive training was to culminate in a forced march, carrying a full field pack, to a bivouac area some twenty miles to the west in the hills.

On Sunday, December 3, 1944, our company was preparing for the march, scheduled to take off in the early morning darkness of the next day. By early Sunday afternoon, I was all ready. My duffle bag, which would be hauled by truck, was packed, as well as my full field pack, which I would be carrying on my back. This included, beside's my personal things, items such as toilet articles, mess kit, one wool Army blanket, a shelter half (one half of a pup tent) with pole, stakes, and ropes, and a folding shovel for digging foxholes. On a webbed belt around my waist, I'd be carrying a canteen of water, first aid kit, and a hatchet.

All clothing I'd be wearing was laid out within easy reach so that when the "fall out" call came in the cold darkness, I could respond in short order. When I was all ready for the next morning's departure, I decided to spend the rest of the afternoon at the post library.

The overcast December day had turned into a light rain. My time at the library reading table was an enjoyable way of spending the afternoon as the water ran down the outside of the library windows. I browsed through some magazines and books and decided to start a letter to Ginny. My mind was on her almost constantly, and writing letters was one way to bring us closer together. Ginny spoke often of us being "together in spirit."

It was about five o'clock, as I sat at the library table, when all of a sudden, an excruciating pain began to build up in my lower abdomen. It was a pain the likes of which I had never had before—nor have I had since. It came on so suddenly and was so severe I thought I was going to pass out. But almost as suddenly as it came, it was gone, leaving me perspiring and a little shaky.

When I had regained my composure and felt I could stand without falling, I gathered up my things and hurried back to my hut. It was good to stretch out on my cot in the warmth of the tar paper hut that housed eight of us GIs. The soft puttering sound of the fire in the oil heater and the rain drumming on the roof was a cozy background to the quiet activity taking place—some of my buddies lying on their cots reading, some playing cards, and one asleep. I was glad to have survived my strange ordeal at the library and to be "home" where I felt reasonably comfortable and secure.

Suddenly, the peace and quiet was broken when the door burst open and the CQ called out, "Telegram for Sergeant Artley!"

I tore the envelope open and quickly scanned the telegraphese for the message:

YOUR DAUGHTER ARRIVED 5:00 PM   GOOD LUNGS
MOTHER AND BABY DOING FINE   DAD

My hutmates, including Belosic and Frazzoni, with whom I'd become friends, shared in my relief and joy of the good news. I put on my rain gear and dashed out into the wet darkness and nearly ran the several blocks to a phone booth where I could send a telegraphed reply. My sobs of joy and tears of happiness competed with the downpour from the sky. After feeding the required coins into the phone slot, I sent the following message:

MY DARLING   WHOOPEE   LOVE BOB

Back in Iowa at the farm, Ginny had been awakened early on that Sunday morning (December 3) with twinges of pain. She had slipped out of bed and tiptoed down the hall to Mom and Dad's bedroom, and, leaning over, had whispered into Mom's ear that she thought maybe she was experiencing some labor pains. Dad got up immediately and went downstairs to fire up the furnace. Mom asked Ginny to crawl into bed and they timed the "twinges." Determining that Ginny was indeed experiencing the beginning of labor, they phoned Dr. Allen and he suggested Ginny be taken to the hospital, where he would call to make arrangements.

The storm system that was dumping all that rain on western Texas was causing an ice storm in northern Iowa. Everything was ice coated and the ground was extremely slippery. Dan, watching from the south dining room window, saw that the car seemed to be stalled on Freie's hill. He put on his wraps and made his way the slippery half-mile to the base of the hill where Ginny, Dad, Mom, and Dean in the old Plymouth seemed to be hopelessly stalled on the icy rutted road.

Little by little, with Dad, Dean, and Dan taking turns at the wheel and pushing, the car and its anxious passengers made their way to the top of the hill and were on their way—with Dan's final admonition to Ginny ringing in their ears that she'd better hold off having the baby until the next day—his birthday.

By the time they had reached the Lutheran hospital in Hampton, about six miles from the farm, the labor pains were coming in close intervals. The nurses were ready for her and got Ginny right into her bed and prepared her for the birth.

But it was a long, exhausting day of intense labor before Ginny brought forth Virginia Jean at 5:00 P.M. (the same time I was having my strange pain). After Ginny had sufficiently recovered from her ordeal, which she soon seemed to forget, she happily inspected the perfect little girl she had produced. And as she wrote to me later, "Daddy, she's beautiful!"

For a day or two, Mom took over Ginny's letter-writing chores, keeping me up-to-date, telling me all about the wondrous happening that had occurred and reminding me how fortunate I was to have such a lovely wife and beautiful baby daughter. She also wrote to Ginny's families, in Detroit and Pennsylvania, telling them all about the birth.

A few days after Jeannie was born, Ginny's sister Laura and her teenaged daughter Chickie came from Detroit to see Ginny and the baby. As was common back then, Ginny was kept in the hospital for two weeks. (It was said that this was *one* time the mother could get her rest.) Laura and Chickie came by train, not on the modern north-and-south Rock Island "Rocket," but from the east, the last hundred miles or so on a bumpy, start-and-stop "milk train." Their adventure, with local color, gave them much to talk and laugh about when they weren't exclaiming over Ginny's baby. They stayed at the farm, Dad and Dan driving them to the hospital each day. (This was especially enjoyable to Dan, who found Chickie, his own age, most charming.) The visit, though short, was a warm, rewarding experience for all concerned, especially valuable for Ginny, who could in this way share her first childbirth with at least *some* of her family.

Back in Texas, the twenty-one mile forced march to our bivouac in the hills was made even more difficult by the steady cold rain. The last hour or so of the march, our company, which had started out in more or less orderly formation, became a rout in appearance, with thoroughly exhausted GIs straggling into the bivouac area by ones, twos, and threes. I thought we must be scattered all over west Texas. Some who fell by the wayside were picked up in trucks to ride the last few miles. However, most of us came dragging in late in the afternoon, making, as the saying goes, "three tracks": our two feet and our rear end.

Making camp that night was extremely difficult. The ground was soaked, our packs were soaked, we were soaked, and the rain had turned to snow. The hillside on which we were to encamp was thick with cedar trees. Though they were wet like the rest of the environment, we cut branches from them to make mattresses in our pup tents.

Campfires had somehow been started out of the wet wood on that soggy hillside and, augmented by more cedar boughs, sizzled and smoked long before they flamed. To this day the smell of burning cedar wood recalls to me that bivouac in the hills of west Texas in that early December of 1944.

When the mail truck (lifeline to our loved ones) arrived the following afternoon, there was a package for me from Ginny containing a pair of new olive drab wool gloves—to replace mine that had been inadvertently burned, along with many other wet gloves, leggings, and socks that had been hung too close to campfires the night before. It was as if Ginny, during the week before she was to deliver the baby, had anticipated my need—a talent she has shown throughout our life together.

It wasn't long before Ginny was again writing to me daily. Her letters had the same warmth and upbeat spirit as before; however, there was a difference. Wanting desperately for me to share the wonder and joy she was experiencing in the growth and develop-ment of our baby, she devoted most of her letters to this new presence in our lives. We, of course, didn't know it then, but this daily accounting was the only way I would experience Jeannie's early babyhood, for I was not to see her until she was five months old.

I hungered for each bit of news concerning our little family that Ginny so faithfully and lovingly shared with me in her letters. However, I also realized that I was having to share my place in Ginny's heart with someone else. Because at that time I had not experienced parental love firsthand, I didn't quite perceive that one did not displace the other, but rather that parenthood enlarged one's capacity to love *more*, taking nothing from one to give to the other. There is ample love for offspring *and* spouse. Here again, through Ginny, I was learning more about love.

It was our second Christmas. Our first apart. I shopped the stores in Abilene for something extra special that I hoped would make up for our not being together. I thought I would like to get Ginny something personal, like an article of clothing—something that would celebrate her figure's return to its cute shape after her pregnancy. Perhaps something like frilly underclothing that would be next to her sweet body. But when I went shopping for it, I lost my courage at the thought of having to deal with the clerks about such intimate apparel and looked instead for something for which I'd feel more comfortable shopping. I settled upon a brass-colored metal music box, with figures of little cherubs encircling it. Its tinkling tune was one that was sung at our wedding, "I Love You Truly."

On Christmas Eve at the farm, with Dad, Mom, Dan, and baby gathered around her (Dean had by then been assigned and called back to the service), Ginny opened her gift, and when it started to play its little tune, she gathered it up in its wrappings and ran upstairs to her room where it could play out its haunting strains while she buried her head in her pillow. No one bothered her. The family went after her only with their hearts, allowing her the privacy she needed until she could compose herself and rejoin them around the Christmas tree.

The training of our outfit was completed at Camp Barkley, so it would be only a matter of time before we would be reassigned and shipped out, with no chance of a furlough for some time. In order for Ginny and me to be together, when baby Jeannie was seven weeks old, Ginny came to Abilene to spend two weeks, which expanded to four.

Dr. Allen encouraged Ginny to go to be with her husband for a while, but advised not taking such a young baby on so arduous a trip. He assured Ginny that Jeannie would be fine with her new grandparents, who had shared with her care from the beginning, thus forming a close bond. Also, in spite of Ginny's wishes to nurse her baby, she had not been able to do so. Thus, with the baby being bottle fed, Ginny's physical presence was not needed.

Ginny took the Rock Island "Rocket" from Hampton to Fort Worth and then came by bus to Abilene, arriving about 8:00 P.M. on January 22. I had been at the station early, not wanting to miss a moment of our time together. But to my chagrin, I almost didn't recognize my wife when I first saw her waving to me through the bus window. I have often pondered the strange phenomenon, in that brief moment, when Ginny in person, didn't quite match the mental image I had been carrying around close to my heart for all of those weeks. It was as if my mental image was Ginny's *essence* and not merely the way light reflected from the surface of her features.

It didn't take long, however, for us to become reacquainted in person. We spent our first night in a room at the guest house. The next day we followed up a lead I'd been given and took a second floor room in the pleasant home of an elderly couple, Dr. and Mrs. Barnet. We were well received there and were very comfortable in the month we spent in their home. Ginny and Mrs. Barnet found much in common to talk about, when I was on duty and she was on her own. She spent her time reading, resting, and writing letters to her far-flung family and, of course, to the folks back at the farm, keeping in close touch with our baby.

This was a wonderful, renewing time for our relationship. However, I was aware of Ginny's absentmindedness when she would be thinking of Jeannie. She tried her best to get me to feel as she did about our little one, but I honestly could not share, to the degree Ginny could, the parental feeling, even though I wanted desperately to do so.

When I came off duty around 4:30, Ginny and I would go to supper, then to the library, art center, a movie, or some entertainment at the USO, sometimes with a couple of my GI buddies, Frazzoni and Belosic, and their wives. We took bus trips of exploration around the city, and on one of those bus trips, we first encountered racial segregation.

We boarded one of the city buses, not far from our room at the Barnet's, to find it nearly empty, with only four or five people seated up at the front of the bus. Wanting a measure of privacy, we made our way to the unoccupied rear, noticing on the way a sign reading, "Colored to the rear." We proceeded without hesitation (after all, we were sort of pinkish in color) and seated ourselves comfortably in the rear of the bus.

to the Air Corps medical group and was on my way to a training session of several weeks at Miami Beach, Florida.

I had traveled by train many times in the service, but this was the first time I was to travel in style—Army style, that is. Frazzoni was put in charge of our group, and Belosic and I were made his assistants, so we had a compartment with berths and "the works." Even though we were traveling on orders, and there were a lot of GIs on the train in addition to our group, it was not a troop train—there were civilian passengers aboard as well.

Going across Georgia, we had a stop of about an hour in Atlanta. Here the wife of one fellow was waiting at the station for him when our train pulled in. The two of them disappeared into the crowd and reappeared only moments before the train was to depart. I took special notice of this couple, identifying with the joy of their reunion and the sorrow of its shortness. This made my longing for Ginny all the greater. However, only a short way down the track, after bidding his wife good-bye with passionate hugs and kisses with which I could empathize, I was shocked to see the same guy with his arms around another girl, "making out" with some unattached woman he had come across on the train. It was beyond my comprehension.

The following letters tell more about the trip:

Miami Beach
April 13, 1945
Friday morning

My Darling—

Well, here I am, my dear, in Miami, Florida. What a beautiful, exotic place. I didn't know there were actually (outside of movie sets) such places. About a block away is the beautiful Atlantic Ocean. My darling, how I wish you were here to see it! I wish the folks could be here, too. But it is definitely no place for poor people like us—living in palatial hotels, that is. However, the majority of the beauties of this place are God-made—the many palms; the strange, beautiful birds; the deep blue sky with tall billowing clouds; the blue, fresh Atlantic lapping the sandy beach. I could go on and on.

But first, dear, isn't it a sad shock about President Roosevelt dying? It hardly seems as if it could be true. We heard it first as we were on the train passing through Palm Springs. We stopped at a crossing and a man opened the door of his car and hollered it to us. We weren't sure we were hearing correctly then and thought it surely just a rumor. Later we heard it confirmed. From then on, all along the way, at almost every stop someone on the platform would ask us if we'd heard. I surely hope his great work toward world unification and peace will continue.

We boarded the train about noon Tuesday in Camp Crowder and soon were on our way. We travelled consecutively through a bit of Oklahoma, Arkansas, Tennessee, Mississippi, Alabama, Georgia, and along the Atlantic coast the length of Florida. We spent two nights on the train, arriving here last night about 8:30.

Upon arrival here, we were brought by bus to a hotel (now in Army hands), where we are put up temporarily until something definite is done with us. (As I write this, it is not yet known, *by us,* what is to be our fate, but it sounds like it might be an assignment to one of the many convalescent hospitals, which in reality are swanky hotels the government is renting.)

It is rumored that, if we are assigned here, we can obtain separate rations, rent for apartments, which during the tourist season (winter) is terrifically high but comes down considerably during the summer months.

It is very hot here. We left April weather in Missouri and have landed smack in the middle of July weather here.

Now, Darling, *if I am* assigned here—personally I can't believe that I am to be—it's too good for one who hasn't been overseas as yet—I shall make arrangements to have you and Jeannie with me as soon as possible. Will write more later . . .

Good morning, my darling.

We are cleaned up for inspection and waiting for further instructions. Sometime today we are to be processed. Monday we are to be assigned.

Some seem to think we are here for a six-week training in parasitology and then will be organized into small units of flying lab men. (We are in the Air Corps now, you know.) According to this report, we will then be flown from island to island in the Pacific, doing survey work in dysentery, etc.

It all sounds very interesting, especially the flying part. That would be much better than to be stationed at some far outpost for the duration. Of course, this isn't official yet. We seem to have taken them by surprise down here and they apparently aren't ready for us. We've been having a hard time finding out anything. But we *have* been enjoying the luxurious surroundings (the Atlantic beach, etc.) while we're waiting for official word.

I'll write more definitely as to our set-up as soon as I know. Last night I sent you a night letter which you should get in today's mail. I hope you do, dear, so you won't be worrying . . .

Last night Belosic and I went to Miami (we're in Miami Beach here) and looked for apartments. We didn't have much immediate luck but were given some suggestions. It seems that after the fifteenth (tomorrow), many of the tourists will be leaving. Belosic's wife is arriving today so he did get a room so they'd have a place to stay until she has time to look for an apartment.

We have been trying to find out all we can about having our wives with us—all information thus far has been more or less unofficial. . . . It seems the wives can eat in the Army mess halls with their husbands for thirty-five cents per meal. And they're good meals. Of course, with an apartment and the separate rations, that wouldn't be necessary. There is a lot of free entertainment for soldiers and their wives, too. The Army seems to have consideration for the Army wife here.

What I am leading up to is this, I'd like very much to have you and Jeannie down here with me. Would it be all right with you, even if it were for only a short while—six weeks? As far as a place to live is concerned, I feel as though, with constant effort I'll be able to find an agreeable place. But what worries me the most concerning your coming is the long train ride. I thought about it on the way down and talked it over with Frazzoni and Belosic. Darling, you'd have to have a pullman, and a lower berth at that, in order to be able to take care of Jeannie and not wear yourself out any more than what you would anyway.

Just how much money do you have available there at home? It will be an expensive venture for rent is high down here.

In making such a trip, you'd have to travel as lightly as possible and have the porter help you. You and Jeannie could sleep in a lower berth okay, I think, and you could have the porter bring the baby's milk from the refrigerator or heat it when it is time, etc.

But, Darling, if you don't think it would be good for Jeannie to make the trip, or if the doctor doesn't think so, or if the folks think it would be too much for you both, I'll un-

derstand. In the meantime, I'll find out what I can about
things and let you know as soon as I do.

I ate breakfast this morning looking out over the Atlantic
(a small portion of it, of course). It was beautiful. After breakfast, I walked down to the water's edge and watched the
crashing breakers surge in on the beach and finally fall exhausted and spent a few feet from my feet. What a noise they
make! How much I love just looking out over the expanse and
watching. The water is such a beautiful bluish green—toward
evening there are streaks of purple in it. How I wish all of you
dear folks could be with me.

Give my love to all the folks, dear. And kiss that wee baby
of ours for her daddy.

And as for you, my little wife—Darling, I love you so very,
very much. I have such a longing for you . . . May God bless
and protect you and Jeannie. May things be well for you, my
darling. I love you—

Your BOB

Eventually, my furlough *did* materialize and on May 10, 1945,
I picked it up at the orderly room and, with several other service
men and women, hitched a ride on a military plane, a C-47 on its
flight to Washington, D.C. From Washington I went by a train to
Des Moines and then on a Jefferson bus to Iowa Falls, eighteen
miles south of Hampton, where my family had driven by car to
meet me.

We must have made quite a scene, there in the street, Ginny,
carrying Baby, and I rushing together in a smothering embrace.
The next thing I knew, I was awkwardly holding Baby in my arms,
while greeting Mom and Dad. Baby was staring at this stranger,
into whose clutches she had been thrust, while I was clumsily
trying to adjust five months of anticipation into this moment of
realization.

Ginny was radiant. Her lovely eyes were moist and wide with
excitement. Dad and Mom, standing back slightly, as if not wanting
to intrude upon our little family scene, were smiling broadly, their
eyes brimming with tears of happiness.

"Darling, isn't she lovely?!" Ginny managed to say. I could
only reply with a vigorous nod and gather them all, Dad, Mom,
Ginny, and Baby, into my arms. Then we removed ourselves from
the middle of the street and entered a nearby cafe where we took
a booth that would accommodate us all, Grandpa, Grandma,

Mommy, Daddy, and Baby, the latter still in her father's arms.

After eating our meal, during which I made my first ungraceful attempt at bottle feeding—I had much to learn—we headed for home.

The next few days, I was involved in a crash course of father's baby care with Ginny, my well-qualified instructor, looking on with amusement as I struggled with changing diapers, making formula, burping the freshly fed baby, and learning how to hold a squirming five-month-old human being, without dropping it.

Jeannie and I had much lost time to make up for, and by the end of the furlough, as she looked from me to her mother for reassurance, she had begun to accept this other being into her family circle of Mommy, Grandma, Grandpa, Uncle Dan, and Ted, the faithful collie. I think by that time I might have come next in line after Ted.

Those few days in May, there on the farm with my family about me (with the exception of Dean, who was serving in the Air Corps), were precious beyond measure. For Ginny and me, our cup of happiness was overflowing, and we drank deeply of it in celebration of our love.

But as is so often the case, our happiness had its flip side. We were all aware of the sadness that was in the air with the knowledge that eventually I would be taking Ginny and Baby from this family circle that had been so wonderfully warm and nurturing. This would be especially sad for Dad and Mom, who had been as close as parents to the baby for five months, and to whom Ginny could not have been any dearer had she been their own child. When coming back to the empty house after taking Ginny, Baby, and me to the station on our departure, Dad went to the empty baby crib and, picking up a small blanket left there, buried his face in it and sobbed piteously. Mom tried lamely to comfort him, reminding Dad that it was inevitable and only right that the little family be off on its own.

However, it would still be a while before Ginny and Jeannie and I could be together as a family—and then for only briefly. But we did ride as a family on the train as far as Chicago. There my wife and baby would be boarding a sleeper for Detroit, and I would be taking another train back to Miami Beach.

Travel during those war years was hectic, to say the least. Trains were overcrowded and schedules were often out of kilter, causing missed connections with accompanying problems. While Ginny and Jeannie had a berth reserved on their pullman to Detroit, the late arrival of our train into Chicago made it nearly impossible for me to get them properly settled in their train and still be able to run up the platform with my duffle bag where my Miami-bound train was about to pull out. Thus, I could only quickly deposit my family and their luggage safely on their train at their reserved berth.

When I first left home for the service after being drafted, Grandpa Crow had given me a silver dollar, advising that, as long as I kept it, I'd never be broke. One silver dollar, by today's values, doesn't seem like very much, but back then it was a coin of considerable worth. I quickly decided this was a time to use it, so I dug into the watch pocket, where I'd carried it since back in 1941, and pressed the silver coin into the porter's palm with the plea to see that my dear ones were taken care of and would get to Detroit safely and comfortably. Ginny later reported that he took very good care of them on that trip, even heating Baby's bottle when needed.

LEAVES IN THE WIND

When I arrived back at Miami Beach, I found that my lab group had already been sent to Camp Davis at Wilmington, North Carolina. Within a few days my orders were cut and I was sent to join them in establishing a laboratory in the rehabilitation center that was being set up there. When I arrived at my new post in the last part of May, the first thing I did was write my "sugar report" to Ginny:

> 1079 AAF BU SQ.E.
> Conv. Hosp.
> Camp Davis, N.C.
> Sunday night
> May 27, 1945

Hello, darling,

Here I am in Camp Davis. I'm not going to try to tell you all the "dope" tonight as my mind is all cluttered up with everything they've been telling me. I can tell you, though, that the first impression of this place isn't very good.

Frazzoni and Smith, another GI friend, went to Wilmington to hunt for apartments. I'm anxious to hear what they have to report. I've been told there is a housing project near camp but that it's full with a long waiting list. I'm going to inquire officially tomorrow.

There is also supposed to be another place on the other side of Wilmington. It's also a housing project. It sounds pretty good, but that's a long way from camp.

I do want you and Jeannie with me so very badly. It's only

fair to warn you, though, that this isn't the beauty spot that I had heard it was. But I'll do my best to get a place that's decent for you and the baby, and we'll at least be together.

One fellow, a lieutenant, seemed to think that, being a sergeant, I could get a pretty good deal in the place near Wilmington. He said I'd probably have to pay about $15 or $20 a month for a furnished place. . . .

What a still, lonely place this camp is. It was closed down once and is just now being reopened. We are way under-strength and, therefore, there are a lot of empty barracks around. . . .

Frazzoni and Smith came back late last night. Their report about housing was the same pessimistic one I'd been hearing. It seems our best chances are in that housing project on the other side of Wilmington. Outside of the distance, it doesn't sound so bad. I'm going to go and check it out today, if I get a chance. . . . Smith is going to try for one. If it looks like a good thing to me, I think I'll do the same . . . I wish I could talk it over with you face to face . . .

How are you fixed for money? I have $12, counting the $10 you gave me. We won't get paid until the tenth of June. Be sure, though, darling, to let me know if you have enough for the trip, etc. When is your government check due? Per-haps we'll have to send home for more money from our bank account in Hampton.

I must close now . . . Go and look in the mirror into those lovely eyes you see there and know that those are the eyes your husband loves, for they're the windows to the soul of his wife—the woman who has all of his love always.

Your, BOB

In the meantime Ginny was busy getting our baby daughter acquainted with her families in Detroit, South Fork, and Philadel-phia. In Detroit, where she had lived with Laura and Bo since she was sixteen, she had the heartwarming experience of getting Jeannie to know Grandma Laura, Grandpa Bo, and aunts Chickie and Jean, the latter being her namesake. Predictably, Baby and Ginny, in her mother role, made a big hit with all of them and were proudly shown off to long-time family friends.

But the time went all too quickly and soon the Ginny-and-Jeannie traveling show was off to her hometown of South Fork, where the reception, because of a larger audience of family members, was even greater. Ginny proudly deposited Baby Jeannie into her aged father's lap. It was especially rewarding for W. H. Moore to hold *his* baby's baby in his arms, and he, along with all the brothers, sisters, brothers-in-law, sisters-in-law, nieces, nephews, and childhood friends, were happy participants of "Little Ginny's" motherhood.

In Philadelphia there was the same great rejoicing over Ginny's new status as a mother and over the little one who had brought it about. While Louise, Web, and Mother Ritchey were actually her foster family, there could not have been any greater capacity for family love than there was between Ginny and them.

This journey, reaffirming family solidarity, was a soul-satisfying experience for Ginny, as well as for her far-flung family. But the physical aspects of the journey were quite unpleasant. During those war years, great numbers of people traveled by trains, and the railroads, not being able to get the needed new cars because of wartime priorities, had pressed ancient relics into service. These musty, dusty old rail coaches had none of the modern niceties that the newer ones had even then, such as comfortable seats and air conditioning. To get any measure of relief from the oppressive, humid summer heat, the car windows had to be open. But the "fresh" air this provided was laden with smoke, soot, and cinders from the coal-burning engine.

About three weeks after we went our separate ways at the Chicago train station, I was sufficiently settled into my new post at Camp Davis to send for my family. I found a place for us to live and made arrangements to meet them at Union Station in Washington, D.C.

The day I was to meet their train I contacted Becky Alinson, a childhood friend from Hampton, who was now stationed there as an officer in the WAVES. She and Ginny had not as yet met, so I suggested that she join me in meeting their train.

It was a miserably hot, sticky day when the train from Philadelphia rolled into the station. The detraining passengers were a bedraggled lot—Ginny among them. As I stepped forward to greet Ginny and take her bags, she, with soot-streaked Baby Jeannie in her arms, stepped down from the car with the words, "I'm pregnant."

I nearly dropped her luggage through the station platform . . . and followed after it. (Then I remembered, that *was* a beautiful time together back at the farm the previous month!) Suddenly, the war news seemed to fade into the background, along with every other concern. We *had* talked of having a large family—but not yet!

After regaining some of my composure, I took my family over to Becky for introductions. Then we walked to the USO nearby. This was a large building of several stories that served as a free stopover hotel for GI travelers. There were accommodations, not only for enlisted personnel but also for their spouses and children. Becky accompanied Ginny and Baby into the area for mothers and children, which was off-limits to even fathers, and helped with the cleanup procedure. After mother and baby were clean and refreshed, we all had an early supper at the USO cafeteria and visited until Becky had to leave.

That night we slept at the USO, Ginny and Jeannie in the part reserved for mothers and children, where Ginny was provided with a real bed and a crib beside it for Baby. I, along with other overnight servicemen, was issued a pillow and a light cover and slept in my clothes on one of several recliner chairs arranged in rows across a large second-floor lobby.

The next morning we were on our way to Wilmington, North Carolina, in a rail car that was of the same vintage and condition as the one Ginny and Baby had traveled on the day before. And as on the day before, the atmosphere became hot and sticky, and the train windows had to be opened. Smoke, soot, and cinders were again a part of the air we had to breathe, and the tiny particles of cinder ash added to the discomfort of the hard mohair-covered seats by making them gritty.

Before leaving the USO that morning, Ginny had taken advantage of the facilities to prepare Jeannie's formula and put it into bottles for the day's feedings on the train. After settling into our seats, Ginny suggested that I ask the dining car steward for permission to stash the bottles of formula in the dining car. He was at first a little hesitant, but after I assured him that I would be responsible for getting the bottles when they were needed, and with him understanding the necessity of special measures on this hot day, he consented. The bag with all the bottles for the day, except one, which Ginny kept out for the next feeding, was stowed in the refrigerator of the dining car, which, conveniently, was the next car behind ours.

One of the tribulations of wartime travel was the priority that freight trains were given over passenger service. This policy resulted in passenger trains being shunted aside to allow a freight to pass. Several times that day, on our way south to North Carolina, we were stopped and made to pull on to a rail siding to await the approach and passage of a long string of slow-moving freight cars.

After one of these stops, in a particularly busy rail yard with several sidings where there was much stopping and starting and shunting of rail cars, our train started to move again. I happened to glance back through the glass in the door at the rear of our car and saw, to my horror, that the dining car—the car in which were Jeannie's refrigerated bottles of formula—was no longer there. I pushed my face against the glass for a closer look, only to see it far down the track, where it had been unhooked, receding into the distance as our part of the train was gaining momentum toward our destination.

The rest of the journey was stressful, to say the least, not only for a starving baby and her parents, but also for the other passengers within hearing of her piteous wailing.

The first order of business, when we reached our apartment, was to build a fire in the coal- and wood-fueled kitchen stove, heat some water, and hurriedly make another batch of formula—all to the accompaniment of Jeannie's screams. This was our first initiation into family life, when "baby makes three."

Our home (thankfully only temporary) was far from what we had fancied in our dreams. It was in a housing development known as Maffitt Village, on the outskirts of the city of Wilmington. Built for the families of workers in the Wilmington shipyard, it consisted of long rows of connected cinder block units with a common roof. Each unit had a front and rear door opening into a yard, not of lush green grass, but of a sandy, desertlike expanse with sparse vegetation, the most predominant being sandburs. But housing was scarce, so we were thankful to find anything.

We had two rooms. The front room was filled with the double-sized bed and a dresser so there was not even room for a baby's crib, if we'd had one. (Jeannie had to sleep in a dresser drawer, set on the floor, or between Ginny and me in our bed.) The kitchen had the small coal- and wood-fueled range, a table and four chairs, a refrigerator, and a built-in cupboard, with a sink in the countertop. Because the bathroom, directly off the kitchen, had only a lavatory, toilet, and shower (no tub), Ginny gave Baby her baths in the kitchen sink.

The inside walls were the same as the outside ones—the other side of the cinder block. Our curtained clothes closet in the bedroom was a space between the chimney and the wall separating us from our next-door neighbors. The floors were bare concrete, with no carpet or rugs. Try as she might, there was little Ginny could do to make the place cozy. And because the unit was furnished, including pots, pans, and table dishes and utensils, the only personal items we had to make it uniquely our home were family photos and a few small items that could be carried in the luggage. Even the bed linen and bath towels were furnished by the Army quartermaster as a part of our living allowance. We remembered, with nostalgic longing, our rustic cabin home back at Possum Lodge.

On about the third morning after we had settled in, Ginny discovered what appeared to be insect bites on Jeannie. She called my attention to them, noting that the bites seemed to be in a row. This revelation raised a red flag in my brain as I recalled my stint as bedbug inspector a few months before back at Camp Crowder. When Ginny was out of the room, I hurriedly inspected our bed and mattress. It was with great reluctance that I informed Ginny of the latest adventure facing us in the "Saga of Ginny and Bob": We had bedbugs!

I was right in feeling reluctant to tell Ginny of my findings. She was ready to leave that place, pronto, and to resign from the war effort. She had never experienced this particular species of the insect world and associated their presence with filth and low living.

I made an indignant trip to the housing development office with a complaint that left no doubt as to how we felt about sharing the place with those unsavory tenants that sneaked out and sucked our blood while we slept. Arrangements were made forthwith to have our unit fumigated. For this to be done, we had to move out early in the morning, taking all the baby paraphernalia that would be needed for the day, such as bottles of formula and diapers. We also had to either remove or be sure all foodstuffs were in closed containers. I had been given permission to be absent from duty so that I could help Ginny with our nomadic day. We rode the city buses, visited parks, the library, the museum, and then rode the buses again until we could again inhabit our place, hopefully, with our unwelcome co-tenants gone.

Whether they *were* gone or not, we didn't know, but at least we were not bothered by them again and no longer scratched, unless we started to think about the bothersome little creatures. In fact, we soon forgot about them . . . until the end of the month when we got a bill from the housing office for twenty-one dollars for fumigating our apartment. Ginny and I considered this adding insult to injury!

If my first trip to the housing office had been indignant, it was nothing compared with this time. I stormed in, and putting the bill I'd received down on the desk in front of the wide-eyed clerk, I informed her in a voice that everyone in the office could hear that I had no intention of paying for the removal of someone else's critters, for they *had* been there when we moved in.

Whether it was the force of my argument or the justice of it that prevailed, I'll never know. At any rate, we did not pay, nor did we ever hear any more of it.

It should have come as no surprise, when, early in August, word came down from on high that all the work and plans for the rehabilitation center at Wilmington, North Carolina, were to be scratched. The military had changed its ponderous mind. Ginny and I were again to be leaves blown about in these changeable winds, this time moving on to Greensboro, North Carolina—a pleasant train trip of only a few hours over the green, rolling hills of the northeastern part of the state. Little Jeannie, with her friendly smiles and pleasant nature, made a hit with fellow passengers.

We arrived in Greensboro early enough to deposit our luggage and start our search on foot for a place to live. This turned out to be a discouraging venture. Because it was a military town, most places were already taken. We also experienced discrimination. Several apartments had signs that read: "No soldiers or dogs," and some, "No children."

Finally, in a neat, well-kept neighborhood, we were fortunate to find a house in which the owner, Mrs. Clement, agreed to rent us a room until we could find an apartment. She was a sad-faced woman, embittered by the death of her only son, a soldier in Europe. She kindly permitted Ginny the use of her kitchen to prepare Jeannie's formula, but we had to take our meals in restaurants. This, of course, was inconvenient and expensive.

On August 14, world events again intruded into our private lives with the welcome news that the war in the Pacific had ended. Japan had surrendered. At the same time we learned of the terrible weapon the United States had used to bring about this victory—the atomic bomb. The following letter home relates what we experienced on that historic day:

Sq. E., AAF ORD.
Reg. Hospital
Greensboro, N.C.
Aug. 14, 1945

Dear Dad, Mom, and Dan,
    The day awaited, worked, fought, and prayed for all these many months and years, has come at last. Like the beginning of the war, it is hard to realize.
    Ginny, Jeannie, and I were downtown when the news came out. We had just had our supper at a restaurant and were leisurely window shopping when we heard someone shout, "It's over!"
    We saw a bunch grouped about a parked car, listening to its radio and we joined them. Soon a car came up the street with its horn blowing. Only a few minutes later, the streets were jammed with honking cars.
    Jeannie looked around in amused wonder at the commotion. As the crowds grew thicker and the noise louder we began to grow uneasy as to what might happen, so returned to our room at Mrs. Clement's. One could write volumes on that street scene—no doubt, being duplicated in towns and cities nationwide. There were expressions of the whole range of emotions. The scene moved one so much, Ginny and I could hardly speak, but just looked and squeezed one another's arms. Ginny borrowed my handkerchief. She said she felt more like being reverent than yelling—I agreed.
    Poor Mrs. Clement—It is rather a sad occasion for her. Her only son won't be coming back from war.
    Wonder what Dean is doing tonight—writing home, I bet. It's funny when some big event takes place, we want to write home about it.

By using Mrs. Clement's room as a temporary base, we

devoted all our free time the next few days to finding an apart-ment. In desperation I finally found a second-floor apartment in a big, old, rather seedy-looking frame house on the fringe of downtown. The apartment consisted of a large room with a dividing wall, that didn't go all the way to the ceiling, making it into two rooms. This provided for a bedroom/sitting room on one side and a kitchen/dining room on the other.

The deciding factor in taking this dingy apartment was its private bath off the kitchen portion. An added attraction was a fireplace, or "grate," in the bedroom/front room portion.

I made the necessary deposit and went to collect Ginny, Baby, and our things at our room at Mrs. Clement's. I was alarmed to find Ginny was not feeling well, so was especially anxious to get settled in our own place. When evening came, we were in our new quarters, with all of our belongings, luggage, and boxes we'd had delivered, piled on the floor around us.

By then Ginny was becoming violently ill, with vomiting and diarrhea. She was much too sick to take to the hospital, even if I'd had the means to get her there. Our landlady said she had a doctor who would make a house call, so I asked her to send for him.

I was no more impressed with this doctor than I was with this place, and our snuff-dipping landlady. The doctor appeared unshaven and generally ill-kept. I perceived him to be a quack and felt uncomfortable with him attending my Ginny. But under the circumstances we had no choice. He thought she must have ptomaine poisoning, and I thought of the chicken we'd had to eat at the restaurant earlier that afternoon.

That night was probably one of the bleakest, most anxious nights I've ever endured. Ginny was desperately ill, and I was trying to care for a nine-month-old baby and keep her off the dirty floor, all the time trying to quiet my fears concerning the possibili-ty that Ginny's illness could bring about premature labor.

The landlady tried to help some with Jeannie, but while I appreciated her thoughtfulness, I just wanted our family to be alone. Whether it was the "quack's" medicine or answered prayers or both, by the next day, Ginny was feeling better, and in two or three days, she seemed to be much like her old self and was able to cope with some new problems that were to emerge.

Three in a bed, when one of them was an active, growing baby, was getting to be less restful for all of us. When things finally quieted down, and Jeannie had been turned parallel to the bed, instead of crosswise, for the umpteenth time, and the little one within Ginny was not kicking, and she and I were drifting off to sleep . . . suddenly Ginny said, "What's that?"

"What's what?" I asked sleepily.

"That scratching sound," she said.

Then both of us were awake and I, too, heard it. It *was* a scratching sound. Upon investigation, we discovered it was coming from the walls. Upon closer investigation, we found it to be caused by cockroaches crawling around behind loose portions of wallpaper. We'd known those loathsome creatures were in our place, as Ginny had first discovered them skittering across our things in the icebox when she'd suddenly opened the door. When Ginny had complained to the landlady about it, she promptly suggested she exchange ours with hers, which was a newer one and on which the doors fit more tightly. Besides, she explained, she was used to cockroaches.

Soon after moving in, we suggested to our landlady that if she would buy the paint, we would redecorate our apartment. She readily agreed to this, and Ginny, Jeannie, and I were soon wading in strips and bits of wet wallpaper as we pulled and scraped it from the walls.

It was a great feeling of accomplishment, when, after several days of living in the mess we were making in the evenings after I came home from work, our apartment had been made clean, bright, and fresh with the water-based calcimine paint, which had no strong fumes. We celebrated with a delicious Sunday dinner that we ate at the table in front of the fireplace. I built a fire of rolled-up newspapers, because we had no other fuel. As we ate our happy meal, the sunlight streamed through the bright, clean windows and laundered, starched curtains, in our freshly painted apartment. This, we thought, was living. "Ginny and me and baby makes three, in our blue heaven."

But, of course, this was too good to last. Within three weeks of our blue heaven, I had been given my shipping orders to Texas again, this time to Randolph Field at San Antonio.

Within the next two days, we had all our things packed up. Some, including a used baby bed we had bought through a classified ad Ginny had seen in the Greensboro newspaper, were shipped to Detroit, where Ginny and the baby were going. The rest of our stuff—dishes, bed linens, pots, pans, and utensils—went back home to Iowa. How many times, we wondered, would we have to send these things back and forth to the farm?

Ginny and I were getting quite good at saying good-bye to one another. But it never became any easier, especially because now there was the baby to part with, too—who we knew would be growing and forgetting her pa.

Only days after Ginny and Jeannie had left for Detroit, I was on my way to San Antonio, Texas. Some of our laboratory group from Miami Beach, including Frazzoni and Smitty, were to be a part of some lab project at Randolph Field there. Once we had arrived, they didn't seem to know what they wanted to do with us. So, within about ten days of being assigned to work on the processing line for soldiers being discharged, Smitty and I were sent on separate trains a couple of days apart back to our old outfit in Greensboro, North Carolina.

My train had a stopover of about four hours in New Orleans, during which I walked to a gift shop on Canal Street and bought a fine china plate, decorated in gold and blue, to have sent to Ginny for our anniversary. The plate arrived safely and served in our family as the "birthday person's" plate at family celebrations. Ginny answered by return mail, "I'd like very much to visit New Orleans with you sometime, dear. . . ."

About forty years later, we did make a short business trip to that fascinating place. But sadly, because of the deterioration of Ginny's mind by that time, we were not able to share the enjoyment we'd once anticipated.

After my return to my outfit, I was reassigned to the lab. But most of my attention and concern was devoted to being discharged. My letters to Ginny the next few weeks ran hot and cold on the possibilities of getting out soon. Our letters, also, for diversion, were the means of sharing our dreams of the return to civilian life.

The bulletin board was posted daily with the names of those eligible for discharge. Eligibility was based on the number of points accumulated, which were determined by years of service, those with overseas service getting extra points.

Greensboro, N.C.,
Nov. 12, 1945
Monday night

Ginny, darling—

What do you know! At long last, after four long years, my name has appeared on the bulletin board on the *right* roster. The orders came through today and our names were posted. There are four lists, one list for each day. Mine is the last name on the last list. (Whew! That was close.) I am to transfer to Squad K a week from today on the nineteenth. Smith goes over Saturday. You see, he has sixty-two points. I shall probably be seeing you next weekend, Darling—what do you know! I would rather be going over with the group tomorrow, but I'm happy to have my name on the list at all.

We shall have to celebrate our anniversary in spirit again this year, dear. But then why not just postpone it a few days until I get there? Oh, my darling, I'm so anxious to live with you permanently.

. . . I've been working on our house plan some more. I like it better all the time. I'm getting quite attached to it. It would be quite easy to make a second upstairs room . . . I'm anxious for when we can be in our own home. . . . I would love to build it with my own hands, with you and Jeannie and the baby nearby, giving me advice and love. . . . Bought two more hand towels today. They'll have some more bath towels and washcloths in Wednesday. I'll try to buy some more then. . . . I bet those dresser scarves you are making with them are nice.

Greensboro, N.C.,
Nov. 13, 1945
Tuesday Evening

My darling,

One day closer to being with you. Now that I know *they,* too, are planning on my discharge and have me on the orders, I can work with a song in my heart. I figure like this: I've done it for four long years, surely I can continue for a few more days—now that I know something definite.

In a letter on the next night, I wrote again of our anticipated reunion:

Before long, dear, this will all be over and our little family will be *together*. . . . I look forward to your laugh and the light and sparkle in your eyes. I love the vibrant love of life in all of you . . . I have three more days of work in the Army. Then Sunday to while away, followed by four days of processing, and then, my dear, I shall be out of "this man's Army," and take off for Detroit and my little family.

While waiting for my time for discharge to come, I was assigned to the separation processing line. Those of us working on the processing line were looking forward to being in the outward-moving line when we ourselves would be processed out.

Eventually, that great day came. I found myself on the other side of the table with the sample bottle in hand and baring my arm for the venipuncture I'd been administering to others. And then on to the other stations of the long khaki line winding its way to the final stop where we were to pick up, in addition to the coveted discharge papers, the much desired "ruptured duck," the emblem that went on the left breast of the shirt and coat, that showed for all to see that we were *veterans*.

But for me it was not to be. In spite of the weeks of our hoping and planning for my release from the Army, and even though the day had finally come when I was seemingly on my way to freedom, it all came to a screeching halt when I was only part way through the processing line.

At one of the stations along the line, my MOS (Military Occupational Specialty) number, designating me as a laboratory technician, recently ruled essential, was spotted, and I was immediately yanked out, thus terminating my separation process from the Army.

The shock of this sudden turn of events, after dreaming and planning for my life together with Ginny as civilians, free of the military dictatorship we'd been living under ever since we had met, was more than I could take without protest.

In the past I'd been inclined to be obedient to authority, careful not to make waves. When it was only myself to be affected by circumstances beyond my control, when I alone was subjected to unfair treatment, I could endure and wait it out. But things were different now—I had a family to think of, with another child on the way. Suddenly, some primitive instinct for family protection was triggered within me. No longer was I intimidated by people wearing little bits of brass on their shoulders or caps. No longer was I impressed by those with more stripes on their sleeves than I wore. I was surprised at the reckless courage that came surging up from within my mere buck sergeant's uniform. I was in revolt and fighting mad.

Immediately after being so unceremoniously taken from the separation processing line, I asked to see a higher authority and went up through the chain of command, maintaining my "battle-field courage."

On Sunday, after about four days of storming through the officialdom of the post and finally seeing that nothing could be changed, I phoned Ginny to give her the distressing news. How much I wished that I could have delivered the message in person so that I could have held her in my arms and let her sob out her great disappointment on my shoulder!

After the agonizing phone conversation, so inadequate a means of communicating when we needed to hold one another close, I fell back upon the device we had come to rely on for some time: I poured my heart out to her in a letter. I wrote a long, detailed account of the whole frustrating experience of the past week, trying to explain the devastating turn of events.

At one point during my spontaneous campaign, it had been suggested that I take my case to the personnel office at headquarters, which I did. Portions of the letter reveal something of the desperate passion that was animating me. I think I must have been temporarily a little crazy.

There I waded through clerks, officers and whomever else got in my way. Still no satisfaction. I wasn't timid at all, Gin, I felt as though I was right and everyone else was wrong. The strange part of it was that there was not a single one who didn't seem to respect my actions. I took advantage of that, too, and told them what I thought of the way things were run. At one point a captain kind of blinked and looked startled at what I said, but no one even *threatened* to throw me out.

The last one I went to see on Wednesday was the Air Inspector. I discovered when I got in the outer office that one was supposed to go through channels to see him—even had to have a request from the C.O. But as I was talking to the sergeant standing in my way, the inspector came out of his office and asked me to come in. I told him my story and, also, as I had told the others, my reason for having to go now so as to get you settled before it was too late in your pregnancy.

After several fruitless phone calls, he suggested a furlough for now so I could get you home. He made some more phone calls and finally got that pretty well agreed upon. However, that, too, is unpredictable as only the Army can be.

This is one of the dark, disappointing times in our lives. We might as well recognize that fact and make the best of it. But *this* we know—Better times will come. A storm, the darkest of them, can only last a certain length of time and then the sun comes out again and things seem even brighter than before the storm and darkness. Please, Darling, it hurts me so to know you are hurt. Please try to think of our many blessings and all that you and I have to be thankful for.

The emergency furlough to take Ginny and Jeannie home was finally implemented and, amazingly enough, did materialize. But in the intervening days, Ginny sprang into action. She wrote and got others of her and Laura's acquaintance to write letters to representatives in Washington. (Those of us in military service were forbidden to write to our congressmen or senators, but Ginny was a civilian.) I pleaded with her *not* to write to the brass in Greensboro, however, fearing that her Irish ire might possibly spoil my chances of *ever* getting out.

With emergency furlough papers securely in my pocket, I hurried to Detroit to gather up my family and take the train to Hampton, hopefully while it was still safe for Ginny to travel in the seventh month of her pregnancy.

As I had feared, little Jeannie did not know me. She had passed her first birthday, was taking tentative steps, and had entered potty training—my baby was growing up, and I had *again* been missing out on the experience!

Ginny, Jeannie and I arrived in Mason City, Iowa, in the early morning of Monday, December 17, 1945. The folks were there to pick us up, and after the thirty-some miles to Hampton and the farm, I could sit back, kick off my shoes, and breathe a great sigh of relief—I had my family safely home, come what may!

That Christmas, my first one at home in more than four years, and the first with Ginny and our baby together, was a blessed time indeed. For Grandpa and Grandma, it was an especially happy time, with a toddler once again as a part of that special season.

When the end of my furlough approached, the thought of the end of our blessed days together became hard to bear, with the uncertainty of when my discharge would be coming. Would I again be absent when Ginny's time for delivery came? Would I not be there for the birth of our second child, too?

With the desperation of a man in the mood to "go over the hill," I sent a telegram to the commanding officer of my unit in Greensboro, requesting an extension of my furlough. The reply came back shortly. The old crank telephone on the kitchen wall of the farm rang with a call from the telegraph office in Hampton, saying they had a message for Sgt. George R. Artley. The lady on the other end of the line said she would put it in the mail to me but would read it to me, if I wished, which, of course, I did. She read: "Extension disapproved. Report not later than midnight Dec 30, '45. Discharge upon return. C.O. ORD"

What an explosion of joy occurred in that old farmhouse as I repeated aloud the last sentence in the message. *Something* had worked, whether it was my storming through the offices of command, Ginny's efforts through her letters to those in high places, or a change in policy. Most likely it was the latter. At any rate, I was soon speeding on the train on my way back to Greensboro, North Carolina, to collect my ruptured duck.

DREAMS ADJUST TO REALITY

Two predominant factors shaped my emotional response to my long-awaited discharge from the Army; one was an overwhelming sense of freedom. I think I have some idea of how those who have been living under a repressive government must feel when given their freedom. For more than four long years *I* had felt repressed, put upon, hounded, ordered here and there to do this and that by those who had been designated my superiors. The other factor that caused my heart to sing—I was *going home!*

I shall not even try to describe the depth of emotions expressed in the kitchen on the farm, late that afternoon in January of 1946, when I set down my bags and gathered my loved ones into my arms, pressing them against the breast of my uniform emblazoned with the "ruptured duck."

The next days, weeks, and months were a wonderful, hectic, and perplexing time of readjustment to civilian life and to the problems inherent in two families living under the same roof, regardless of how loving and kindly disposed the members are toward one another.

Dean got his long-awaited discharge from the U.S. Army Air Force and came home to live for a while before enrolling at Iowa State College in Ames. Dan, having graduated from high school the previous spring, had a job in town but was living at home. So the old farmhouse was alive with several levels of interest. Each of the four upstairs bedrooms was occupied. Ginny, Jeannie, and I were given the large southeast bedroom—the one that had always been my parents'.

On February 5, just a few weeks after my military discharge, the population of our young family and of the farmhouse was increased by one when our second child was born. Again, as fourteen months before, the birth occurred during an ice storm. About midmorning Dad came into the kitchen where Ginny was sitting, busily ironing some laundry. He commented that Ginny seemed to be pretty busy so we'd better watch her, because sows, when they were about to farrow, became busy "making nest." At this, Ginny threw a piece of rolled-up laundry at Dad, and we all joined in the fun of Ginny's being compared to a pig.

About noon, when her first contractions began, Ginny and I were driven to Grandma Artley's house in town, so we'd be near the hospital in case the freezing rain worsened, which it did. About 5:00 P.M., at Ginny's suggestion, Grandma drove us the five or six blocks to the Lutheran Hospital. Just as we got there, the storm caused the power to go off, and Grandma, always her best in an emergency, hurried home to get some candles.

In spite of the power outage and with the help of the hospital's auxiliary power, Grandma's candles, and nature's irresistible forces, Robert Moore Artley came into this world, protesting loudly.

But while new life emerges on the growing edge of a family, death comes to the mature portion. In the spring of 1949, Grandma Artley, whom we'd all come to depend on always being there, was diagnosed with cancer and died soon after. In February of 1950, Uncle Wayne Artley, Dad's younger brother, died, widowing our much-loved Aunt Lavina, who, as a lab technician in the Hampton hospital, had served as an inside friend and help to Ginny both times she gave birth there. These two family losses helped us to realize anew that we were in a world where death as well as birth was an ongoing reality.

Ginny and I had dreamed of having our own place where I could be the artist-farmer I'd asked her to marry and where our children ("lots of 'em") could grow up. However, there was no way financially that we could get a farm of our own. In addition to this practical matter, Dad's health had been deteriorating over the past year. He was gradually losing the strength and use of his lower legs, making it increasingly difficult for him to do farm work. Thus, we decided to work the farm together with Mom and Dad.

In the last year or so of Army life, Ginny and I had been developing plans for our dream house. Now, we thought, we could put these plans to use. The folks deeded us two acres of the farm on which to build, and full of starry-eyed dreams, we went to the bank for a GI home loan. The banker, however, in his financial wisdom, helped us realize that our plans were far beyond our present means, so we went home and revised them. With the help of a GI home loan we built something that was more realistic. What was to have been the garage/studio was redesigned into our house: two large rooms, a kitchenette, a bath, and a large, centrally positioned "heatilator" fireplace, which furnished our heat that first winter. The plans allowed for further expansion as needed and as made possible by improved finances.

Ginny, probably the least materialistic person I have ever known, entered into the spirit and planning for my sake, but as far as she was concerned, all that was required in a house were four sound walls, a roof, and a loving atmosphere to make a secure home for our family. As she repeatedly told me, she didn't care where we lived, "as long as we can be together and are happy."

Dan did much of the field work on the tractor that season, while Dad, Dean, and I worked at building the house. The following February, Ginny, Jeannie, Robbie, and I moved into an unfinished but livable home. While the house we actually built fell far short of the plans we had dreamed on paper, we *did* manage to salvage the features we considered most important—two large windows (living room and bedroom) through which we could watch the seasons change on the rolling hills to the west of us and view the magnificent Iowa sunsets. After we put the kids to bed, we read to one another far into the night as the fire crackled and the ancient Seth Thomas clock on the mantel ticked.

That Ginny didn't put much importance on the material things for our home was fortunate, because our cookstove that first year was kerosene, and a makeshift cupboard on the back porch served as our refrigerator during the cold months. In the meantime our names were added to a long list of those waiting for a wartime economy to convert to making home appliances.

That spring we established a windbreak of spruce, planted some apple trees, and put up the white picket fence Ginny had envisioned for "our home out in the West," where, according to the old song we had liked to sing, we could "let the rest of the world go by."

Ginny entered wholeheartedly into her new life on the farm,

Jeannie, Ginny, and Robbie at grass-roots level on the farm, summer 1948.

Ginny, Robbie, and Jeannie in front of Ginny's picket fence on the farm, 1949.

wanting to immerse herself in all aspects of it. She even volunteered to help me clean the gutter in the cow barn one time. Afterward, she decided she'd rather change the baby's diapers.

Ginny also asked me to teach her how to milk a cow. So while she balanced herself on the one-legged milk stool beside the huge brown body of one of our gentlest cows, she succeeded in extracting a few squirts of sweet, warm milk from the udder of the patient critter. Ginny was delighted by her accomplishment in her one and only milking session.

In spite of our seemingly idyllic situation there on the farm and in spite of the loving kinship with Mom and Dad nearby that cemented their bond with our children, after a few years Ginny and I realized that we were not making it financially and we could not continue farming. Even with our frugal life-style, our expenses were exceeding our income. We agonized over these matters, seeing our dreams crumbling. Eventually Ginny, perceiving things better than I and seeing what must be done, urged me to make use of my GI benefits to go back to school and further my art education.

Once we had made our decision we informed the folks and started making plans for our new life. They were saddened by the thought of our leaving, of no longer having their first two grandchildren nearby; however, they were understanding of our motives and were supportive and helpful as we made preparations over the next few months.

Helping to alleviate the concern Ginny and I felt over abandoning Mom and Dad in the farming operation was the knowledge that Dean, who shared my love for the farm, would be taking over our part. He also agreed to buy our house.

The four-and-a-half years we lived on the farm were important to the founding of our family. These were peaceful, comfortable years that served as a time of family bonding.

In January of 1950, our last winter on the farm, Ginny bought a hardbound notebook with a black leatherlike cover. In this she started keeping a journal of our growing family. One can see from her own words her appreciation for the value of life and the inevitable brevity of each living moment.

January 18, 1950
   Bob and I went to Mason City today. The children stayed

with their grandparents. They would much rather stay with "Mama" and "Papa" than go to Mason City. . .

It was a very cold day. We had trouble with the car windows frosting over. It took us an hour to get there. I got my eye glasses first. The glasses plus the treatment cost $26. We had lunch in the drug store and afterwards went shopping and had a good time mostly looking. Bob and I never tire of one another's company.

We did buy a wall-mounted can opener for Mom and Dad. We also bought the children each a small hot water bottle shaped like a kitten.

January 20, 1950

Bob, Jeannie, Robbie and I went to Grinnell today. It was a nice day for traveling—not too cold . . . It took us two and a half hours to get there. Bob felt right at home in his old college town. He seemed to be brimming over with an inner excitement combined with a nostalgic sadness. Bob took us all to the Dixie Inn where we had tasty tenderloin sandwiches. From there to the Registrar's office to get a transcript of his grades to send to Iowa University. Then we joined him and went to the third floor of Magoun Hall to see Miss Sternfeld in the art studio. She was Bob's art instructor when he attended Grinnell. She introduced us to her class which was painting a picture of the janitor. Jeannie was especially interested in watching the students work at their easels . . .

January 21, 1950

It was a fairly warm, cloudy day. The children played outside most of the time. I spent some of the afternoon with Mom. She was interested in hearing all about our trip to Grinnell. Jeannie and Robbie burst in frequently to ask their Grandma for a cookie. It's good for them that their Grandma is the old-fashioned type.

January 25, 1950

Towards night it got terribly cold. After chores were done Bob read to the children while I baked bread.

January 26, 1950

After lunch the children were playing in the bedroom while Bob and I were in the living room. We overheard bits of their conversation: Robbie: "Don't spank him (Cactus Pete, the doll), he'll think you don't love him." Jeannie: "Oh no,

Robbie, we love them when we spank them because we want
them to be good."

February 8, 1950
   Bob's cousin Ruth Evans called to ask if we would like to
have an orphan ewe lamb. Bob made a pen for it in our basement. Later on in the day, John Evans brought the lamb. She
was so sweet and we all became attached to her immediately.
John had brought a bottle and nipple and told me how to fix
the formula.

February 9, 1950
   A resonant quavering ba-a-a echoed from the basement. I
had been lying awake for some time thinking of the previous
day's happenings, but Bob was still sound asleep. I was startled
to hear Jeannie from her bed say, "Did you hear that?" Robbie, teasingly from his bed next to hers, "I wonder what that
is?" His voice had a touch of laughter in it. Jeannie laughed
"Oh yes, what is that?" Another "ba-a-a-a" quavered and
trailed off. It sounded like a newborn baby. Then Jeannie
called out, "Daddy, we want our little lamb up here." Bob
stirred some as I nudged him, "Hey, you, we need someone to
fix the fire." A yawn, "Yeah." He slowly arose, "You wanted
that lamb for the kids, I didn't."
   After Bob fixed the fire and the heat began to permeate
the rooms, the children again asked for the lamb. "You can't
have the lamb until you get dressed," Bob told them. So I got
the clothes they were to wear, and they dressed faster than
I've ever seen them. Usually I have to coax and scold, hurry
them up each step of the way. Right then and there I decided
the lamb was worth the trouble she made for us. The children
named her Mickey.
   She began to "baa" some more. Jeannie held her like a
baby and comforted her while I fixed her bottle of one and
one half oz. of milk and an equal amount of water. She
chewed and tugged at the nipple and in no time flat had
consumed the entire amount. Afterwards, since she doesn't
wear diapers, and since she isn't trained, Bob returned her to
her basement pen.
   Before Bob started chores, he came back in and suggested
that we all take a walk. His eyes were shining as he told us,
"It's really beautiful out. Look how the hoarfrost clings to the
branches of the trees. Everything is covered. Better hurry,
though, because the sun is shining and it might not last long."

So we donned our outside clothing—leggings, boots, coats, scarfs, hats and mittens and ventured outside. Bob had not exaggerated one bit. The colors were white, blue and gold. The white of the snow and frost, blue of the sky, and gold of the early morning sunshine. The grove looked like a white fairyland. The countryside was still and beautiful. We walked around in the grove, snapping pictures now and then.

We popped in to say "good morning" to Grandma. (Grandpa and Daddy were in the barn milking.) Jeannie was anxious to tell Grandma about the lamb. Jeannie asked Grandma if they would take care of the lamb when we went to Iowa City. Grandma said that they would, and then added, "Then when you come back, you can play with your lamb." Jeannie quickly answered, "We'll come back to visit—not stay." Robbie piped up quickly, "And we will eat too."

Later in the day our kitchen chair came loose at the joints. Bob mentioned fixing it. Robbie had been given some toy tools for his fourth birthday, just a few days before, so Jeannie said, "Robbie can fix it!" Robbie heard and dashed into the closet, grabbed his tool chest, ran back into the living room, yelling, "Let me fix it, let me fix it!" So while Robbie hammered, Bob squeezed the joints together and it was fixed.

Friday, February 10, 1950
The children had bad colds today so I kept them indoors . . . Bob read a chapter of *Winnie the Pooh* to them. (We all enjoy it.) Just as we were starting to eat our evening meal, the folks returned from town and dropped in. They brought coloring books for the children. We had them eat with us.

After they left and Bob went back outside to finish chores, Jeannie, Robbie and I worked on Valentines.

Saturday, February 11, 1950
What a good feeling of security and warmth, to kiss my children goodnight as they lie in their beds asleep, and then crawl under the covers beside my husband. Too often I take this for granted, but the realization of this privilege came to me tonight, as I tucked the children in before retiring. I feel like I want to hang onto every moment of this precious life . . . I have so much to be thankful for.

Sunday, February 12, 1950
We stayed home all day today. We didn't even go to Sunday school or church. The children had bad colds and it

took a lot of effort and patience to keep them in bed. Bob read to them and I kept bringing them different things for them to play with! They got so restless toward evening that dear little Jeannie said "Mommy, please get me something to make me happy—something I haven't played with for a long time."

So I gave them some of Bob's old water color paints. That kept them occupied for a long time—until Bob read a chapter of *Winnie the Pooh,* and then turned out the lights for them to go to sleep. Our dear little children. I love them so much. I hope with all my heart that I can be a good wife and a good mother.

Monday, February 13, 1950
Both children giggled and acted like they enjoyed the crazy story I told them before they went to sleep. Earlier Jeannie and Robbie took turns giving the bottle to Mickey . . . Another precious day goes into memories.

In the following entry Ginny makes reference to feeling blue or depressed—a condition she referred to as "the vapors" which seemed to recur from time to time:

Tuesday, February 22, 1950
I had the "vapors" today. But after Bob bought me a new dress and a pair of shoes, they didn't last long. It's a good thing he doesn't do that every time I have the vapors or I would be spoiled.

In the morning Dad and Bob went to town to get the folks some coal. Then in the afternoon Dad stayed with the children while Bob and I went to Hampton. Besides buying a dress and shoes for me, we bought the folks a picnic basket for their thirty-fourth wedding anniversary tomorrow.

Wednesday, February 23, 1950
Robbie got a hair cut at the barber today. Grandpa took him. Dad said that as soon as Robbie took his hat off, the barber looked over and yelled, "Who cut your hair?" Then he asked, "Did your Grandpa cut your hair?" Robbie said, "Who?" I guess they finally found out that his mother was the one. I don't think I'll ever darken that barbershop's doorway. Dad said that if I had been there, I would have had to face a lot of razzing. . . . Jeannie helped wash the dinner dishes for me while Bob, Dad and Robbie were in Hampton. We played

for a while in the doll house, then I washed both our hair. Afterwards, she ironed her doll clothes while I ironed our clothes.

Thursday, February 24, 1950
Today is Bob's folks' anniversary. Thinking it was yesterday, we gave them the picnic basket yesterday. So . . . today I put a potato in a box and a celery stalk in another box and wrapped them separately and took them over. I wanted them to have *something* to open *today* . . . While Bob was in the house with the children, I took a few minutes to walk through the heavy snow down towards the pasture. I wanted to be out in the silent open spaces alone for a bit. That always gives me a spiritual satisfaction.

Friday, February 25, 1950
Mom asked us over for supper. She had some of her delicious buns . . . The other day television came to Iowa for the first time. They telecast from Ames. Jeannie and Robbie were on television over a year ago when we were in Philadelphia . . . talking to Santa Claus . . . Tonight while Bob worked on our dresser, I read aloud to him, *Remember the End.*

Wednesday, March 1, 1950
Had the old-fashioned flu. Poor Bob did the chores and the farm work, the housecleaning and took care of the children. Mom sent the dinner over. Dad came to see how I was this morning.

Thursday, March 2, 1950
Still sick. Bob was kept busy doing all of the work. He's a good cook. The children have been so good. I don't know what I would do without Bob and the children. We couldn't afford to hire help. I'm so rich having them.

Friday, March 3, 1950
Dad came in to see me this morning, then he and Bob delivered seed corn. Bob didn't want to leave me, but I insisted that he go as Dad is late in getting his seed corn delivered to his customers. The children were good while they were gone. I read to them and made paper hats and paper airplanes for them. Mom sent over the dinner. Afterward, Bob spent a couple hours doing up the dishes while I read to him. Bob was late doing chores tonight. Against his protestations, I warmed

up something for supper and Jeannie and Robbie set the table. My three loved ones can manage a home very nicely.

Saturday, March 4, 1950
  Dean came home from Ames today. I did the dishes today, sitting down now and then, when I got tired . . . Bob cleaned the hog house, Mickey's pen, and took care of the house besides. Mom sent over a good supper which consisted of Spanish rice and her delicious buns and a pie . . . Dean stopped in to see how I was feeling. Jeannie and Robbie are getting restless from being indoors so much. I read quite a while to them yesterday and also indexed my recipes.

Sunday, March 12, 1950
  A week has passed since last writing in here. Since Bob and the children had the flu, I was kept very busy. It was wonderful to have friends to call upon to do the heavy morning chores. Mom sent some meals over and did some patching (clothes) for us. Dad came every day. I learned how to make and bank the fire in the furnace. Bob is still a little weak and is having trouble with his sinuses, but he's carrying on with the work again.

Wednesday, April 19, 1950
  Everyone is very tired tonight. Bob didn't get in until after 8:30. Long hours these days. He and Dad have been seeding oats.
  It was a windy chilly day. The kids and I cleaned out Mickey's pen and carried the manure out into the field . . . We cleaned the basement, giving it a good scrubbing . . . Bob brought in a thick bedding of clean straw for Mickey's pen. She seemed so happy . . . Jeannie and Robbie brought me some lovely pussywillows. The dear little kids. I love them so much!

Thursday, April 20, 1950
  A letter from Meriam today saying that Dad (Moore) was very sick. I knew he was staying with Renna so I called up there. Renna said that he was much better today but had been seriously ill with the flu and it had settled in his lungs. Dad talked to me a little. His voice was so feeble that my heart ached for him. I still feel uneasy about him. . . . I washed clothes today. The wind was terrible. The sheets wrapped themselves around me as I was hanging them up to dry . . .

While Bob was doing chores I helped fix up the children's doll house . . . Robbie was wishing he had a barn as big as Jeannie's cupboard. I told him I would bring up the mill that Daddy had made for him. He could use that for a barn. Bob made their cupboard, doll house, bed and mill. Grandpa made them their table and chairs.

Bob and I had an interesting evening. He read to me while I washed my hair and patched his overalls. Then we had a good time playing Chinese checkers.

Friday, April 21, 1950

A beautiful day. Jeannie and I went to town. We bought her a little red coat and a blue skirt for me . . . Robbie stayed with Bob. He likes to be in the fields with the men . . . I'll always remember Robbie and Jeannie dashing in the house the first warm day last month, happily yelling for me to come out, that they wanted to show me something. I followed them out and Robbie grabbed his little rake and vigorously raked aside some old grass. He told me to lean down, grinned and Jeannie grinned, while I examined. It was a little green shoot of grass springing out of the ground.

Mother's Day

Jeannie, Robbie and Bob all wished me a happy Mother's Day this morning. Jeannie and Robbie together carried out a small package. Their faces were aglow and they seemed so tickled about giving me something. It was a bottle of Coty's cologne (Lily of the Valley). Bob gave me a lovely yellow handkerchief. My wonderful little family! . . . Bob did a beautiful lettering job of the poem, "Mom's Apron," for his mother and I made her an old fashioned apron . . . We took Dad and Mom on a drive to the Little Brown Church and out to dinner. We had a very nice time in spite of car trouble—the generator. Had to get the battery charged up in Fredericksburg.

It was not easy to pull up our roots from the farm where we had planned to raise our family in a lifestyle with values in which we both believed and to start over in a university setting, and I probably wouldn't have done it without Ginny's gentle urging. For a long time after we left, when we would go back to the farm for a visit, Ginny could not bear to even look at our "little house" through the grove. The hurt remained for years.

Nevertheless, amid tearful good-byes in June of 1950, Ginny and I loaded the secondhand Chevy we'd purchased with my Iowa soldier's bonus and set off for Iowa City to become residents of that academic community. Grandma and Grandpa would bring the children to join us in a few days, after we'd settled in.

We had been preparing for this move for several months but had seen only floor plans of the former barracks that had been converted into two-bedroom apartments in the student housing area known as Stadium Park. So Ginny and I spent several evenings, after the children were in bed, measuring the furniture we would be taking and fitting it into the cramped space we were allotted according to those floor plans. There were two bedrooms, a bathroom with shower stall, a storage closet, and a long room the width of the barracks. Behind the partial wall at the end of that long room was the small kitchen, with the larger front part our living room.

Because there were no built-in bookshelves, I bought some lumber and made an open-faced bookcase, with doors at the bottom for storage. Another set of shelves I made for the children's room. The third piece of furniture, made specifically for our new adventure, was a three-shelf unit to mount on the wall over our table between the kitchen and living room. It has hung on a wall in each of our homes since.

The place that was to be our home was quite a comedown from our airy, new white cottage on the farm. If Ginny was as daunted as I was when we first stepped into the dark, dismal interior, she said nothing, but, typically, threw herself into the task of cleaning and scrubbing the place so we'd have it ready when the van arrived with our belongings. By the time Dad and Mom had arrived with Jeannie and Robbie a couple of days later, they found a cozy "make-do" home.

Though our budget was tight, Ginny bought a good 35-mm camera, making arrangements to pay for it in monthly installments that we could handle. As she explained to her somewhat chagrined husband, it was important to record our growing family *now* and not wait until we "could afford it." How thankful we have all been that she had this foresight. We made good use of the camera to record our family's growing years.

We found ourselves in the midst of the baby boom, with kids spilling out of the doorways of these temporary places—homes for former GIs like us, all intent on making use of GI education benefits. Dad suggested that the procreation of the place might be caused by the close quarters. At any rate, in September of the following year our third child would be born.

Almost immediately after settling in, summer classes began and I busied myself with courses in life drawing, painting, and engraving. And Ginny, after getting her household settled, brought her journal up to date:

July 3, 1950

A lot has happened since I last wrote in this book. I am sitting here at the table in our barracks home right back of the stadium (142 Stadium Park). Bob is studying and Jeannie and Robbie are in their beds.

Jeannie and I went to Pennsylvania the week before we came here. Bob and Robbie stayed home to do the farm work. We went with the purpose of seeing my Dad and Mother Ritchey. They are both in their eighties and it might be the last time I ever see them.

Dad seemed so old and feeble. It put a lump in my throat to see him that way. He was always so active, full of life and spirited. He was staying with Renna and Chauncey. I stayed with them and all my brothers and sisters came there to see me . . . We went over to the cemetery at South Fork on Memorial Day. Dad went along. Dear old Dad. He had such a rough life . . .

Jeannie and I went from South Fork to Philadelphia by train. Louise met us at the station. It was good to see Mother Ritchey again. She is so full of fun and everyone is crazy about her. "Wees" and Web have a lovely home . . . It's always so hard leaving those you love when you know you won't see them again for a long time.

Jeannie and I spent two nights on the train coming back. We were so happy to see Bob and Robbie again.

The following week was spent in preparation for moving. It saddened us to leave a place where we had spent four years of our lives. . . . The folks brought the children down Sunday evening and spent a few days with us. It was especially hard for them and the children to part when the folks had to return . . . I am so happy to be here. I wanted Bob to finish his schooling.

The children adjusted very quickly. They've made lots of friends and have had a lot of fights. . . . I have become acquainted with many of their mothers.

When fall classes began, I took a full academic course load
toward the B.A. degree that had been interrupted at Grinnell
when I was drafted ten years earlier. Ginny, too, became actively
involved in our new life in Iowa City, not only as a busy wife and
mother, but also as a participant in the University:

Oct. 9, 1950
    I wish I had written more in this book this past summer.
We have been so busy with Bob going to school and so many
things coming up that were unforeseen . . . Jeannie fell from
the bar of a swing . . . and suffered a crushed vertebra. She
had to wear a body cast for six weeks . . . She was such a
brave little thing . . . very little complaining. When it happened, I felt like the world had fallen from under me . . . she
was lucky that she didn't become paralyzed . . .
    Bob became a cartoonist for the *Daily Iowan* (student
newspaper). I keep telling him that this is the field he should
enter . . . of course he doesn't receive pay, but he has the
satisfaction of getting his work in the paper and he may get
recognition that may lead to a paying job. I'm so happy for
him. He has so many subjects to carry . . . math is his hardest
subject and he must carry a semester of that.
    Another thing that's happened is my becoming a co-ed. I
thought I would like to take advantage of living in a university
town and take a couple of courses. I am carrying eight
hours—English and history. It's very interesting.
    We visited the folks at the farm often this past summer.
Bob helped with installing the bathroom and painting the
house. . . . The folks came down last Friday and stayed until
this afternoon. We're always glad to see them come. . . .
    When football season was in full swing, our court neigh-
bors had a wiener roast the night Iowa played Southern California . . . We huddled around the campfire, sang, ate apples
and popcorn and listened to the game on the radio. Iowa
defeated California.

November 4, 1950
    Interesting but busy times these days . . . Halloween we
dressed the kids up to go begging in our court . . . I had a
party for all the children in our court . . . We made hats out
of paper and Bob painted black cats on them. . . . Jeannie
comes home with things that her little friend tells her, like,
"Cheryl says that a girl who chews gum after a boy has chewed
it will turn into a boy."

Ginny wrote about the Christmas of 1950 in March of the next
year:

March 3, 1951
It's about time I wrote in here. . . . I must tell about our
nice Christmas and the preparation for it . . . Jeannie was one
of the angels in the Christmas play at school . . . They sang
"Away in the Manger." I think that song will always be my
favorite song because every time I hear it, I think of Jeannie's
sweet, clear, bell-like voice singing it. . . . The week before
Christmas was spent making cookies, candy and popcorn balls.
All four of us worked on this project and we all enjoyed it so
much. Friday night I took some of the children caroling . . .
One of the neighbors had us in for hot chocolate and cookies.
Christmas Eve, to my way of thinking, is the most beautiful part of Christmas . . . We had been talking about and
preparing for Christmas for a long time . . . we wanted to
make the last few minutes of expectation linger. . . . There is
nothing more beautiful than the inner spiritual feeling of
Christmas eve. . . . Jeannie put on her new red nightgown and
Robbie his new blue and white striped pajamas. They were
delighted to see us place a cup of apple cider and cookies on
the table for Santa Claus. . . . We lit the candles on the front
window sills and turned on the tree lights. Bob read some
Christmas stories to the children. Then we took some pictures
of them hanging their stockings on the bookshelf. When we
put them in bed they were so excited. . . . All night long the
children would awaken and ask us if it were "time to get up
yet." Finally we all got up, blindfolded the children and took
them into the living room. When we took the blindfolds off,
Jeannie made a bee-line for her doll and Robbie for his cow-
boy suit. They received many gifts. They were anxious for Bob
and me to open the gifts that they had given us. Robbie and
Jeannie gave me a sewing kit and all three of them gave me a
pretty flowered sewing box. Bob gave me a pretty blue nightgown. The folks and Dean came down Christmas night and
returned home the next day. They brought arms full of gifts
and food. We had such a nice time. It was one of the loveliest
Christmases we've ever had.

Feb. 12, 1951
The doctor told me today that there is no doubt that I am
pregnant. The baby is due the first part of September. I am so
happy, even though our finances are very low. But I'm sure
that we will manage as Bob and I are happier than we've been

"The week before Christmas was spent making cookies, candy, and popcorn balls. All four of us worked on this project and we all enjoyed it so much." Stadium Park in Iowa City, 1950.

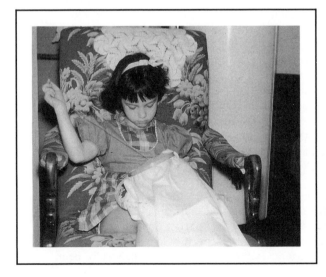

Ginny wrote in her diary: "I've been teaching the children how to embroider. I gave them each a pillow slip and they embroidered their names on them." Jeannie at Stadium Park, Iowa City, 1951.

for a long time. Money troubles are such little troubles. Bob and I have always thought so much of one another and a love like that will overcome many obstacles. I want to do my own sewing and buy as little as possible as prices are really soaring. Everyone's wages have been raised but the veterans' allotments, so we must be very careful. [During this time we had bought a used, old-fashioned, treadle-style Singer sewing machine, and Ginny put it to good use. Beside clothes for Jeannie and herself, she made matching, chocolate-colored sports shirts for Robbie and me. He, of course, outgrew his, but I wore mine for several years, until it was ready for the ragbag.]

March 10, 1951
   I've been teaching the children how to embroider. I gave them each a pillow slip and they embroidered their names on them. They do very well. . . . Bob and the children went to McBride Museum while I went to the doctor and afterward shopped. Bob said they had a good time. He said that the children asked very intelligent questions about all the stuffed animals. We have been reading different animal stories to them and they wanted to know about them.

March 16, 1951
   The four of us had a nice time playing games this evening. We played "Black Magic," "Hide the Imagination," and "Pantomime." The children were very good in acting out different stories and Mother Goose rhymes for us to guess.

March 19, 1951
   This evening I baked cookies and worked on my maternity smock . . . Robbie and Bob were boxing and Robbie gave Bob a bloody nose.

Not long after Ginny and I were married, her father told me how much she reminded him of her mother, Renna. He said there was not only the physical resemblance, including black hair and a pink-and-white complexion, but also the similarity of their gentle, loving natures . . . as well as their high sense of fun—their loving to play tricks on family and friends.
   What a fresh breeze Ginny brought to our family—keeping us all a little off-balance, never knowing just what to expect from the leprechaun I'd brought home from the war! But her little shenani-

gans were filled with fun and always perpetrated with a loving concern for her victim. I remember the time she prepared one of the family's favorite desserts with shaving cream for whipped cream; the time she tried to serve me a dish of clay that looked remarkably like chocolate pudding (but I turned the trick for her, making her think I'd licked up every delicious drop); the time, unbeknownst to me, she kept changing the blades in my razor to make me think the much-touted, long-lasting blades were even better than advertised. How merry her laugh was.

Then there were the bricks she'd packed in Dan's suitcase when he went to church camp; the rocks she'd put in the teakettle to fool Dad into thinking it was full of water when he made the morning fire in the kitchen range—and then how she'd worried that the April Fool's joke might backfire if the kettle boiled dry and the bottom melted.

What a rich marriage Ginny and I shared, generously seasoned with her sense of fun and laughter! How I always loved her rollicking, love-filled laughter! If I didn't know better, I'd suspect that Ginny had invented April Fool's Day—she enjoyed it so much!

April 2, 1951

While Bob studied all evening the kids and I planned how we would fool him on April Fool's Day . . . so early the next morning Jeannie came into our bedroom and whispered for me to get up . . . I told her to awaken Robbie so she and Robbie, a little sleepy, but nevertheless excited, waited while I lifted the receiver and called for Bob to get up, that he was wanted on the phone. The kids expectantly stood by . . . Bob sleepily toppled out, took the receiver from me and grunted "April Fool," put the receiver down and went back to bed. All that day the children were trying to play April Fool jokes on one another and on us. It was fun even though it did get tiresome. . . . That afternoon we visited the art museum . . . We then went to the Student Union where we had ice cream . . . When we came home I took some money out of our piggy bank for Bob to get some wieners and buns. I fixed a tray for each of us with cocoa and cake . . . Bob read to the children and they went to bed. I helped Bob a little with his Spanish and then to bed—the end of a happy and busy day . . . I'm so happy and do wish the time wouldn't speed by so fast.

The summer of 1951, I graduated. We have in our collection of slides of that time one showing our family group with me in my cap and gown, and Ginny, very pregnant, in a brand new maternity dress bought especially for graduation. Dad and Mom came for the great occasion.

I intended to continue for a master's degree in art with an eye toward teaching. I still had almost three years of schooling coming to me under the GI bill. However, so many former service men and women were availing themselves of the educational opportunities provided by that government program that it was cut back, and I was one of those who had to make a sudden shift in plans when funds were cut off. Not only did we lose my school funding, but also our housing and living allowance—I had to find a job and another place for us to live.

Ginny and I, with her suitcase, went to Mercy Hospital in Iowa City in the wee hours of September 14, 1951, where our second son (third child) was born soon after our arrival. Mom and Dad had driven down from Hampton a week earlier to be with Robbie and Jeannie while Mommy was in the hospital. As recorded in Ginny's journal:

September 15, 1951
    Steven George Artley was born yesterday at 5:21 A.M. He weighed 9 lbs. 9 oz.—our biggest baby. Jeannie was 7 lbs. 2 oz. and Robbie was 8 lbs.

While mother and newborn were still in the hospital, the rest of us moved to a house on an acreage near Solon, several miles north of Iowa City. There we lived until March, and it was there Ginny brought Baby Steven home when her time was up in the hospital.

After the loss of GI benefits, housing, and subsistence forced me to drop out of the university, we endured an acute financial crisis during the fall and winter of 1951 and 1952. I had a part-time night job as engraver at the *Daily Iowan,* which was the student newspaper to which I had been contributing editorial cartoons for several months. However, my salary was not enough to cover our expenses. If it had not been for Ginny's family sending cash and Dad and Mom keeping our fuel barrel filled, Christmas that year would have been pretty bleak. A day or two before December 25,

Ginny, in her new maternity dress, with Jeannie and Robbie and Bob, ready for graduation exercises, summer 1951.

Ginny and brand-new baby Steven at our country home near Solon, autumn 1951.

while I stayed at home with the children, Ginny drove our ailing old '37 Chevy to Iowa City. After taking advantage of some clearance sales and buying some slightly damaged toys at reduced prices, she came home all aglow with a joyful spirit that resulted in a Christmas that our two oldest kids remember as one of their happiest. Ginny and I that year gave each other gifts we'd given in past years, rewrapped in new Christmas paper.

The head of the university's journalism department arranged for me to have an interview with the executive editor of the *Des Moines Register and Tribune.* This eventually led to a job as editorial cartoonist on the *Des Moines Evening Tribune* for a salary of seventy-five dollars a week plus benefits. We felt we were on our way up—I had a job I'd dreamed of since I was a boy and a wife and children any man would value.

In March of 1952, our family moved from our country home near Solon, where Jeannie and Robbie had been attending a one-room country school for the previous six months, to a rented house on Twenty-fourth Street near Drake University in Des Moines. We were reasonably comfortable for the year we lived there; however, it was not a particularly happy time for Ginny.

Soon after Steve was born, while we were living in our home near Solon, she experienced a period of severe depression. The doctor said it was something mothers often suffered after giving birth. After a time she seemed to have recovered from these debilitating attacks, but every now and then Ginny would go through periods of depression, crying for no apparent reason. When Robbie would discover his mother in distress, he would put his arms around her and with an understanding beyond his years, ask what he could do to comfort her.

In retrospect, I think Ginny suffered bouts of depression throughout our years together. At the time, I was never aware of what the problem might be and could not fully appreciate her plight. We didn't seek professional help because we did not recognize that her "moodiness" could be an illness. At such times I wondered if maybe I had unknowingly said or done something to cause her "blue spells," or "vapors" as she called them.

Only in recent years have the children and I come to the conclusion that Ginny did, indeed, suffer from some form of depression. I look back now with a new understanding and realize that what I thought was just her "being difficult"—not her usual warm, happy, vivacious self—was possibly a manifestation of a clinical condition.

On a winter day in 1953, word came from Pennsylvania that Dad Moore had passed away. This sad news was particularly hard on Ginny, who felt that she had not spent enough time with the one she and the rest of the family had not only loved but looked to as a mainstay in their large family.

We managed to scrape together enough money for her to make the train trip to be with her family for that sad time. Once again, as it had been since she was a child, Ginny was reminded of how widely scattered her loved ones were. As she told me one time, she felt she was "always saying good-bye."

After her return, Ginny gathered the children around her and explained to them about the funeral. She also spoke of how much she wished they could have been there with her, and how sad she was that they could not get to know their Grandpa Moore and the rest of their family in Pennsylvania and Detroit as well as they did those in Iowa. Ginny's large family meant a lot to her. However, in giving her heart to me, she had left them to come to Iowa to become a part of my family, thereby separating herself from her own. While we did make the long drive east several times through the years, and some of the family from the East managed to visit us occasionally, the distance and the shortage of money kept it from being often enough for one as loving and family-oriented as Ginny. This, too, caused her hurt.

While living in our rented house in Des Moines, we were searching for a place to buy that would be out of the city but within commuting distance:

April 20, 1953
    The folks took us out to look at a couple of acreages this
morning. One is in Johnston Station and one in Altoona. They
both are in the eleven to twelve thousand bracket—we
couldn't find a decent looking place for less than that. We
have only $1500 for a down payment which isn't enough, as
one place wants $3000 and others more than that.

*Ginny's large family meant a lot to her. Her brothers
and sisters gathered in the winter of 1953 when their
father died. Left to right, first row: Bob and Ed; second
row: Ginny, Meriam, Renna, and Laura; third row: Art,
Bill, and George.*

*The Artleys at home in Waukee, Iowa, circa 1954. Left
to right: Jeannie, Ginny holding Steven, Robbie, and Bob.*

Finally we were successful in our search and bought a two-acre plot in the village of Waukee, in Dallas County, about eighteen miles west of Des Moines. We moved to Waukee in July of 1953. Ginny commented on this in her journal:

September 10, 1953
These are beautiful fall days, but we need rain badly. We've had to buy water from Adel (for our cistern)—12,000 lbs for $7.00. There is no city water here in Waukee. Waukee is a very small town, about 18 miles from Des Moines. It has three churches, two groceries, a hardware store, bank, a bar-lunch counter, a garage, a library that is open twice a week, and a consolidated school. It is a good school but overly crowded. There are about forty pupils in each of Jeannie's and Robbie's rooms. . . . We had an open house at the school last Friday night. Some of us mothers were asked to bring a cake. I had baked a chocolate cake that afternoon. . . . I left it to cool and came back to it to find some taken out along the side. Robbie confessed. It was too late to bake another so I patched it with icing . . .

We do like this place so much. It's a huge house with a screened-in porch across the front facing the street to the east. There are about twenty-seven different fruit trees and a grape arbor. I like the tall pine trees that border the back of our two acre lot. The barn is as well built as the house.

Jeannie has the small back bedroom with all the windows, and Robbie and Steve have the large front bedroom. Ours is the master bedroom at the head of the stairs. There is another small bedroom Bob uses as a studio.

September 14, 1953
We celebrated Steve's second birthday. He received many cards and presents from relatives. I baked him a cake and Jeannie decorated it and set it in the middle of the table. I was out of the room for a while and when I came back, half the cake was gone and the decorations torn off. We had previously told Steve it was his cake so we didn't feel we could scold him for eating half of it.

January 10, 1954
So far since last winter, one good snowfall and that didn't last over two days. I think we're going to have to buy more water for our cistern.

I had the flu last week and the house gathered dirt and dishes . . . After Thanksgiving Robbie had scarlet fever and Jeannie had to stay home from school, also . . . We had a lovely Christmas. This is the first year the two oldest didn't believe in Santa Claus. Jeannie got a black female cocker she named Boots, which we had bought from the animal rescue league. . . . Robbie got an electric train and Bob made Steve a cute little circus wagon with his name on it.

Ginny became more and more wrapped up in the increasing demands put upon her by her active, growing, community-involved family, leaving precious little time or energy to devote to keeping a written record. However, as hectic and often stressful as those years were, Ginny looked back on them with loving nostalgia.

While we lived in Waukee, our fourth and last child was born. The next to the last entry in Ginny's journal noted the event:

November 15, 1955
Time has passed again. Joan Louise Artley was born yesterday about 5:30 p.m. She is a picture of Jeannie when she was born.

On the morning of November 14, 1955, Ginny informed me that this *might* be *the day,* so I phoned in my "regrets" to the paper, and we made arrangements to have the kids go to the neighbors after school until Dad and Mom could come later that night.

About noon, I drove Ginny to Des Moines. But first Ginny said she wanted to stop at a drive-in for a hamburger. With some trepidation on my part—remembering how fast Ginny was getting at giving birth—I complied and we each had a sandwich and a milk shake. Then noticing Ginny wincing, I suggested we get going to Methodist Hospital "now."

But she had another matter to attend to before that—winter coats at Younkers for the boys who were outgrowing last year's. I was dismayed at such an idea, but Ginny insisted she *knew* there was time.

Because of heavy traffic and no parking spaces, I let Ginny off at the west entrance to the store, where I was to pick her up shortly with her purchase, and then I made my way in slow-moving traffic around and around the block several times. After an alarming lapse of time and several passes by the meeting place with no Ginny in view, I parked the car illegally and dashed into the crowded store, expecting to see an emergency ambulance crew attending a woman giving birth. But instead, among the throng of shoppers, I spotted Ginny, sauntering along, carrying her purchases, and seeming mildly surprised to see me inside the store. She suggested that maybe we *should* be getting along to the hospital now, as the contractions were coming more frequently.

Before the end of the afternoon, Dr. Robinson came from the delivery room into the fathers' pacing room to tell me I had a beautiful baby girl. Soon I was with Ginny, who proudly introduced me to our second daughter, Joan Louise Artley. I determined right there that I was going to get to know *this* daughter from the beginning and not wait until she was five months old. Then I found a phone and called to tell the good news to our other three. We had what we considered a complete family—two of each gender.

With her family of four growing children, spanning eleven years in age, Ginny's time and energy was devoted to nurturing rather than writing. This is regrettable, for it would be so much more fulfilling to have her heartfelt words about the early years of our two youngest as we do about our two older children.

Each of Ginny's children, in their diversity, was precious to her beyond measure. She loved each of them "the most." Each held a special place in her heart that was expressed in her solicitous concern up into their adulthood.

There is no doubt in my mind that had Ginny been given music training when she was young, she could have become at least modestly accomplished in a talent that was present throughout her mother's family, the Georges. As it was, she loved to sing to herself as she went about her housework, but was self-conscious if there was anyone to hear her. How I loved to hear her contralto voice beside me, untrained but sweet and full, as we shared the hymnal in church or around the piano at family gatherings. But I especially loved to hear her sing lullabies to each of our babies in the little rocking chair that Dad and Mom had given to her when she went home to the farm to have our first baby.

She loved these special times of closeness to each of her babies

Ginny and her four children, spring 1956. Each of Ginny's children was precious to her, and she devoted her time and energy to nurturing her family.

Ginny and Rob, aged fifteen, in 1961.

when she could celebrate her motherhood by holding them close to her breast and sing out the fullness of her heart in thankfulness. Three of these lulling songs to our babies stand out in my memory: "Twinkle, Twinkle, Little Star," "While the Angels Watch Over Thee," and a little tune that Dad also sang when he rocked them, which was adapted from the song "Every Little Movement Has a Meaning All Its Own."

As the family grew, Ginny would sometimes sing messages to the older ones or to me, admonishing us to be quiet or requesting assistance in putting the baby down in its crib. Sometimes these operatic messages brought smiles or snickers, or quiet replies in the same tune and tempo.

In 1957, after about five years of producing a daily cartoon for the editorial page of the *Des Moines Tribune,* our hopes for my career as a cartoonist on that paper came to an end. A fruitless search for other cartooning jobs on dailies in other cities prompted me to accept work as art director for a Des Moines advertising agency. But the atmosphere of the place and the employer-employee relationship was so intolerable that, after less than a year, I made my escape and went to work in the art department of Plain Talk Publishing Company on the east side of Des Moines.

This was a congenial workplace where the employees were treated with dignity and respect, making me glad to be a part of that organization. And while it was not newspaper cartooning, my chosen work, I still found the nine years I spent there to be a good time, during which I learned much and honed my graphic skills.

During these years, as before, Ginny was busy being a mom and homemaker. She was usually the one to take the children to the doctor for childhood emergencies and illnesses and nurse them back to wholeness for everything from diaper rash to stomach upset, sore throats, chicken pox, measles, and more.

Ginny chauffeured the children to piano lessons and then stood over them to be sure they practiced. When they were in school band, she also oversaw their home practice on trumpet, flute, and drum.

At the same time she was involved in community programs and projects relating to the children's activities. She served as den mother when Robbie and Steve were in Cub Scouts, just as she'd helped out when Jeannie was a Bluebird during our year in Des Moines.

Ginny and I also attended Cub Scout meetings when I served as cubmaster, PTA meetings, parent-teacher conferences, and school programs in which our children took part, culminating in each of their graduations. She even helped the girls plan for slumber parties at our house (which we *all* had to endure).

When the boys were in Little League, Ginny was an enthusiastic booster of our Waukee team and shared in transporting the players to the games. As a girl, she had herself played in neighborhood sandlot games, instructed by her brothers. Later, in Detroit, she'd attended big league games where she saw famous ballplayers like Lou Gehrig and Babe Ruth and became conversant with their names and memorable achievements. With her keen interest in the game and her background experience, it was Ginny, not I, who tutored our boys (and girls) in how to throw a curve ball and scoop up a grounder.

Ginny also taught Sunday School for several years in Waukee. She was so adept at it and related so well to the children that she was given a problem junior high class, with whom she had such success she was asked to shepherd them on through their high school years in Sunday School. They became fond of their teacher, some even coming to see Ginny when they returned to visit their hometown after graduation.

In her role as mom, Ginny was there when the children came home from school, to share in their joy at a bit of happy news or to hug them close and listen when they told of an affront or disappointment.

Ginny always showed appreciation for whatever the children brought to her as gifts or mementos—childish drawings and school papers that were displayed on the cluttered bulletin board or taped to the refrigerator door. And when each of them was small, they plucked violets and dandelions and brought these crumpled little bouquets as trophies of spring to their mother. Each was lovingly received from her children's little hands and placed in a cup or small glass of water on the windowsill over the kitchen sink.

Through the years, there moved with us from home to home a crudely crafted plywood cutout of overlapping hearts with hooks on which to hang keys, a gift brought to her mom when Jeannie was in the lower grades. Incised in the wood in childish lettering were the words, "To Mother, With Love, Jeannie."

In later years, looking back, Ginny often referred to our fourteen years in Waukee as her happiest. This was no doubt because those were the years when our children were all under our roof, and we were secure in familial love, expressed and demonstrated. And she felt secure in the love she and I shared.

However, with my changes in employment and a chronic shortage of cash, those were also difficult years, even unpleasant at times, especially for Ginny.

Those years in Des Moines and Waukee, like our months on the acreage near Solon, represented a time of stress for Ginny in dealing with the needs and concerns of our growing children. She had to keep them clothed, as they kept growing, and try to be reasonable in meeting their wants in light of the wherewithal. Our cars were always used ones (our only new car being a '63 Plymouth), so when Ginny needed to go shopping, she had to load all four of the children into a car that invariably had something wrong with it, then drive to Adel or Des Moines.

There were also stresses resulting from the complications and demands inherent in a neighborhood filled with about ten children besides our own. She refereed squabbles, sometimes using all the diplomacy she could muster. There were even fistfights, upon occasion, in which Robbie sometimes became involved when he stepped in to rescue his feisty little brother.

And Ginny became bogged down in the humdrum of the day-to-day sameness that can be the fate of a mom and homemaker. There were times, no doubt, that she must have longed for her laboratory days when she had been involved in challenging work amid co-workers with whom she could share mentally stimulating conversations.

Ginny sincerely enjoyed having coffee with her friends and neighbors, but often they, too, were immersed in a world that limited conversation to topics of child-rearing, recipes, and helpful hints for homemaking. So when I came home from work, Ginny would often meet me with a kiss, all freshened up in a clean dress, as was her custom, and then, sitting down beside me, seek to share something of what she perceived to be my interesting day "out there," with her gentle plea, "Let's talk."

Adding to the stressful conditions, no doubt shared by most mothers, was her sense of inadequacy as a mom. She was unsure of herself, feeling inferior in this respect to her peers in the community. As I sat hunched over the drawing board in my home studio, preoccupied with the free-lance work that, hopefully, would stretch our income to cover our growing expenses, I wasn't a very good listener when she tried to tell me, in her quiet way, how much she was hurting inside. It is only now with the help of our adult kids that I have become aware and sensitive to her suffering then, due to her self-doubts. The kids and I now ask ourselves, could it be that Ginny suffered thus because she didn't have her own mother as a role model? For in spite of the love and nurturing she received in the homes of her beloved Mother Ritchey and her older sister Laura, she often spoke wistfully of missing the loving contact with her own mother who was only a sweet legend in Ginny's life. And soon there was to be another loss to which Ginny and all of us would have to adjust.

Late in the afternoon of August 21, 1964, I answered the phone in the art department of Plain Talk Publishing Company to hear the choked voice of Dean's wife Reggie on the other end saying that Dad had suddenly passed away only minutes before.

He had been in deteriorating health for twenty years, but bedridden only in the past six months—paralyzed from the waist down. The doctors told us that Dad's heart had simply stopped beating, thus gently releasing him from the creeping paralysis that soon would have caused him to choke to death.

Going home was not quite the same for some time following his death. However, after Mom had rallied from her loss, she once again made the old home a loving, nurturing place. For the next fifteen years—until she had to move to a nursing home—she continued to be mother, grandmother, and great-grandmother—our connection to our heritage on my side of the family.

In April of 1965, Ginny made a final entry in her journal:

> My how time flies! We're a little older now. Jeannie is a sophomore at the University of Iowa in Iowa City; Robbie is a freshman at Drake University in Des Moines (he lives at home and commutes); Steve will go to high school next fall, and Joni is nine and in third grade.

Soon after this, we started the *Waukee Journal*, and Ginny had no more time to make entries in *her* journal.

JOURNALISTS, PRINTERS, AND PUBLISHERS

During our last years in Waukee, Ginny began to expand her talents outside of the home. With her full-time job as the nurturer of our home and family, she had not sought other work. We both felt it important for Ginny to be there when the kids (especially when they were small) came home from school and called out, "Mom, we're home!" However, she did earn a pittance, writing a column for the *Waukee Citizen,* a weekly newspaper. She enjoyed writing the column and did a good job of it. But when the *Citizen* ceased publication a couple of years later, her in-the-home job was gone.

I came home from work one evening to find Ginny excited about a new idea. She suggested that we start a newspaper for Waukee—something we could do together in our spare time at home.

Ginny's enthusiasm for the idea was infectious. Over the next several days, we discussed and dreamed aloud until we had a concept for our publication pretty well formulated in our minds. I drew up a rough layout so that we could visualize it together. We imagined it to be a weekly, tabloid-sized newspaper of no fewer than eight pages. After batting several suggested names back and forth, we finally settled on the *Waukee Journal.*

What fun those dreams were! But to realize them, we had to be realistic. There was no way we could start publication of a newspaper on our own. That would take capital we didn't have. So we went to Adel, the county seat, and presented our idea to George DeFord, editor of the weekly paper the *Dallas County News.*

Mr. DeFord liked our idea. As a result, the *Dallas County News* became the parent organization, the publisher, of the *Waukee Journal*, taking over the business end of the project—selling advertising, billing, collecting, printing, distribution, etc. This left the fun part to us—the news gathering, writing, editing, composition, and preparation of the camera-ready paste-up sheets.

A room in our basement, one that had variously served as a playroom, a little theater for the neighborhood kids, and a place for stringing up wet laundry during inclement weather, became the newsroom of our dream paper. There we set up a desk and a telephone extension, and there Ginny worked at an old Underwood typewriter, gathering, writing, and editing the news of Waukee. George DeFord provided us with a Polaroid camera and all the film we needed, which Ginny used to good advantage, recording photo images of people, places, and events in our community. Besides the news stories, she wrote two columns, "Our Town and Countryside" and "The Pantry." The latter featured a local homemaker of the week with a photo and her favorite recipe.

The *Journal*, on Ginny's insistence, also included an editorial cartoon produced by her erstwhile editorial cartoonist husband, as well as a comic strip and a crossword puzzle. We also saw to it that our paper had at least one editorial in each issue—something we considered necessary to express its soul. And we encouraged letters to the editor, with Ginny prevailing upon a couple of the town's residents to contribute columns on a regular basis. These became quite popular, enjoyed by the writers as much as the readers.

Ginny did all the typing—news, columns, photo captions, and headlines, which someone from the *Dallas County News* picked up late on Tuesday afternoon. Late on Wednesday, galley proofs of type, layout sheets for paste-up, with the ads already composed and pasted in position, a portable waxing machine, and other accoutrements for paste-up were delivered to the editorial office of the *Waukee Journal* in our basement. That evening, after supper, my studio, adjoining the newsroom, became the composing/paste-up room, where Ginny and I, and sometimes one or two of our kids, worked until the wee hours, getting the camera-ready paper finished, to be picked up early Thursday morning. For all of this, Ginny was paid forty dollars a week—and she could do it in her own home.

Late Thursday afternoon, the printed and addressed *Journal* was delivered to the Waukee post office, and a bundle of extras

THE WAUKEE JOURNAL

POSTAL PATRON LOCAL

BULK RATE
U. S. POSTAGE
PAID
WAUKEE, IOWA
PERMIT NO. 2

VOL. 1   Waukee, Iowa, Friday, May 27, 1966   No. 1

OUR TOWN AND COUNTRYSIDE

Who do you wish would come to live in the new green building up-town? Perhaps a good bakery? A dry cleaner? A day nursery?

-x-

BOOB OF THE WEEK: The women who go to the laundromat unprepared with correct change, then pester the Uptown Cafe for quarters and dimes.

-x-

I have a neighbor who feels so comfortable with me that she calls my name and walks right in. I like the informality of it all.

-x-

Does Waukee have a "haunted house" that the kids are afraid to walk past? The process of maturing into a healthy adult receives a giant boost the day you actually walk by and find that all your fears were groundless. Re-learning can take place, and re-learning is the perfect remedy to rid of us of many of our useless anxieties. Every town should have a haunted house.

-x-

Do you do do you not miss the Sunday morning music from the Methodist loudspeaker?

-x-

DOUBLE YOUR PLEASURE: Use the peck of the children's school papers to write a letter to Grandma--she gets news on both sides; use your garbage pail as a scrub bucket--when the floor is done, your pail is clean; squirt liquid detergent straight into the jar you use for salad dressing, then shake a few times before adding it to the rest of the dishwater--the concentrated detergent cuts the oil in the jar, then goes on to do the other dishes.

-x-

Time Magazine had an item about a retiring sportswriter who commented, "My life has been one long vacation because I have been paid for doing the thing I like best." Here is the real showdown between a man and his work. Would you do it even if the salary were not a consideration? I know a few who probably would. Who in town enjoys his work more than Doc Charlie Howe?

-x-

Ah, youth! Children delight in the strangest of things. One of mine remembers a bad sunburn I had last year, and that she helped remove the blistered layer. She notices summer coming and asks anxiously, "Hey, when you gonna peel again?"

-x-

I wish I needed to see a lawyer about something so I would have an excuse to go into Gill and Huscher's charming place of business. So far I only nose-press against the window.

Poppys for Sale On May 27th

Winnie Shaffer and her Cub Scouts will be selling poppies in Waukee about 3:30 p.m. Friday. Winnie has been doing this for over 10 years. She is a member of the American Legion Auxiliary and is assistant chairman of the poppy committee.

Vandalism Acts

Vandals, early Saturday morning, damaged several pieces of property in Waukee.

The glass in the bulletin board of the Methodist Church was broken, and the letters were arranged to spell vile words. The bulletin board had been presented to the Methodist Church from the people in the community as a memorial for Mrs. Glenn Copeland, killed in an automobile accident nine years ago.

The vandals also upset a bottle of gas at the Church, kinked the gas lines and broke a window in the southeast side of the basement.

Also in the path of destruction was the glass in the handsome Town Crier bulletin board, which was broken for the second time in two weeks.

Jack's Grocery Store was another stop of the vandals, where three windows were broken, and the glass in the door into the base of the water tower was shattered on the same mission of destruction.

Town Marshall, Ray Bainter, said that all this was done after 2:00 a.m. Saturday.

$800 Taken in Van Meter

The Dallas County Sheriff's office reports that between $800 and $850 was taken from a safe at the Jungman Oil Co., in Van Meter. The break-in was discovered about 7:15 a.m. Friday morning by Burt Stanford, an employee at the firm. Officials said that entry was gained, apparently, by tripping the lock in the front door.

The Denniston & Partridge Lumber Co. was also entered through a window, but nothing was found missing.

POST OFFICE
CLOSED ON
MEMORIAL DAY
MAY 30th

Welin Elected In School Vote

The voters in Waukee and Dallas County elected Harold F. Welin of Boone, as Director for the proposed South Central Vocational-Technical School and Community College.

Mr. Welin will be one of nine members representing nine districts of about equal population, serving on the area Board of Education. The vote in Waukee was light, with only 33 voting.

The school will train interested persons in many and various skills.

There are many questions concerning the proposed Area School that are yet to be answered, but briefly, it will meet a wide variety of needs on technical, vocational and academic levels.

The campus will be located so that it will be convenient for all nine Counties, serving the following Counties: Dallas, Marion, Boone, Story, Guthrie, Polk, Jasper, Madison and Warren.

HOPE IT WON'T MAKE HIM SICK

END OF SCHOOL FESTIVITIES

Highlighted By Commencement

Nineteen girls and sixteen boys were awarded diplomas at Commencement Exercises held Tuesday, May 24, 1966, in the gymnasium of the Waukee Community High School. For each recipient, these diplomas signify the completion of prescribed high school courses of study. Academic awards were made to the class members by high school Principal Vincent Mayer. The Valedictorian of the class was Peggy Smith, while Mike Aldrich was named as class Salutatorian. The scholastic averages of the Valedictorian and Salutatorian were very similar, with the final semester grades able to determine the one-two order.

Recognition was given for those students who had maintained a B

or better scholastic average throughout their four years of high school. Those so honored are as follows: Martin Smith, Roberta Wright, Mike Baker, Linda Henderson, Carol Allen, Cisal Johnson, Chris Lewis, Jane Haberman, Peter Rahlson, Connie Anderson and Karen Tollari.

The Danforth awards went to Roberta Wright and Mike Baker. Berry O. Burt, representing the American Bar Association, presented the Citizenship Award to Connie Anderson.

The Commencement speaker, Ray Pugh, was recently named Vice-Principal of Callahan Junior High in Des Moines. His thought provoking address entitled "A Challenge for You," was directed to the graduating class and provided much food for thought.

Walter T. Giles, local Board President, awarded the diplomas to the graduating seniors after Superintendent Eason had presented the class and recommended that the group was prepared for such recognition.

BACCALAUREATE

On Sunday evening, May 22, the Baccalaureate Service was conducted in the school gym, with Joe Turek delivering the address. The Awards Dance, the Baccalaureate Service and the Commencement Exercises were most of the Junior-Senior Banquet decorations still in place. Commencement, as usual, provided a capacity crowd in the auditorium.

JUNIOR-SENIOR BANQUET

The Junior-Senior Banquet was held on Saturday, May 14, in the school auditorium. Under the direction of their class sponsor,

Cont. On Page 5

LAST DAY OF SCHOOL

This is the last day of school for Waukee Community School. The official dismissal is set for 1 p.m. The first day of school this fall is scheduled for August 29. Final registration for the 1966-67 school year will be on August 25 and 26.

SET IMMUNIZATION CLINIC ON JUNE 2

An immunization clinic, 7 to 9 p.m., will be held on Thursday, June 2, at the Waukee School. Doctors and nurses will be in attendance for smallpox, polio, tetanus, dyptheria and whooping cough. Margaret Felton, County Public Health Nurse advises, "Protect your family."

580 Increase

Since 1960

The result of the Federal census, just completed in Waukee, shows an unofficial population of 1,267. The official results will not be available for some time as they must be tabulated by the Census Bureau in Washington.

Waukee's population in 1960 was 687. The unofficial increase therefore is 580. This means that Waukee will receive at least $5,000 per year more revenue from road use tax and liquor profits tax. This will be a substantial help in the Town's street program and for other improvements. Streets can be improved only as fast as funds are available for such purpose.

The two local women who did all the counting on the census were Mrs. Marilyn Davis and Mrs. Donna Steffen. Federal census supervisor, Gladys Bell, reported that the ladies did a fine job.

Adel Pool To Open Sunday

The Adel Municipal Swimming Pool will open Sunday, May 29, for the season, according to Manager Bob Anderson. Prices are as follows: Single admissions, through 12 years, 25c, and over 12 years, 50c. Season tickets through age 12 are $4.00, and from 13 to 18 years, $6.00. Family season tickets (no swim limit), $15.00, and adult season tickets, $5.00.

Bill Sumny will be senior life guard. Other life guards are Dottie Fredregill, Kris Mitchell, Roger Schmiedeskamp and Tom Caudron.

The Water Safety Program will start on Monday, June 13.

Margie Giles Taken by Death

The community was saddened by Margie Giles' illness and death. We can say, "She made the world better by having lived."

She leaves her husband, Bill, and three children, Dick, Linda and Marlene. She also leaves her parents, Mr. and Mrs. Samuelson of Boone; three sisters, Mrs. Dorothy Heathlin of Kansas City; Mrs. Nadine Hoffman of Miami, Okla., Mrs. Alice Larson of Dallas, Tex., and three brothers, Walter Samuelson, Robert Samuelson and LaVerne Samuelson, all of Boone.

She was active in the Maple Grove Methodist Church, a member of W.S.C.S., a member of the Guild, Sunday School Superintendent, and also played the piano for the Church. She was chaperon for the girls basketball team at Waukee High School for two years. She was also a member of the Women's Club in West Des Moines. Services were held in the McLaren Funeral Home in West Des Moines, Wednesday afternoon at 3:00.

The first issue of the Waukee Journal. Ginny did all the typing, wrote the "Our Town and Countryside" and "Pantry" columns, and shared the tasks of editorial writing and paste-up with Bob.

was dropped off at our place—for us to either exalt or agonize over.

There were at least two community issues in which we became involved and which, because of our editorial position, made some enemies. One occurred when we bucked a powerful faction on the school board. The other was when we championed the cause of the village of Waukee versus the powerful utilities company regarding natural gas for the town. There was to be a vote to decide which entity would be allowed to sell and distribute gas. Our *Journal* waged a vigorous campaign. When the votes were counted, our side had won and the village of Waukee was able to be the purveyor of natural gas and keep the profits at home.

All of this was enough to get newspapering into our blood to the extent that after a little over a year, when the *Waukee Journal* folded for lack of advertising revenue (there were not enough businesses in Waukee), we looked for other publishing possibilities.

Ginny found a classified ad in the *Des Moines Register,* telling of a county weekly for lease. Upon investigation, we found it to be in the town of Adrian, in southwest Minnesota, about fifteen miles north of the Iowa-Minnesota border.

We drove to Adrian one Sunday to look the town over. We liked the looks of the little community and decided the commercial area looked viable enough to support a newspaper, so we returned home to Waukee to discuss the whole concept. After much family discussion, agonizing over the pros and cons involving the move, Ginny and I finally decided to launch into this new adventure. I gave notice to Plain Talk Publishing and we signed the papers leasing the *Nobles County Review* for two years. We were able to sell our house to a family we felt comfortable to have living in the home that had meant so much to all of us.

Once these decisive moves had been made, with papers signed and commitments made, the irreversible machinery was set in motion and moved forward relentlessly, regardless of the groans and second thoughts as our family lived out the final days in our home in Waukee. Rob, then a student at Drake University in nearby Des Moines, wrote a piece, "The House on Sixth Street," for one of the final issues of the *Journal,* which was a heartfelt farewell to our home there.

Our move from Des Moines (where we'd lived for only about sixteen months) to the big white house on Sixth Street in Waukee was probably the happiest move our family ever made. In contrast, our move to Adrian, Minnesota, was probably the hardest and most traumatic.

When we left Waukee after fourteen years, we were leaving a place that we had all thought would be our home "forever." In this home Ginny had presided over the nurturing of her family through the shank of their childhoods. Here she had become involved in and made good friends throughout the community. In fact, all of us found that our roots went deep into the nourishing soil of the community of Waukee.

The move that wrenched us from the place that Ginny often looked longingly back upon as her "true home" was one that was to cause us much agony during our first few months in Adrian, that summer and fall of 1967. There were times when we regretted the decisions that led to the move, but, as we had discovered in the past and were to know again in the years ahead, we were being "looked after," for this move, as painful as it was, proved to be one that, in many ways, made a positive difference in our lives, just as had our move from the farm to Iowa City back in 1950. Both were largely due to Ginny's initiative.

We were to take over publication of the *Nobles County Review* in the middle of August. This would allow us enough time, we thought, to get out the final edition of the *Waukee Journal,* pack, move, and settle in Adrian before having to put out the first issue of the *Review.* But things didn't work out that way.

In the last week of July, we received a frantic call from Jim Wilson, the owner of the Adrian paper we were leasing, to say that there was some misunderstanding between him and the publisher currently leasing the paper. The publisher had walked out, leaving no one to produce the paper. Wilson explained that it was important for a paper to publish continuously, without any break for even one issue, in order to maintain its status as the legal paper of the county. If a paper lost its legal status, it would be losing a considerable portion of its income through the "legals" the county was required to publish periodically. Thus, it was imperative that we somehow spread ourselves between Adrian and Waukee to get *both* papers out.

Of course, the distance between the two places was too great to allow for commuting. So after some hurried, distressing discussions, Ginny and I came to the painful decision that Steve and I should go to Adrian and attempt to keep the paper legal there, while she and Rob and Joni put out the final issue of the *Waukee Journal* . . . and pack for the move to Adrian.

I was not a part of the Normandy invasion on D day in June of 1944, but from what I've learned of that stupendous operation, I think probably those days in early August of 1967 were not far below it in scale, as family, friends, and neighbors helped us make the transition from Waukee to Adrian.

On a previous trip to Adrian, we had rented a house where we planned to live until we could get something permanent. (We later bought it and made it our home for the fourteen years we were there.) Bill and Toni Boeker, our landlords, had freshly painted the walls and varnished the hardwood floors. Because we as yet had none of our furniture from Waukee, they loaned us a couple of folding cots so Steve and I would have beds until our move was complete and Ginny and Joni joined us.

By the time Steve, Joni, Ginny, and I (Jeannie was married and in her own home, and Rob was attending Drake University) were reasonably settled into our house in Adrian, we were well into the weekly hassle of getting out the *Nobles County Review*. And it *was* a hassle.

The previous publisher had left a mess, not only within the walls of the newspaper office (which we had not been able to inspect before signing the lease because Mr. Wilson, the owner, had "forgotten the keys"), but also, more seriously, because of the legacy of bad feelings the publisher had left between the town and the paper. Living in the town of Pipestone, about thirty miles from Adrian, the publisher had been in town only one or two days a week—to sell ads and pick up news items from correspondents and to collect bills. He apparently did nothing to make himself felt as a part of the community. Thus, he was perceived instead as being interested only in how much money he could take from it for himself. This, understandably, made for a feeling of bitterness toward the paper that we, as the new publishers, had unwittingly assumed along with the lease. We were seen as more of the same—outsiders intent only on making money at the community's expense.

Thus, the reception we received from the business community

was, at best, cool. The first few weeks were discouraging to the point of despair as I went from business to business, trying to solicit advertising space for the paper.

The scene within the newspaper office itself was one of long neglect. When Wilson had first purchased the *Nobles County Review,* it was being printed by the letterpress method. Because he was converting it to offset, he had sold or hauled to the junk heap all of the old letterpress equipment, including cases of metal type. However, a large sheet-fed flatbed press on which the paper had formerly been printed was still taking up a great deal of much-needed room.

Copies of back issues of the paper were stacked helter-skelter along the walls. Two or three cast-off chairs, a small writing desk with two small drawers, a four-drawer metal filing cabinet, and an antique brass cash register that only partially worked made up our office furniture. The only new piece was a stand-up bench at which to paste up the camera-ready pages for the paper. A thick coating of undisturbed dust and grit covered everything in our new workplace. In this setting, we were to produce a weekly paper that would make the citizens of the community glad to have us as the new publishers. The prospects were not bright.

However, as Ginny had done in times past, she set about to make the most of things as she found them. Our primary task each week was to get the paper out, regardless of the difficulty. Little by little, we cleaned the place and put it in some semblance of order. We convinced Wilson, the owner of the paper, to finish his project of clearing out the letterpress equipment by having the large flatbed press dismantled and hauled away. Then we persuaded Mr. Thompson, the owner of the building from whom we were renting, to remodel the interior (it was all one large room) into two front offices, an adjoining paste-up or composing room, and a back room for storage where there was a sink for washing up (the toilet was in a corner room of the dark, dank, dusty, limestone-walled basement). This back room was also where we ran the week's issue of the paper through the foot-operated addressograph machine, on its way from the printers to the post office, before its closing time on Thursday.

Soon after we started our stint as publishers of the *Nobles County Review,* Ginny started writing a weekly series of historical pieces on the Adrian area. She had always liked history and enjoyed doing the research for it. This series not only served to remind the residents of their past, but it helped us to come to know something about the town and the countryside of which we were now a part.

The readers responded favorably to this series. This, along with Ginny's "Pantry," featuring local cooks' recipes, and her column "Village Views" proved to be popular. The "Grapevine," salvaged from our *Waukee Journal* days, provided the "locals" or gossip column—material furnished by correspondents from throughout the community.

We saw to it that we always had an editorial, an original comic strip, and an editorial cartoon. Steve drew some of the latter now and then, and Joni furnished occasional spot drawings as "space fillers." These contributions, besides the children's help around the office, made publishing the paper truly a family project. We used our Polaroid camera to provide many photos (one of the advantages of the offset printing process) to record the happenings and personalities of the community. We worked closely with and covered all the activities of the schools in our area, public and parochial. This also helped our paper's readership and increased subscriptions.

One of the favorite features Ginny came up with was called "Office Cat." In about a two-column-by-five-inch area was a photo of our stub-tailed cat, Wooley, who had moved with us from Waukee and taken up residence in our newspaper office (his fringe benefit was all the mice he could catch). Ginny would take Polaroid shots of him in different poses, each with a caption line beneath it quoting some remark he'd supposedly made pertaining to a variety of subjects. As a result of this newspaper exposure, Wooley became famous in the area—inspiring at least one scrapbook of clippings of his photos and "learned sayings."

By the end of 1967, we were beginning to hear favorable things about the paper, and advertising inches were increasing. One woman of the community came into our office one day to express how nice it was "to have our paper back." And on one of my regular calls to an advertising client, the manager, who in the past had hardly given me the time of day, called me into his office to tell me he liked what we were doing with the paper and wanted to increase his advertising space.

This positive response was pleasing to us. We were also

beginning to feel more accepted into this community of naturally reserved people who generally seemed to find it difficult to accept outsiders into their midst. When they realized that we were sincere in our interest in the area and were making our home there, we began to feel the warmth coming through the rather cool exteriors of this predominantly northern European stock. And by the end of the fourteen years we lived in Adrian, we had made some good friends there.

But it didn't take fourteen years for us to realize we were among many kindly people. Bill and Toni Boeker, the owners of our house and down-the-street neighbors, showed us many kindnesses, beginning when we first moved into town. We had barely settled into our Adrian home when our next-door neighbors, Alice Bergman and her mother, brought us a beautiful, fragrant loaf of home-baked bread. This was but the beginning of a continuing show of neighborliness. Here again, Ginny and I realized that, in spite of the pain we had gone through in leaving our Waukee home and the hardships of taking over the paper, we *were* being watched over.

Our family was not alone in our attempts at putting out a weekly paper. When we first entered the dreary office of the *Nobles County Review,* we were greeted by a young college girl, Maureen Taylor. She said that, if we were willing, she would be happy to work part-time for us as she had for the previous publisher. Having grown up in the area, she was his one connection to the community. Maureen worked for us until she returned to college in the fall and proved to be of invaluable help in our early days in Adrian.

Because publishing a weekly, as we well knew from our Waukee experience, involved a concentrated flurry of work on the first two or three days of the week, and because much of my time was spent selling advertising space, we needed extra part-time help. We hired a young mother of the community who helped with the typing on the first few days of the week and then with the paste-up. Besides having Steve and Joni's help after school, we hired one of Steve's classmates who had a talent for such work. She also helped with paste-up and putting the finishing touches on the paper before it was ready to be "put to bed." As with the *Journal* in Waukee, this could call for some late-night work on Wednesday so that the camera-ready paste-up sheets could be taken to

Worthington, eighteen miles east of Adrian, to be printed on the *Worthington Daily Globe*'s large web offset press. Because the *Globe* printed several area weeklies, in addition to their own daily, it was important that we get our material—paste-up sheets and photos, cropped and marked for size and place—into their plant on time to fit into the slot provided for us in their schedule. This arrangement made for some frantic last-minute scrambling—especially if a photo or other item was discovered to be missing when the printing plates were being made.

There were many times, when making the return trip from Worthington, with the car loaded down with freshly printed papers (smelling of printing ink and newsprint), that I wondered why we had ever gotten ourselves into such a stressful business.

In addition to the editorial aspect of putting out the paper, there was the business side. This, along with selling advertising, was something we hadn't had to deal with in the *Waukee Journal*. But because we were the publishers of this small country weekly, all aspects of publishing fell to us—even sweeping up the place.

Ginny took naturally to the business end of our venture, and, to her surprise, found that she liked and was good at the practical side of our adventure—billing for ads, paying the bills, and keeping track of all the details that gave me fits.

Thus, in the demanding, hectic world of a country weekly, Ginny was finding an outlet for her innate sense of organization and attention to detail that had been buried for the most part in her previous years. These talents, along with her untrained sense of design and her warmth with people, made the newspapering experience a time of fulfillment for her.

Toward the end of our two-year lease of the paper, we decided to exercise our option to buy it. Subscriptions had increased and advertising inches and revenue had gone up to where the paper was becoming a profitable venture. With Ginny's good business sense and management skills, we were, for nearly the first time in our lives, beginning to see a comfortable margin left over when balancing the checkbook. It was a hectic life, but we were beginning to feel we could adjust and enjoy.

However, probably because of the successful turn the paper had taken, its sale price went up to what our banker advised us was too much. He suggested that we dicker for a lower figure. While this process was going on, I received a phone call from

Wilson, the owner, who informed me that he had sold the *Nobles County Review*. He said that it was to be taken over by the new owner at the end of our lease in just a few weeks.

This sudden turn of events left us in shock. What would we do to make a living? Where would we go? For the last few weeks remaining of our lease of the paper, it was hard to give our "all" to the *Nobles County Review*. We felt betrayed. In addition, much of our time and energy was given to wondering what the future held for us.

The man who came to our aid when we discovered we would no longer be publishing the *Nobles County Review* had sauntered into our office one summer morning in 1967. He was a tall, slender man with a friendly face and was dressed in the black garb, with its "backward collar," of a Catholic priest. This offbeat clergyman took a bit of getting used to. But in those early days in Adrian, when we were regretting the decisions that had brought us into such a situation, we soon made the happy discovery that this original was "on our side." In his off-hand, maddening way, Father William Anderson offered us his friendship, and we soon discovered we had much of common interest, including printing. He had his own printing shop in the basement of the manse at St. Adrian Catholic Church. There he printed the Sunday bulletins and many other pieces, both religious and secular, for his parish and for the community at large.

Not only did he have a keen interest in the craft, but he was good at it, with an artistic talent that was expressed beautifully in the many printed pieces that came out of his parsonage printery, all seasoned with a delightful sense of humor. So Ginny and I, as well as our kids, spent a lot of time in our newspaper office, our home, his home, and on picnics with this man of the cloth who was not of our church. We came to value him as a true, lasting friend.

In 1969 as we pondered our future, Father Bill, as he was affectionately known in the Adrian community, suggested we open a print shop in Adrian. There had not been one in town since the time Mr. Thompson owned the *Review* and printed it by letterpress there in his Adrian shop. Since then, any commercial printing was done out of town with the local newspaper office acting as broker. This was a role I had not been much interested in so we hadn't pursued job printing. Now, however, the idea of running a print shop with hands-on production did appeal to both Ginny and me.

With the guidance of Father Bill and his expertise in the craft, we started making plans for a new business in town. He helped us negotiate the purchase of the old (1891) Adrian State Bank building for a reasonable price (the banker was of his church) and arrange for a business loan at the same bank (now in a new building), where we had been doing business since coming to town.

Father Bill also helped us pick out the minimum equipment and order the paper stock, printing ink, and other supplies needed to start a small offset printing business. He even gave us presents of small items he considered surplus in his own shop.

It was with a great sense of adventure when, on the first week of September 1969, we opened the doors to the Print Shop in the old bank building on probably the most prominent corner in town.

In our last issue of the *Review,* we ran a full-page ad, announcing the opening and services of our shop. Some of the loyal *Review* readers vied to be the first customers. However, unknown to us, the sale of the newspaper had included a deal to set up the new owners with a job printing shop. As a result, a town that had been without a place to get printing done now had two . . . to scramble for printing jobs in an area where there had not been much need in the first place.

This situation put us in a desperate position. It also created bad feelings between the new owners of the newspaper and us. We felt we were victims of a shenanigan, and the new owners saw us as mean-spirited villains out to steal what had been promised to them.

At any rate those first few months of the Print Shop were rough. I found it necessary to do what I'd often had to do in past years—go back to the drawing board. So I scrambled not only for the printing jobs but also for free-lance art work. I managed to get some but found it necessary to also take a night job doing unskilled work at the Sailor Plastics plant in town. This extra work helped but wasn't how we'd envisioned running a printing business.

Then new hope arrived in the form of a full-time job offer at the *Worthington Daily Globe.* I was to do some editorial cartooning in addition to servicing an advertising account for a supermarket. Eventually, I was taken off the advertising job to devote my full time to cartooning. This turn of events saved our printing business.

The century-old
former Adrian
State Bank build-
ing where we
opened our Print
Shop in 1969, "on
probably the most
prominent corner
in town."

In front of our
home in Adrian,
Minnesota, circa
1975, when Ginny
was running the
Print Shop.

At about the same time the Nobles County librarian approached Ginny with the offer to run the branch library in Adrian. This would mean closing down the shop, selling off almost new equipment at a loss, and paying off the business loan at the bank. It was very tempting to have each of us on a salary, with no responsibilities for running a business, but in the end Ginny chose to stay with the shop. She continued to run it for the ten years until 1979.

Those years were productive, with business increasing and Ginny dealing with all aspects of running a print shop. She liked working with clients, helping them to plan brochures and other printed pieces. She worked with several businesses and organizations, doing their newsletters. Even after we had closed the shop in 1979, one client expressed the wish that Ginny continue to help them produce the newsletter.

Ginny would arrange to do a printing job and then go to the bank for a loan to buy the necessary paper stock. She dealt with the paper merchants and other suppliers that made calls. After the job was completed—a process that involved typesetting on a new IBM Selectric typewriter, on which she became very proficient, and the photo composition machine for larger display type—she did the layout, composition, and intricate task of paste-up, which included the placement of the black patches for photos and then sizing and cropping the photos to be "dropped in" with the blocks of type. Then she made the offset plates on the plate-making machine. After the printing was done, she would cut and trim as necessary, fold, gather, and staple, and then package for delivery. After the money had been received for the job she had billed, she went to the bank to pay off the loan for the paper. Thus, Ginny was becoming a respected businesswoman in the community.

Because Ginny was essentially alone in the shop, with my full-time work at the *Globe,* we found it necessary to hire a part-time printer to run the Multilith offset press. We chose Wilfred (Freddy) Winter, a rural mail carrier, who came to the shop on a part-time basis after making his daily mail run. Freddy was a loyal, resourceful worker who had previously been a letterpress printer at the old *Nobles County Review.* He and his wife, Matty, were some of the good people of Adrian who became our friends.

I did help out some at the Print Shop when I'd finished my day's work at the *Globe,* but Ginny carried the brunt of the work.

It was her industry and good management that made it possible to pay off our mortgage on the shop and close it at the end in the black, and with a sense of accomplishment.

Not only was the venture a modest financial success, but it also allowed us to get into some small-time publishing. With the opening of Interstate 90, which skirted the edge of Adrian on its way across southern Minnesota, we conceived of a publication specifically for that highway community. This small magazine was printed in two colors on the cover, with inside feature articles and photos and drawings of points of interest along the local segment of the highway. It was passed out free at rest stops and businesses catering to travelers and was supported by advertising from those businesses. We called it *The I-90 Traveler*. We thought the idea was a good one, but after a few issues, we had to cease publication. For it to pay, we would have had to expand both ways up and down the interstate, and that would take capital, which, alas, we didn't have.

We also printed a book, *The Tale of a Table*, by George Knips, and another, *Slade, a Hotel and a Family*, by Fred Slade. These were both written by local people and were fun projects in which I did pen illustrations. A long-time friend from childhood days, Mac Allinson, who taught English literature at a college in Iowa, collected some of his poetry into a book, *Categories*, which we printed and I illustrated with some pen drawings.

These publishing ventures whetted our appetites for more. In 1978 our Print Shop imprint was on *Memories of a Former Kid*, a book I had written and illustrated with my cartoons from the newspaper series by the same name. This particular project was our own publishing venture—we stood the cost and reaped the profits. It was successful beyond our expectations, so much so, in fact, that we could not handle all the added work it entailed, so we sold the publishing rights to Iowa State University Press.

All in all, the Adrian experience, in spite of its early hardships and pains, was something that, with conscious planning, could not have been better for us. In particular, our time in Adrian gave Ginny the opportunity (in addition to her work in the Print Shop) to give further expression to her latent artistic talent. We both took part in a watercolor workshop conducted in the Adrian library by the nationally known wildlife artist Jerry Raedeke. Ginny displayed a feeling for that medium; had she pursued it, I think she could have done some nice paintings.

Back when we had lived in Waukee, Ginny and I had taken some night classes at the Des Moines Art Center. She chose a class in ceramics, which she thoroughly enjoyed. There she produced a small, rectangular ceramic box, about three-by-five-by-two inches. She inscribed a subtle design on the lid and her initials on the underside. It was fired with a beautiful light blue glaze. I now keep postage stamps in it on my desk.

With her interest whetted for working in clay, Ginny was eager to join me in a night class in sculpture at the Worthington Community College in the late 1970s. There she produced the figure, about six inches high, of a squirrel sitting on its haunches eating a nut it held in its forepaws. She fired it in a brown glaze and gave it as a gift to her sister Louise.

In 1982, after we'd moved back to Hampton and had been apprised of Ginny's affliction, I built her a modeling stand with a turntable and bought her some clay, hoping she would again find pleasure working in that medium. But when I tried to get her started with it, she showed no interest.

WHAT'S THE MATTER WITH MOM?

It is hard to put a date on when the insidious disease that stole the mind and vibrant spirit away from Ginny first began to show itself. As we look back, we can now detect, from the perspective of what has transpired over time, different isolated episodes or incidents of peculiar behavior that were manifested perhaps as far back as 1978.

In 1980 Jeannie first noticed something being wrong when we were visiting her in Washington, D.C., when little Jennifer wanted to play the game of "Clue" with her grandmother and Ginny could not manage it. But those of us who had been around her more back home had been noticing other disturbing things about her behavior before then.

When the children, all gone from home, would come back for a visit, they would take me aside and ask, "What's the matter with Mom?" I, trying to deny my own fears, would be almost angry in replying, "What do you mean, what's wrong with Mom?" It was almost as if I considered them disrespectful of their mother. However, deep inside, I knew that their questions were legitimate, that there *was* something wrong.

Through Ginny's diligence and management skills, the debt on the Print Shop was finally paid off. In view of this, we thought we would like to sell the business and passed the word through our suppliers, as well as through some ads in trade papers. There were a few inquiries over several months in 1979, but nothing came of them. In the meantime Ginny, with the help of our part-time printer, Freddy Winter, and her other part-time help kept the business going.

However, during 1979, the last year the Print Shop was in business, an increasing number of printing jobs had to be done over because of some unexplainable errors that showed up in the finished work. This could prove quite costly, an expense that, of course, had to be borne by the Print Shop. Ginny felt terrible about these "goofs" for which she was responsible, and in my blindness I became impatient with her.

"Why in thunder did you do that?" I'd ask in exasperation. "I don't know *why* I did it!" she would reply, nearly in tears.

Little by little, the Print Shop seemed to be getting to be too much for her. The work was making her nervous and tired her more than before. Finally, we decided that, if we couldn't sell the shop as a going business, we would simply close it up, sell off the equipment, and put the building up for sale.

It was a relief, once we'd made up our minds, to finally deliver our last printing job. Yet with a feeling of sadness, too, we closed another chapter on our life together.

Unfortunately, we could not enjoy Ginny's retirement as we'd hoped. Her mental problems gradually became more evident. She would forget things that I, in my chronic forgetfulness, had depended on her to remember for me. She became easily confused, whereas she had been the one of us who knew what the score was. Ginny had been the one to take care of the monthly bills, write the checks, keep track of appointments and, in general, keep her home, husband, and business running on track.

Sometimes she did inexplicable things that were foreign to her usual way. On one occasion, putting on a new pair of pants for the first time, I discovered the button missing that would have fastened the little tab and held the front closed before pulling up the zipper. I asked Ginny to sew on the button when she had time, and I wore another pair that day. To my chagrin, when next I put on the new pair of pants, I discovered that, instead of the button being sewed on, the tab had been cut off, thus eliminating the need for the button.

This discovery was quite a shock. It bothered me to the extent that I never mentioned it to Ginny. Knowing that such behavior was not akin to Ginny's nature, I didn't want to confront her with it. I simply wore the new pants sans tab, with no one being the wiser. But every time I put them on, I saw Ginny's handiwork and was reminded that something *was* wrong . . . not only with the pants.

Other aberrations began to appear more and more often. When Ginny and I were visiting with friends, she would suddenly interject a thought that was entirely foreign to the topic of our conversation. This broke the thread of our intercourse and caused puzzled embarrassment to all of us, especially to Ginny, who realized she'd said something wrong.

Through the years, even though she was naturally shy and had a tendency to hold back, Ginny had always made worthwhile and even witty contributions to a discussion, so this verbal misstep was but further evidence that something was not right with her mental process. Sometimes she would use wrong words in a sentence. This could be humorous, and we all, including Ginny, would laugh at it. At first we poked good-natured fun by calling her Mrs. Malaprop, a character in a play who makes ludicrous blunders in her use of words. But, after a while, instead of laughing at these malapropisms of Ginny's, we'd try to overlook them, realizing that she was not *trying* to be funny.

One evening Ginny had invited friends for supper. As the time for their arrival drew near, Ginny, who loved to have people in for meals, seemed ill at ease and reluctant. As I helped her with the last-minute details, when it was necessary to rearrange some of the table settings, it seemed almost too much for her.

The meal was fine and our guests seemed to enjoy it, but Ginny seemed to not be really with us—to be somewhat in a fog. Years later, after Ginny's condition had been diagnosed, our friend, referring to that supper, confessed she had thought maybe Ginny was a closet alcoholic.

During the early stages of Ginny's mental problem, before a name had been put on it, these strange behavior patterns were stressful for all of us—certainly for Ginny, because, as yet, she was still aware that she was apt to say or do something "stupid," and this only compounded her sense of insecurity and her suffering.

In addition to Ginny's mental condition, I had experienced a siege of phlebitis, and in the fall of 1980 I had prostate surgery. In view of the emerging health problems of their parents, our kids began a campaign to get us to move back to Hampton, which we had left thirty years before. There, they argued, we would be near family. Our son, Rob, and his wife Kris were in the forefront of this movement because they were now living there and felt they would be able to "look after" us. The rest of our kids were in agreement.

The prospect of again living in our old home territory among family and old friends (those still around after our thirty years' absence) was appealing. So in midsummer of 1981, we added our house to a list of twenty-one others that were not moving on the market in Adrian. In spite of the poor real estate turnover, by the next weekend we had an interested buyer. This was a happy surprise to our real estate agent, as well as to us, because we had expected to sit for months with a "for sale" sign on our lawn. However, the buyer was unable to get the necessary financing, and our euphoria collapsed as we prepared again for a long wait before getting another nibble.

In the meantime I had been talking with the management at the *Globe,* trying to sell them on the idea of my continuing to work for them by mail from Hampton. After some reluctance on their part, but understanding the concerns of our family, they generously agreed, and tentative plans were made so that, by phone and by mail, their staff cartoonist could continue to be a part of the *Globe* family, at the same salary. However, in view of the fact that, in about two years, I would be sixty-five, Jim Vance, the publisher, wanted me to agree not to retire until "you are eighty." This was fine with me for I was happy in my work there and hoped to continue for many years.

With the *Globe*'s blessing we felt secure in our prospective move, and, when in about a month after first listing our house we had another prospective buyer, we set about making definite plans for the move. This time the house transaction went through without a hitch, at our asking price, and we suddenly realized we would soon be without a place to live. On the next weekend we drove to Hampton to look at some houses Rob and Kris had lined up for our inspection.

In all our years together, Ginny and I have had the feeling we were being looked after. In spite of rough going at various times along the way, there was always a greater wisdom that seemed to direct and sustain us. And this was again the case. It was as if we were hurried along on our way to Hampton. Everything clicked and fell into place in one-two-three order. The house sale in

Adrian and our purchase of the Hampton house could not have moved more smoothly, and everything progressed so rapidly that we were hard-pressed to get our things sorted and packed in time for the movers.

In spite of the happy anticipation of moving back home where we'd be near Rob and Kris, their children, Mom, and all our other relatives, there was a deep sadness, again leaving a house that had been our home for fourteen years. There were many things we were leaving in this house. In this home we had dreamed dreams and had seen some of them realized, such as having our Print Shop become a publishing house—and then the successful publication of my first book, *Memories of a Former Kid*. Within these walls we had entertained friends, and now we were leaving many of those friends—some for the last time. (As it turned out, they'd never see Ginny again as they had known her.)

Also in this house, when Ginny and I realized that it was just the two of us again, we had talked of how we'd spend our "golden years." Ginny dreamed of our buying a motor home and becoming nomads, visiting our far-flung family. She said that way I could devote my time to drawing and painting the places along the way and could sell some of them to help meet expenses. Her eyes were bright and dreamy as she told me of these things in her soft, throaty voice, the same as during our courtship when she had dreamed aloud about our future home and family.

We didn't realize it then, but we were leaving what was to be our last home in which Ginny would be a vital force. If we *had* known, our grief would have been inconsolable.

Our arrival in Hampton in October of 1981 was a joyful occasion. Joni had come from Minneapolis to help us move. She and Ginny and Simon (our cat) were in the Ford Bobcat, while Kelly (our huge Irish setter) and I led the way in the Buick. Our little caravan pulled up in front of our new home to find the moving van backed up to the front porch and being unloaded, with the help of Dean and Dan.

Dan and his wife, Esther, had invited us to stay with them until we had our things in place. However, after school let out, Kris and Rob and their children, along with Dean's wife, Reggie, showed up to welcome us and assist in getting things moved into place; with all their help, we soon had our bedroom set up, so we accepted the supper portion of the invitation but elected to spend our first night in town in our own bed.

The next days were happy, exciting times as Ginny and I made almost daily visits to Mom in the nursing home nearby, visited family and friends, and received callers who welcomed us back home. We shopped for curtains and other things to make our place comfortable. Before long, Ginny and I, working side by side, had made this snug, two-bedroom bungalow built sometime during the teens of this century into an unpretentious but cozy home in which we were reasonably settled. Soon I was even at my drawing board in my basement studio that Dan was constructing around me as I worked to meet deadlines for the newspaper back in Worthington.

The rest of that autumn and into December, Ginny was functioning about as she had been in Adrian. But there was increasing evidence that she had a health problem. She still drove the car occasionally but began to show signs of confusion and even got lost once or twice in our small town. Without making an issue of it, I gradually took over all the driving, until her Minnesota driver's license was no longer valid. However, she did ask me to pick up an Iowa driving test booklet for her to study in preparation for taking the test. She tried valiantly, for she had every intention of passing the test to get her Iowa driver's license. She spent hours going over all the driving rules and regulations and traffic sign recognition. Then she asked me to quiz her. However, those sessions were not successful at all and only caused her further frustration.

It was sad to see one who had always been so diligent in her studies and able to absorb facts, who had put me to shame with her ability to memorize, now not able to remember the simplest things in the book. When she would miss a question, she'd ask to take the book and study it again, but to no avail. Finally, she would put the book aside, determined to go at it again when "my mind is clearer."

This went on for quite a while. Ginny had always liked to read in bed; now, if she retired before I did, I'd come in later to find her asleep with the Iowa driver's license booklet propped up on her chest. As I'd always done, I would carefully remove her glasses and book and lay them aside. And, as always, if she was not in a deep sleep, a faint smile would flicker across her face.

So the weeks went by, with Ginny always preparing for the test that was given at the courthouse every Saturday morning. But, as Saturday arrived each week, I helped her forget the appointed time. I felt guilty in this subterfuge, but I had no intention of letting her suffer through the humiliation of trying to take a written test she was bound to fail miserably. Nor, for that matter, did I want her to attempt to drive again with her obvious state of confusion and erratic behavior. After a while, she forgot about taking the test, and I sadly put the little booklet away, realizing this to be but another part of Ginny that was in the past.

Christmas, that first year after our return to Hampton, was a bittersweet time for all of us. It was good getting together with Rob's and Steve's families and having Joni home for the holidays from the University of Minnesota. Jeannie and her daughter, Jennifer, could not be there, because they were in the Philippines, where Jeannie, now divorced, was serving as a diplomat in the U.S. embassy. We brought Mom from the nursing home for Christmas Day, and Dean's and Dan's families joined us, too. However, because of Ginny's condition, a dark cloud hung over what otherwise would have been a happy occasion.

To Ginny, the Christmas season had always been a special time. She would start preparations weeks in advance, cleaning and decorating the rooms, baking Christmas goodies, and writing greetings to all those friends and relatives who lived away; her shopping for Christmas often began in early fall. She had always wanted to get all the preparations done early enough so as not to be rushed during the last few days before the holiday, thereby not spoiling the joy of the season.

But now, sadly, these formerly fun activities for Ginny, like everything else she tried to do, were confusing and difficult for her. I worked with her, trying in vain to inject the same old spirit into the season. But Ginny's fogginess prevented her from full participation.

Granddaughters Rebecca and Heidi, always close to their grandma's heart, tried to help her make Christmas cookies. But this formerly fun-filled pre-Christmas activity, because of Ginny's limited participation, was a disappointment to all involved.

For her Christmas shopping, of course, I was with her. But it was far different from former times when Ginny had done it with purpose and enthusiasm. Now I had to become much more involved than when I had accompanied her in the past. Then she had led the assault into the crowded stores with a singleness of purpose that had left me trailing along behind as a dumb beast of burden carrying packages, and maybe our coats and Ginny's purse. Back then, when she had tried to consult me and make me enthusiastic about a particular item, I could not fully take part, being in my shopping stupor. Now, as I led Ginny from store to store, trying to rekindle her former spark, I longed with sadness for those shopping trips with her that I had once considered boring.

Rob took his mother to help her buy a gift for me. He, too, was frustrated and saddened by her inability to get involved in the process. She either vetoed or simply showed no interest in anything that Rob suggested. Sometimes she picked something he didn't think I'd appreciate or that was more expensive than she could afford. Finally, she chose a pair of fleece-lined, leather woodchopper's mitts and seemed pleased with her choice. But when they went to pay for them, Rob saw the one who had helped him countless times with his math homework now completely confused and unable to comprehend the amount required, shoving all her money into the startled clerk's hands.

THE DIAGNOSIS

Not long after settling into our home in Hampton, Ginny and I made an appointment at the local clinic with Dr. Dorothy Heuermann and took with us our medical records from the Adrian clinic. We were acquainted with Dr. Dorothy, as she was affectionately known in the community, because she had been my parents' physician and friend for many years.

We explained the problems Ginny had been having and asked whether she could help. After studying Ginny's records and visiting with her for awhile, Dr. Dorothy gave her a thorough physical examination. Then she suggested that Ginny go to Dr. Sant M. Hayreh, a neurologist in Mason City, and made an appointment for us there.

Dr. Hayreh, a kindly man, wore a turban, which made him an imposing Indian figure in a Midwestern clinic. He gave Ginny some tests in his office, beginning by asking her her name, where she lived, who her husband was, what was the name of the president of the United States currently in office, etc. Then he observed her as she walked and did other physical movements. When he had finished, Dr. Hayreh said he wanted to do a complete neurological work-up to rule out several possible causes for her confusion and memory loss. Hopefully, the process would narrow the problem to a specific cause—something that could be corrected with medication or, if needed, surgery. The tests, he said, would have to be done in the hospital and would entail about a three-day stay, so he made an appointment for Ginny to enter St. Joseph's Mercy Hospital in Mason City on the December 29.

Late in the afternoon on that day, we drove the thirty miles to Mason City, and Ginny was admitted to the hospital. She had spent time in hospitals several times in her life, so this was neither new nor very stressful for her. I helped her settle in, and we spent the evening visiting quietly and trying to cling to the hope that the tests she would be undergoing in the next couple of days would reveal that there was nothing seriously wrong—that it was only something that could be easily corrected by medication or by simple surgery. I recalled Dr. Hayreh mentioning the chance that a blockage of blood vessels to the brain might be cutting the flow of oxygen to that vital organ. If that were the case, that problem, it seemed, could be corrected. The more frightening possibility was a brain tumor that surgery might be able to alleviate. If it were arteriosclerosis, medication and diet could possibly restore her mental dexterity to that of the vivacious, witty Ginny we had all known. Thus, we kept our hopes up—after all, didn't we have faith in medical science and the wonders it could perform?

Those thoughts preoccupied my mind as I kissed Ginny good night in as jovial and nonchalant a manner as I could before driving home. The same hopeful sentiments were expressed at the table those days as I had meals with Rob and Kris and family—at which times I was painfully aware of Ginny's empty chair beside me.

Each day after Ginny's tests, I went to her room and we talked of our activities that day. Ginny had difficulty relating just what she had been involved in, but was always glad to see me and sorry when it was time for me to leave.

On the final day, when the tests were completed and Ginny was to be discharged, I was at the hospital early to bring her home. I thought of times past when I had brought her home from the hospital (three times with new babies, for I had been away in the Army when Jeannie was born) and the joy I had felt to know I would have her at home again. I had the same feeling this time—but with an apprehension, too, as to what the tests would have revealed.

I went first to the nurses' station on the neurological floor to attend to the necessary paper work for Ginny's release. When the nurse handed me the papers to sign, I quickly scanned the form, stopping at the space labeled "Diagnosis." In the blank was typed the word "Alzheimer's."

It was as if a lightning bolt had struck my innermost being. I broke out in a cold sweat. Suddenly, I was aware that Dr. Hayreh was standing beside me. In my dazed disbelief, I pointed to the dreaded word. He nodded and went on to explain that the diagnosis had been determined by eliminating, in the tests given, all other possible causes for Ginny's mental problems. The only positive way to diagnose Alzheimer's, he said, was in an autopsy after death, when the brain tissues could be examined for the telltale signs of the disease.

Dr. Hayreh told me, as gently as he could, that medical science, as of that time, neither knew the cause nor had a cure for the increasingly prevalent disease. There were drugs he could and would prescribe to help alleviate some of the symptoms. But he said that the irreversible deterioration of the brain would continue until Ginny would become completely helpless and require total care. The doctor could not give me a time frame in which this would occur. Individual cases varied, he said. Some had been known to go on in a slow decline for ten, fifteen, or more years, while for others the deterioration was much faster. And usually, Dr. Hayreh explained, death was brought on by heart or kidney failure, or pneumonia. He said that, as the brain lost its power to send signals to various parts of the body, their functions would gradually shut down. Eventually, in many cases, the patient would no longer be able to swallow and would literally starve to death.

With this heavy knowledge weighing me down, I went to Ginny's room with as much cheer as I could muster, to find her ready and waiting patiently, all smiles, in a chair by the window.

I had asked Dr. Hayreh, when he told me about the disease and what to expect, not to tell Ginny . . . at least not yet. He had looked at me in a way that said he thought I was wrong in making the request, but he had acquiesced. I wanted some time to assess the effect of this frightful knowledge and felt I was right in not telling her just then. We had known of a case of that horrible affliction when we had lived in Minnesota, and had been appalled by it.

She was to find out, of course (I had every intention that she would . . . later), but, as it happened, it would be inadvertently in August of the next year. Ginny and I were visiting Joni and her husband, Bob, in their St. Paul apartment. Joni and Ginny and I were sitting in their living room when Ginny commented that we all seemed worried about her and said, "I have brain cancer, don't I?" Joni was first to respond and told her the truth, thinking I had already done so.

Even though the knowledge that she had Alzheimer's was distressful to her and she cried as Joni and I tried to comfort her, before long she seemed to forget even that.

I tried to justify what might have been seen as my cowardice in not having told her earlier of the true nature of her affliction by rationalizing that she had had those months, at least, without suffering the awful knowledge of what lay ahead of her. And what difference would it have made anyway? I asked myself and Joni, who seemed to think her mother should have been told before. What was there that she could have done differently had she known? No affairs had to be settled, no large estate had to be portioned out to the children. Ginny, all her life, had given the most any of her loved ones could have wanted—herself and her love—and she had long since made her peace with God.

No, the ones for whom Ginny's affliction did require a settling of affairs were the rest of us—especially me. I was determined that I would be by her side for as long as she needed me—or for as long as she was aware of that need. That, of course, is the gray area in this whole matter that continually tortures me, even as I write this. Is Ginny aware when I *am* with her? Are there moments, no matter how brief, when she is aware of my absence— and aches for me as I do for her constantly? How cruel a fate for those who love!

At any rate, my keeping the name of Ginny's affliction from her was meant to shield her from hurt, just as I would have shielded her from a missile with my own body.

That day when we came home from the hospital with the diagnosis, the family was anxiously awaiting the results of the tests. If this had not been so, I might have delayed telling them and kept the awful secret to myself—for a while, at least. But although I was reluctant to reveal to family and friends the nature of the tragedy that was slowly engulfing us, it *was* a relief to be able to share the burden of this awful knowledge and to experience the love and support given in return.

Even with the word out, I tried to deny the reality of it. I had the prescriptions filled and saw that Ginny took her medication on schedule, but in the meantime I tried stubbornly to live as we had been, in spite of the cloud that enveloped us. While Ginny and I attended our church meetings, Bible studies, and took part in some community and family functions, I was at her side to guide her, cover up, or laugh off her malapropisms and erratic behavior. And every day I kept watching for any change in her behavior that I might perceive as indicating her decline. Mercifully, we were spared seeing what was ahead—the grim details of the horrible nightmare that was slowly engulfing us.

COPING

When we attended social gatherings, we felt especially exposed. Once in a while, after moving to Hampton, it was necessary to go back to the Worthington *Globe* on business. The first two or three years Ginny accompanied me on these trips. Our friends at the *Globe* always made us feel welcome and were loving and protective of Ginny in her illness, as were our friends around town.

I wrote to Jim Vance, my boss at the *Globe,* trying to explain my home situation and the way I was afraid it was affecting my work.

Hampton, Iowa
March 1, 1984

Dear Jim,

Would you please share this with Owen, Paul and Ray?

When I was talking with you on the phone yesterday, Ginny walked into the room, and I was not able to respond truthfully to your question concerning her health. The sad truth is that it is deteriorating, and she is becoming more confused as the weeks go by. Much of the time, of late, she does not recognize me as her husband. At such times she is looking for "his" return and wonders, with sadness, why "he" has gone away "as we have always done things together." And she has shed many tears over the awareness of her growing limitations and the problems it brings upon the rest of us. She doesn't want to cause hurt to anyone and worries about it. It is hard for her to carry on a sensible conversation and she can't write letters any more, or even a check. This is the same person who, among all her other accomplishments, did our income tax returns and helped our children with their math homework. (I couldn't do the latter!)

We're told the future holds only worsening conditions, not better. But whenever things are better, for even a few moments, we enjoy and even have good laughs, occasionally, and continue to hope—and pray, and pray.

I do appreciate your kindness in going along with us in these times, and I am hoping the time may come before too long when I can again do more work and be worth my keep on an increased basis.

I then ended the letter with "P.S. We both thank you for the warmth with which Ginny is greeted when we 'go home to the *Globe.*' "

Jim wrote a warm, supportive reply, trying to assure me that the quality of my work was not slipping as I had feared it might be. And he expressed the sympathy they all felt for the suffering we were experiencing and of their friendship:

> Your extraordinary devotion to each other during so many years together has been a beautiful, enviable love story which your many friends couldn't help but note (because it was so obvious, wondrous and real), couldn't help but admire (because from both yours and Ginny's aspect, it was so selflessly dedicated and lovingly sustained). Know this, Bob, for certain truth now—yours and Ginny's loving example is not forgotten by your friends, nor will it be ever so long as they live in sound mind. I hope this knowledge can be some consolation to you now, Bob. Know, too, that both you and Ginny are in our prayers constantly.
>
> As for your work, Bob, be absolutely assured that Owen, Paul and I are of one mind: You have our fullest backing, support and understanding for the duration of this difficult situation, longer, if necessary.
>
> Florence joins me, and Mom and Dad, too, in sending our love to the whole Artley clan.
>
> JIM AND FLORENCE

As time went on, social exposures became more difficult, and we withdrew more and more into our shell. One time when I realized that Ginny's condition had brought us to this stage was at

Ginny and I in our home in Hampton, 1983.

Our Japanese guests, Mr. and Mrs. Kato, at the impromptu tea Ginny prepared in the Hampton house, autumn 1984. "Even when Ginny was having increasing trouble with her homemaking skills, if guests would drop in, she would try to be a good hostess and serve them something."

a function to which we had been invited at the Methodist church. It was a buffet supper with the food laid out on tables before the call to start the line. As we waited, Ginny and I were visiting with someone when I suddenly realized she was not beside me. Instead, she was at the food table, going from dish to dish, picking up and sampling morsels of food. As discreetly and quickly as possible, I went to her side and gently moved her away to where, hopefully, we could melt into the background.

Much is made of small towns as places where everyone knows everyone else's business. This is generally true and can be quite irksome, but at the same time this trait can be of help when there is trouble or need. Ginny had always cherished her privacy and, wishing to keep a low profile, had chafed at the nosiness of small-town people. So it's ironic that, when the knowledge of Ginny's affliction soon became community wide, people's awareness actually helped to make our situation easier.

As time went on and Ginny's condition deteriorated percepti-bly, people made allowances for her strange behavior or her inappropriate or incomprehensible speech. Even the Hampton police were aware of our problem and kept an unobtrusive watch over her. They were actively involved a couple of times.

Usually, when working at my drawing board, I would hear her moving around on the floor above me, going from room to room in a restless state. Sometimes, if I didn't hear her, I'd go up to find her lying on the couch or sitting quietly in a chair. At other times, she might have gone outside. This, of course, was my constant concern.

One time, as I was working in my basement studio, the phone rang, and a woman, whose voice and whose name I did not recognize, said that Ginny had come into her house and seemed confused, not knowing where she was or how to get home. I was shocked, for I had not even been aware that she was out of the house.

Just as I arrived at the home of the woman who had made the call, about three blocks from our place, a police car pulled up. The officer said that he had received a call, too. I assured him that I would take care of the situation and thanked him for his concern. When the woman of the house let me in, she said that Ginny was in the kitchen. I went there to find her standing in the middle of the room, quietly crying. Taking her in my arms, I kissed her, thanked the lady for her kindness, and we went home—Ginny in confusion and humiliation and I in sadness for my dear wife. I realized anew how vulnerable we were.

Some months later, Ginny again slipped out without my knowledge. Again I was alerted by a phone call. This time she was at a convenience store and gas station at the intersection of highways 3 and 65, about two blocks from our home. I took the car, and as I drove up to the store, I saw Ginny standing by a police car, talking to the officer inside. My nephew, George, was standing beside her.

It seemed that when Ginny had appeared in the store, quite confused and not able to make much sense to the clerks, someone called the police. When they had realized that she was Mrs. Artley, they had phoned my brother Dan's house. George, being the only one at home, had jumped in his car and come to see what help he could be to his Aunt Ginny.

Ginny's tendency to slip out of the house and wander away kept us all on the alert and on edge. Our next-door neighbors, Kevin and Becky Carlson, were constantly coming to our rescue in one way or another—such as the time I was gone on a short errand and Ginny hurried over to their house to tell Becky to come quickly, because something was wrong with the stove. Becky rushed into our kitchen with Ginny to find the electric timer sounding off. Ginny, in her confusion, had apparently turned it on and then had not been able to shut it off.

Little Alyson Carlson, then about five years old, would often join Ginny when she saw her start off down the sidewalk, take her hand and walk with her, bringing her back home. Or seeing Ginny out in our yard, she would stay with her until I came out to check Ginny's whereabouts.

Another who watched over us in our vulnerability was Cousin Ruth, a retired RN who had become friends with Ginny in the early years when we had lived on the farm. Now, she lived down the street and across Highway 3; whenever she saw Ginny wandering, Ruth would join her and walk her home.

A most dependable source of help and comfort were Rob and Kris and their kids, whose house we could see from ours. Many times I breathed a prayer of thanks that at least one of our children's families was nearby. Sometimes, during Ginny's wanderings, Rob or Kris or one of the children would phone me at my drawing board to say that Mom or Grandma was at their house and not to worry, they would keep her there for a while and see that she got home.

Dean's wife Reggie, who taught a special education class in a residence that the school leased across the street from us, was also vigilant as to Ginny's wanderings and saw that she got home.

Ginny also "visited" the middle school, a half-block north of us, where she had previously befriended the secretary. Both of them were natives of Pennsylvania and had ended up in Iowa as a result of marrying servicemen during World War II.

Although all of this wandering about and suddenly appearing unannounced could in itself be disruptive and disturbing to those being visited, Ginny never did anything that was in any way antisocial or unfriendly. She was, as she had always been, soft-spoken and kindly disposed toward people. Thus, rather than antagonizing her surprised hosts, she elicited from them sympathy and concern for her well-being.

Going out to the farm, a place we had lived so long ago, was something of an emotional strain now that Mom was no longer in her house, and it sat empty and sad. We were glad when arrangements were made for Basil and Ila Rowland, who were old family friends, to move into the house so that it would again be filled with light and warmth. Yet, even though these were friends, it felt strange to me to go into the house that had been home for more than sixty years, where my brothers and I had been born and grew up, where Ginny had lived for about seven months when she went home to have our first baby, where we had lived with my folks after my discharge from the Army in 1946 while we were building our own house nearby, and where we and our four children had come home to visit countless times—now occupied by others. I was reluctant to cross over the threshold, even though I was always made to feel welcome.

However, sometimes when Ginny and I would go to the farm for some purpose and I would be visiting with Dean in the barn or about the sheds, I would suddenly realize that she was not beside me. There she would be, in her confusion, entering the back door of the farmhouse as she had often done over the years. Of course, Ila knew her and, understanding Ginny's problem, kindly made her feel welcome.

Ginny, in her aimless wandering about our house, sometimes would come up to me to ask that we "go home." I would gently explain to her, "Ginny, we are at home—*this* is our home." But she would only look confused and turn away. I wondered if, by "going home," she might actually be saying she wanted to go back to when she was *whole*. This thought saddened me—for isn't "home" where we feel comfortable and secure? Did this mean she was suffering for lack of these feelings? My heart ached at the idea.

Though I was thankful that Ginny's illness had not caused her to become mean and abusive, as with some victims of Alzheimer's, there was a personality quirk that did distress me. During a period of our time in Hampton when we were constantly being confronted with and further frustrated by new aberrations in Ginny's personality, an unexpected and surprising facet appeared. Jealousy reared its ugly head.

Throughout our years together this had never been a serious problem between us. I did sense that Ginny kept a watchful (but discreet) eye on me when we were in the company of particularly beautiful, charming women. She would sometimes make, under her breath and for my hearing only, a teasing remark about my awareness of some such woman. And, with her eyes sparkling mischievously, she would other times remind me, "You can look, but don't touch."

This jealous tendency in Ginny was not at all irksome to me. In fact, I was rather flattered. I also felt comfortable in knowing that Ginny considered me *hers*, which is just what I wanted to be.

However, I felt differently when, along with Ginny's other abnormalities, she suddenly became jealous of a close mutual friend. As far as I know, no one besides me was aware of her paranoia in this area. She still was discreet, but when this woman and her husband would drop in for a short visit, Ginny kept an eye on us, and afterward, when we were alone, she would make snide remarks about the woman, who she perceived was trying to steal me away.

This behavior I did *not* like; this was *not* Ginny. Also, in spite of myself, I felt self-conscious when this friend was around and felt a restraint in our usual casual manner toward one another at gatherings where she was present. This situation was especially ironic because Ginny and she had always been close. However, eventually this phase of Ginny's troublesome disease also passed.

In spite of the problems that seemed to be accumulating with an ever-increasing momentum, I was still stubbornly determined that we were going to live as normal a life as possible, for as long as possible. We went on long walks around town. We drove to Beeds Lake, about two miles northwest of town, and walked the footpath around the lake, through the woods and along the edge of the western marsh area, enjoying the birds, waterfowl, and other wildlife we sometimes encountered. I tried to get Ginny to take a ride with me in a rowboat or paddle boat, but she seemed terrified at the suggestion.

We visited close friends and relatives, often having meals with them. Aunt Ethel had her own apartment in a senior citizen complex in Latimer, and we went to see her frequently. We also made visits to Dean and Reggie out on the farm, to Dan and Esther in town, to John and Helen when they were home at their farm for the summer, to Ruth just down the street from us, and to all our other cousins and aunts and uncles in the community at large.

Of course, we were constantly popping in on Rob and Kris; at their table we had our regular places. Whenever possible, we made trips to Minneapolis to visit Steve and Denise and their family, as well as Joni and Bob in their apartment.

We visited Mom in the nursing home two or three times a week. She and Ginny had always been close, and Ginny usually wanted to go with me when I went to see her. Ginny had always been particularly empathetic to the old and infirm, so she always took special note of nursing home residents. On one occasion, when we went to visit Mom in the care facility of Franklin General Hospital, I took along a watercolor painting that I had done and wanted to show her. As we went through the hallway on the way to Mom's room, we passed a woman in a geri-chair, whom I knew to have the same affliction as Ginny—only in a more advanced state.

Ginny, in her usual friendly manner, went up and spoke to her, then turned to me and asked me to show her my painting, remarking that this woman had been an artist and might appreciate seeing it.

Ginny's impulsive action took me by surprise, but, in spite of my reluctance to do so, I unwrapped the painting, and Ginny took it from me and handed it to the woman. She carefully took the watercolor in her hands, as an artist might do, and studied it with obvious pleasure—while I marveled at Ginny's perception of that woman's need and the Alzheimer's victim's positive response.

Ginny had always been fond of games—card games, board games, crossword puzzles—any type of game that was a mental challenge, and she was a formidable opponent. When we visited the farm, soon after our arrival Mom and Ginny would be engaged in a Scrabble tournament that might continue, off and on, for the duration of our stay. They were evenly matched so the tournament could end in either's favor, to be renewed on our next visit. Ginny loved to play the game with any of her family who had the courage to do so. She and I spent many evenings, after the children were grown, playing Scrabble. I was a good loser—I had a lot of practice.

One evening, during her mental decline, Ginny suggested we play a game of Scrabble. Reluctantly, I set up the board. After each of us had drawn our seven tiles and placed them on the racks, I started the game by forming most of my tiles into a word on the starting area of the board, drew out tiles to replace those I'd used, and leaned back for Ginny's turn. She stared at the board and the tiles on her rack and finally looked to me in helplessness. I offered her help. She had some tiles she could play, but she didn't seem to comprehend how to go about it. After another attempt or two to play the game she had always been so good at, she pushed back from the table, realizing she was defeated before she even started.

As I folded up the board and put it, the tiles, pencils, and score pad into the dog-eared box, I suggested we do something else that I felt she could handle. Then I put the Scrabble box at the back of the closet shelf where Ginny was not likely to see it.

Soon after we had arrived in Hampton, Helen, my cousin John's wife, invited Ginny to attend an HOA (Help One Another) Club meeting with her. Ginny was happy to go with her dear friend and came home with the happy news that she had been invited to join.

The HOA Club was a home-grown club, started in 1911 in Aunt Bertha's and Aunt Nina's farm neighborhood northeast of Hampton. (It is the oldest club still in operation in Franklin

County.) I know little about the organization, only that several of my aunts and female cousins were members over the years. (My mother, not being a "joiner" and not driving a car, had declined the invitation.) As far as I know, the group was not only for social purposes but performed community service, as well. Each month, responsibility rotated to one of the members for the program and to someone else for refreshments.

When we had lived in Waukee, Ginny had been active in the women's club, and when her turn had come round to have charge of the program, she had delighted in spending hours in preparation. She would thoroughly research the chosen topic in our home library and encyclopedias, as well as at the public library. Without fail, she would put together a presentation that resulted in compliments and expressions of appreciation from those present.

Thus, knowing of Ginny's mental decline, my apprehension for her, as her turn for the program came around, made me a willing participant when she and Helen suggested that Ginny have *me* for her program. So I entertained the group with a chalk talk that seemed to meet Ginny's obligation to the organization and please everyone, especially Ginny—for whom I had done it.

Every month Ginny looked forward (as much as she could anticipate anything in her growing confusion and fading memory) to when Helen would come to take her to HOA, where the women, knowing of Ginny's condition, were supportive and made her feel included.

One day, about noon, the phone rang, and Ginny beat me to it. I had been trying to take phone calls, because Ginny would have a hard time relaying any message that might be involved. But this particular time, when I realized it was Helen calling, I relaxed, glad that Ginny could visit with her. When she had hung up, she said that she would have to get ready to go to the club, as Helen was coming to pick her up at two o'clock.

After lunch, Ginny bathed and dressed in one of her nice outfits, so she was ready for Helen quite a while before the appointed hour. When I realized that some time had passed and I had not heard Helen come for her, I came up from my studio to find Ginny sitting quietly on the sofa, waiting patiently for Helen. I asked if she was sure Helen was coming for her, and she assured me she was. I suggested that maybe I should take her to the meeting, but Ginny was adamant, so I went back downstairs, with my ear cocked for the sound of Helen's arrival.

About fifteen minutes passed with no Helen, and I went up to find Ginny still waiting, with her hands folded as they had been for the last hour, not doubting in the least that she was to be picked up at any moment. At this point, knowing that this month's meeting was to be held at the public utilities building, I phoned the place and asked for Helen, who was quite distressed as to why Ginny had not arrived.

The phone call that Ginny had taken from Helen at noon was to tell her that, because Helen had to take the refreshments, her car would be crowded; she had wondered if I could drive Ginny to the meeting that day.

I rushed her right over, getting there just in time for the refreshments. The rest of us felt bad for Ginny because of the mix-up, but she didn't seem chagrined in the least, and when Helen later brought her home, Ginny said she'd had a nice time. Her friends in the club had gone out of their way to make it so.

As a result of that incident, another in my learning process about this baffling affliction, I became especially jumpy when the phone rang, wanting to be sure I got any important message before turning the call over to Ginny.

There were countless stressful, embarrassing situations brought about by Ginny's growing confusion and memory loss, which, had it not been for the kindness and understanding of those around us, could have become even more painfully complicated. One such time was when the minister of our church surreptitiously handed me a check Ginny had given her—written for an amount much larger than we had been giving. I don't recall how I handled that situation, but I appreciated the minister's understanding, and the incident served as a flag, alerting me to keep track of the checkbook.

Ginny had always found eating out a special treat, something we hadn't been able to do very often when our family was growing. But when we became just the two of us again, we indulged in that luxury often. This was especially true when Ginny's condition no longer allowed her to prepare meals, and that task fell to me.

Often, we made a foursome with John and Helen. Sometimes Ginny would suggest that she and I go to "Smiley's" for spaghetti and Texas toast, one of her favorite restaurant dishes. Actually, the place, which was on the north side of the courthouse square in

Hampton, was known as Stanley's Pizza and Steak House, but Ginny insisted on calling it Smiley's, so I did, too.

During the first four years in Hampton, we made annual trips to Pennsylvania, to Holidaysburg where we saw Louise and Web Jones, and to South Fork, where we visited Ginny's brothers and their families. Ginny's sister Meriam, whom we had used to visit in the nearby coal mining town of Dunlo, now was with her daughter, Ann, in Florida. Ginny always seemed happy at these reunions with her family.

The first of our trips after Ginny's diagnosis was in May of 1982. Louise had arranged a surprise for Ginny by having the South Fork relatives all gathered at her house when we arrived. Ginny *was* surprised, to be sure, but characteristically seemed to take it in stride. She still recognized everyone and went from one to the other, quietly and warmly greeting and talking with each of them. It seemed, for a while, as if she were her normal self.

That happy day was filled with talk, laughter, and food. However, beneath it all was concern and sadness as, little by little, the realization came to each of her family members that their beloved sister and sister-in-law, as they had always known and loved her, was indeed slipping from them in a way that could not quite be comprehended.

The first two or three years, we made those trips to Pennsylvania by bus, which worked out well for us. We could board in Hampton, change in Chicago, and be met by Louise and Web only a few blocks from their home in Holidaysburg. The last time we traveled by bus, however, the trip was very stressful. By that stage in Ginny's condition, changing buses in the noisy, crowded confusion of the Chicago station was extremely upsetting for both of us. And when the bus ride took us along the steep, undulating, curving roads of western Pennsylvania, through the very hills she had always loved, Ginny was terrified; she tensed up and kept muttering, for my hearing only, very uncomplimentary remarks about the bus driver's ability. I tried to calm and reassure her by diverting her attention, pointing out the beauty of the scenery through which we were traveling—just as she had delighted in doing for me in years past. But she showed no interest. By the time Web and Louise met us at the bus stop in Holidaysburg, we were both nearly nervous wrecks.

A few days later, when they drove us to South Fork to visit Ginny's family there, her reaction was the same as it had been on the bus, so that none of us enjoyed what had always before been a pleasant auto trip. More and more when I had driven her in the car back home, Ginny had been showing some of the same symptoms, but it was getting worse. It was as if all the objects she saw hurrying by her were more than she could handle.

Our last trip by bus had been such a negative experience that the next year we decided to try the train. We made arrangements to go by Amtrak. Although it was not as convenient, we found this way of traveling much better than by bus. The train was roomy and comfortable, allowing us freedom to move about. However, Ginny's illness still made for stressful situations. In order that she not get lost, I walked with her to the ladies' toilet where I waited for her outside the door, worrying about how the swaying car might cause her to fall.

Inevitably, each trip, by whatever means, was more taxing than the previous one. Each time we arrived in Holidaysburg it was a blessing to be able to fall into the welcoming arms of our hosts and relax for a few days. But each time we arrived at their home, they could see the toll this insidious disease was taking on their beloved Ginny.

When we four had been together in the past, the three of them would often play cribbage, while I, not caring much for card games, would sit nearby and read, delighting in the happy background sound of their play. I'll not forget the sadness we all felt the time we realized Ginny could no longer participate in this game with Louise and Web. For old times' sake, they had gotten out the cards and the cribbage board in preparation to play. However, it was soon evident that Ginny could not comprehend the cards she held in her hand, or how to play them.

As part of our stay in Pennsylvania, Ginny and I would spend time in South Fork, visiting her family there. Sometimes Louise and Web would drive the twenty-some miles from Holidaysburg and accompany us to see Art and Laura, Ed and Vera, Margaret, who was the widow of Ginny's brother George, and Bill and Mary, who lived in the old home place where Ginny had been born. Her oldest sister, Renna, had died several years earlier.

During the third year after our move to Hampton, word came

from South Fork that Bill had suffered a massive, paralyzing stroke. However, his mind was unaffected, and although he had difficulty making himself understood, he did respond to those around him with his smiles, or tears, and one hand with which he could grip.

The first time we visited him after his stroke was quite emotional. As we all sat around trying to bring some joviality into that afflicted home, Bill managed to let it be known that he wanted Ginny to read something to him from the Bible. Ginny, even in her sickness, was then still able to read, although with difficulty.

The room was so quiet one could have heard the proverbial drop of a pin as Ginny was handed a Bible and, sitting beside Bill's wheelchair, she slowly opened it to the book of Psalms. In a quiet, steady voice, she read from the Ninety-first Psalm, one of her favorites:

> He that dwelleth in the secret place of the most
> high shall abide under the shadow of the Almighty.
> I will say of the Lord, He is my refuge and my
> fortress: my God; in Him will I trust.

I doubt that there was a dry eye in the room as brother and sister, both ailing, sat side by side, sharing the bit of comfort and strength that the psalm could give them, as Ginny, in her soft voice, full of love and concern for her brother, read on without a hitch to its conclusion.

During one of our visits to Pennsylvania, we learned that Ginny's brother Art also had been diagnosed with Alzheimer's. This, of course, was an added blow to the family, not only for Art's and his family's sakes, but because of the implications it presented as being a hereditary disease.

Art, true to his nature, tried to joke about his condition, and we tried to laugh with him. But it was no laughing matter, as his condition caused him to become abusive, on occasion, to his wife Laura. They had always been close, and, as the disease progressed rapidly in his case, he was taken to a nursing home near their home in South Fork, where Laura visited him daily, fed him his meals, and in other ways helped take care of him.

Louise and Web drove Ginny and me to visit him there. To

those of us aware of the situation, the visit was a poignant occasion—brother and sister, both afflicted, trying to relate to one another. Our last view of Art was of him on Laura's arm, waving good-bye to us. A little over a year later, he contracted pneumonia and died.

As Ginny's condition deteriorated, even the comparative comfort of the train was wearing on her because of the time it took, so for what turned out to be our final trip to Pennsylvania together, we flew.

Even this speedy way was not easy—mainly because it was so complicated. It involved a car trip to Des Moines, where we left our car with friends in nearby Waukee. Early the next morning we caught our plane for St. Louis, where we changed to a flight for Washington, D.C. Jeannie and Chris met us there, where we stayed for a day or two with them before taking a shuttle flight to Harrisburg, Pennsylvania, and from there a bus to Holidaysburg.

Near the end of our stay, Jeannie and family drove up from Washington for us. Saying good-bye this time was especially hard for Louise and Web, because we all could see that it was probably Ginny's last trip to her beloved Pennsylvania. The only thing that made it easier was Ginny's incomprehension of the situation; she seemed not to be suffering like the rest of us were.

The next couple of days spent in Jeannie's home should have been enjoyable, and would have been, except for Ginny's increasingly erratic behavior. Ginny and I were to sleep on the rollaway in the study, just off the front hall. This was a comfortable accommodation with a half-bath just a few steps away and all of the books we could possibly want. However, I spent more than an hour one night, after everyone else had retired, trying to get Ginny to come to bed. She stood in the center of the front hall, stubbornly refusing to budge from the spot, no matter how much I pleaded and cajoled her. Talking in whispers, so as not to disturb the household, I tried every trick I could think of, to no avail. I did everything but pick her up and carry her to bed—which would have been so much simpler and less frustrating.

Finally, after I'd given up, she came into the room on her own and got ready for bed. Neither of us said anything more about the incident, and she went right to sleep. Though both physically and emotionally exhausted, I could not sleep for some time. I lay there feeling bewildered and hurt by a fate that could deal so meanly with us. Ginny had never behaved like this before. I was certain this was our last long trip together—things were simply getting too difficult.

If Ginny's mental deterioration had happened all at once, as with a stroke, I think it might have been easier for us. Of course, there would have been the initial devastating shock, but later, faced with the reality of the thing that had happened, we would have resigned ourselves to the fact that all we could do was adjust to it.

But such is not the case with the insidious nature of Alzheimer's disease. Instead, especially in the early stages, one is not quite sure whether there is something wrong or not. It teases, and even, at times, dangles false hope before one. There were times when I would tell myself that Ginny was seeming better and that she was going to beat this thing that was destroying her while we who loved her stood by helplessly. Then there would be a cruel relapse and I knew the nightmare was real.

In 1983 or 1984, during one of our annual visits to Louise and Web in Pennsylvania, I awoke one morning to find Ginny, lying beside me, already awake. She smiled and gave me her familiar "good morning" with a kiss. For a few precious moments it seemed as if she were her former, whole self, as we conversed briefly. My heart leapt with joy and disbelief. But then, just as suddenly, the sun disappeared behind the cloud of our despair, and we were again in its shadow.

I will not soon forget the first time I experienced Ginny's not knowing me. She had gone to bed, and after my usual nighttime rounds, locking the front and back doors, checking to see that the fire was okay in the fireplace and that Simon and Kelly (our cat and dog) were in the basement, and turning off the lights, I went into our bedroom to get ready for bed. As I entered, Ginny, with an expression of alarm on her face, said, "What are *you* doing here?"

Perplexed, I told her I was going to bed.

"Not in *here*, you aren't!" she said, and drew the bed clothes up tight around her.

I suppose Ginny and I have had our share of marital fights.

But our differences never, even remotely, approached anything like violence. And if our arguments deteriorated into a frigid silence, which was the worst that happened, we made it a practice not to go to sleep in such a state. Usually, after lying with our backs toward one another on far sides of the bed for a long time, each waiting for the other to first seek a truce (which sometimes made for a short night of sleep), we were eventually in one another's arms, exchanging assurances of our love. Even in anger, we could not bear being apart.

Never in all our married life, up until that fateful night, had I been denied entrance to our marriage bed. Thus, this harsh order from the lips of my loving Ginny struck me to the heart in total disbelief. Even though I knew that "this was not Ginny," still I felt profoundly betrayed and hurt.

After getting an extra blanket from the closet, under the stern, watchful eye of a Ginny I did not know, I retreated to my recliner in the darkened living room, wallowing in self-pity and with a sense of great loss of the closeness we had always shared.

At a very late hour, after Ginny had finally gone to sleep, I crept quietly back to our room and very carefully, so as not to jiggle it, lay down on my side of the bed. When morning came, at long last, Ginny had apparently forgotten about the "strange man" who had tried to invade her privacy and seemed to accept my presence for whomever she might think I was.

Another time when the chagrin of being perceived as a stranger by my loving wife was brought home to me, I was working in my studio, thinking Ginny was upstairs, when the phone rang. It was Rob, saying that his mother was there and for me not to worry, that she was fine but maybe, after a while, I should come for her. Then he went on to explain: Ginny had appeared at their door, about two blocks from our house (across busy Highway 65) to say that there was a strange man at her house and that she wanted her children to know that she was "not *that* kind of woman."

After a while I walked over to Kris and Rob's house and we visited quietly. Then Ginny was content to go home with her husband of many years—but who nonetheless felt quite insecure in his position.

There were several more episodes when I was a stranger in my own home. It was always boggling and, in spite of my reasoning, it hurt. One time when discussing the situation with Rob, he suggested that maybe, if I would go out and come in again, I might, by interrupting her train of thought, be recognized as myself. So the next time Ginny showed that she didn't know me, I tried Rob's suggestion.

I came upstairs from my basement studio to find Ginny pacing from room to room, a familiar pattern now, "looking for Bob." I confronted her, saying, "I'm Bob."

"No," she said, "I mean my husband."

When I tried to convince her verbally, she just looked at me as though I were trying to pull her leg. So, remembering Rob's suggestion, I told her that I would see if I could find him for her and went out the back door. After a little while, I walked around to the front of the house and rang the doorbell. (I didn't want to just walk in with the chance she still didn't know me and would think I was an intruder.) Ginny opened the door and greeted me warmly as her husband. There were times when I felt I was acting a part in some weird drama, keenly aware of the tenuous position I held in Ginny's lucidity. There were other times when I pretended to go along with Ginny's strange perceptions. This tactic seemed to work better than trying to tell her she was mistaken, which might upset her.

In 1984 she began to have hallucinations. This didn't get to be a real problem in Ginny's case, but she would occasionally indicate that she saw something or someone in our house that none of the rest of us could see. But what she "saw" did not frighten her or cause her any concern. Here, too, we did not tell her she was "only seeing things" or try in any way to dissuade her. Instead, we either ignored her remark or acted as if we too saw what she saw. This could make for some fun in which Ginny seemed to enter.

Ginny and I usually walked about a mile every day—sometimes more. We most often took the same circuitous route, going south from our house and returning from the north. (I had calculated this way to be about a mile.) It took us through residential areas, past some homes of people we knew, past two school yards and the old Waterworks Park. It was a pleasant walk and we sometimes, if I felt up to it, took Kelly, our rambunctious Irish setter, along on a leash. But most of the time, it was just Ginny and I, walking briskly.

We walked mostly in silence, as Ginny's speech was increasingly becoming incoherent muttering. But sometimes, as we approached a fire hydrant, she would say to me in confidence, "Isn't he cute!" and then say "Hi" to it as we walked by. Eventually, if there was no one else nearby, I, too, not wanting to be left out of the camaraderie, would also greet the little iron fellows. We even stopped, sometimes, to briefly visit with these friendly fire hydrants that we were getting to know on our daily walks.

This all seemed to please Ginny. Now I look back, with a mixture of humor and longing, on those walks as another phase of our togetherness.

Accompanying Ginny's restless wandering was her inclination to pick things up and put them elsewhere. During this period, she was constantly rearranging and stashing items about the house. Maybe one shoe would be missing, or something from the kitchen would show up in the bedroom. I opened the refrigerator door one day to find the electric iron sitting on a shelf next to the butter dish.

Her diamond ring came up missing and we both searched throughout the house without success. I kicked myself for not being on top of the situation and not having put it away for safekeeping. Months later, when we moved from our house in town to the farm, one of the women helping us found it while wiping a cleaning cloth along the top shelf of the kitchen cupboard. Evidently, Ginny had *herself* put it away "for safekeeping."

Ginny also had a small partial denture that disappeared. However, it was never found. Before her illness she was very secretive about it and would even attempt to keep me from seeing when she cleaned it. I could only speculate as to what happened to it.

Ginny's penchant for rearranging things was not only limited to inside the house. She was out in the backyard with me one sunny day while I was mowing the grass, when I noticed she had a garden trowel and was kneeling by the flower bed next to the garage, apparently planting something. Upon investigating, I found she had dug up an iris from a bed in front of the house and was replanting it there.

Ginny had always liked working in the garden soil, but she had not done so for a long time. She was working diligently at her task, obviously enjoying it, so I said nothing about this one perennial being snuggled in the bed of annuals I had recently planted there. I felt certain, however, that it would not survive.

But Ginny's green thumb was apparently still vital, for the lone iris flourished and put forth a beautiful fragrant flower that far outshone those in the bed from which she had taken it. I praised her for her bit of gardening, and as one might guess, that iris was my favorite in our entire flower garden.

In the first years after the diagnosis, Ginny's mental condition, compared with the way it is at this writing, was good. How happy we all would be, if, by some miracle, her mind could be restored, if only to what it was *then!* During that time we could still communicate, although with some difficulty, and could be together in our home and enjoy most of the little things that had made our life together so rich. Even though there was the realization that these treasures were slipping away, there were still the remnants to savor.

Sometimes Ginny's loving concern for her family resurfaced in little ways that helped remind us of the loving wife, mother, and grandmother we had been blessed with. One time, on one of our excursions downtown, she led me into the furniture store, insisting that we buy a recliner chair she had been wanting me to have. Later she encouraged me to buy a particular style of studio painting easel I had been wanting for years. She showed pleasure at my having these things.

Some of these "awakenings" of Ginny's seemed to depend on her medication. One time, for instance, we discovered that one of her medications was causing her to be too sedated. When that was adjusted, her mind cleared to some degree and her mental powers and awareness seemed to resurge slightly.

Joni and Bob came from Minneapolis for a weekend visit at that time, and when Ginny greeted them at the door, Joni was amazed at how much better her mom seemed. But these tantalizing bits of encouragement were short-lived. While we all tried to extract the most we could from them to feed our diminishing hopes, each such "revival" only left us in more despair, when we realized again that it was only, for the most part, the vacillations of a cruel disease.

The strange behaviors of some people suffering from dementia include disrobing—sometimes in public. Thankfully, Ginny was spared that humiliation. Instead of taking *off* her clothes, she *added* to what she already had on, layer upon layer.

At such times, when she would slip out of the house for one of her wanderings, she was literally overdressed. This gave her a ludicrous appearance, like a circus clown before he takes layer upon layer off in his comic act. I felt embarrassed for her to be seen this way before I could get her back into the house, but I was thankful I didn't have to rush out with a blanket to cover her nudity. However, one time I *did* rescue her before she went out the front door with an extra bra over her blouse.

One night during this period of overdressing, I went to help her get ready for bed and found her to have on three or four blouses and a like number of skirts, as well as underwear and stockings, one over the other. After peeling off her things, a layer at a time (similar to what the circus clowns did) until I got down to the real Ginny, I helped her get into her nightgown and into bed. Then I went into the bathroom to prepare myself for bed. I couldn't have been gone for more than three or four minutes, but when I returned I found Ginny out of bed and almost completely dressed again . . . with all her layers. In exasperation I blurted out, "Ginny, what are you doing?" and set about to get her ready for bed again.

Apparently, Ginny saw the humor in this situation (not far different from what she might have pulled on me as a trick in former years) for she burst out laughing, her familiar joyful laugh. We ended up by falling across the bed in one another's arms, in a paroxysm of laughter—the kind of deep, joyful laughter we had shared many times in our years together, but something we had not enjoyed for a long time.

When we first moved from Adrian to our home in Hampton, Ginny was still preparing our meals. She was able, for the most part, to practice the skill she had so diligently taught herself early in our marriage and so devotedly practiced over the years. But as Ginny's mental powers declined, so did her proficiency in the kitchen. I came up from my basement studio one evening, about suppertime, to find Ginny in the kitchen, apparently trying to make one of her vegetable stews that had become a family favorite. On the counter was a cooking pot in which were some cut up potatoes and carrots, in a condition more resembling something for the garbage than for the table. Things on the counter and on the stove were in disarray and she seemed confused as to what to do next. As I recall, that evening I suggested we go to Smiley's for Ginny's favorite, spaghetti and Texas toast. After that, I took over the cooking as unobtrusively as possible, so as not to hurt her feelings. We ate out a lot, which Ginny had always considered a special treat.

Even when Ginny was having increasing trouble with her homemaking skills, if guests would drop in for even a brief visit, she would try to be a good hostess and serve them something. This could sometimes create a problem or make for embarrassment.

One day, Dean appeared at our door, bringing friends, a Japanese couple he wanted us to meet. A few years earlier, this young couple had spent a few days on the farm with Dean and Reggie, through sponsorship of the U.S. State Department. This had been arranged through a family friend who was then an employee of the department; he had also brought other foreign guests in the past so they might experience an American family farm. These arranged visits were enjoyed not only by the guests but by the hosts as well, and some international friendships had resulted.

Junichi and Setsuko Kato were two of those friends. This time, being in the United States on business, they had come on their own to see Dean and Reggie at the farm. Reggie was teaching that day so Dean had brought the couple that we might meet them before they stopped across the street to tell Reggie good-bye on their way to catching their plane in Minneapolis.

After introductions we visited a while, and Ginny, always glad to have visitors, showed smiling pleasure at their presence. They asked to see my studio, so I took them down and showed them my work. Presently, I realized that Ginny had not accompanied us to the studio so, while Dean and the Katos were visiting, I slipped upstairs to see why she hadn't.

Ginny was busy preparing some refreshment for our guests. She had placed some cups, saucers, and spoons around the table, as well as some other kitchen utensils not appropriate for the occasion. There was also a plate of Oreo cookies—our usual stock for the grandchildren—on the table. She even had our large ceramic teapot in the center . . . filled with cold water.

Ginny was obviously enjoying preparing something for her guests so, without being obvious about it, I exchanged the cold water for hot from the teakettle on the stove, removed some of the superfluous items, and tried to rearrange some of the place settings in a way I thought more appropriate—as Ginny would have wanted. Then returning to the studio, I told our guests Ginny had prepared a little refreshment.

Dean and Reggie had previously told Junichi and Setsuko about Ginny's illness, so they were understanding and kind as Ginny tried to be a gracious hostess at her spontaneous tea party.

Another time, when some unexpected guests dropped in for a short time on their way through town, Ginny startled the man by suddenly bringing in from the kitchen and presenting to him a tray on which was a spatula, a serving spoon, and some other kitchen utensils. This, too, was her attempt to be the gracious hostess she had always been. The incident, like many situations brought about by the disease, was not without humor, yet not without pathos for the sensitive victim.

The guest, who had not previously known of Ginny's illness, handled the situation with aplomb, and nothing was made of it. But at such times I longed to gather Ginny in my arms and shield her sensitive nature from *any* hurt, even unintentional ones.

When our kids were urging us to move back to Hampton from Adrian, Minnesota, one argument Kris gave was so that they might "look after" us. At the time I was amused and pleased by her sentiment but thought to myself that we were quite capable of taking care of ourselves. But now, as Ginny's condition was worsening, I began to feel less self-sufficient. Furthermore, I realized that Ginny and I not only needed but that I *wanted* to be "looked after"—to a certain extent, at least.

So when Rob, who, living nearby, could observe and be involved in the increasing problems attendant upon our deteriorating situation, suggested that I hire outside help to care for his mother, I listened. However, I was reluctant to act. This to me seemed like a radical step and further admission that we were letting this monster get the best of us. I was painfully aware of the increasing stress building up, caused by our trying to handle things on our own. I acknowledged that it was always a welcome relief when family members or friends would drop in for even a brief visit—to be with Ginny a bit so that I could run an errand without having to worry about her. I could not really rely on those occasional visits to meet our increasing needs. Nor could I expect those benevolent others to restructure their busy lives to fit ours—even though that was what they were doing.

The situation was becoming such that I feared to leave Ginny alone for even a few moments. She, who was becoming more like a two-year-old than a grandmother in her sixties, might get into something or leave the house while I was gone and disappear down the street. To take her into the store with me was getting to be a hassle, as she picked things up constantly. And if I left her in the car, with the admonition to "stay put" because I'd be "right back," to run in for a loaf of bread or a carton of milk, she might be gone when I returned, wandering around downtown. This possibility made for some anxious moments, especially if there was a long line at the check-out.

It got so that I waited to run errands after school was out for the day. Then I'd ask grandchildren Rebecca, Heidi, or Andy to run over from their house, only two blocks away, to sit with their grandmother for a few minutes while I was gone. This they did willingly, but even though their love and concern for their grandma was profound and they wanted to be helpful, the increasing demands put upon them were becoming ever more an imposition. I was allowing Ginny's illness and my resulting frustrations to take their toll on *all* of us.

Rob, realizing that his dad, as well as his mother, was part of the problem, became quite emphatic that I must get at least part-time assistance with Ginny's care.

Thus it was that I engaged the first of Ginny's caregivers. Betty Gunderson, who came highly recommended for the work, consented to give us some time from her busy schedule. It was arranged that she come to our house two days a week, arriving soon after breakfast, which I continued to get for Ginny and myself, and take over for the rest of the day, leaving for her home right after calling us to supper, which she put on the table. Betty's primary duty was caring for Ginny—keeping watch over her, giving her her bath, and being a companion to her throughout the day.

Before Betty came, I helped Ginny with her personal care as help became increasingly needed. I helped her with her bath and with dressing, but I did not attempt to give her a shampoo. Instead I'd take her to Marguerite's Beauty Salon. Marguerite, whose late husband had also been a victim of Alzheimer's, was understanding of Ginny's condition and was gentle and kind—another one of those good people on this planet who help to ease the pain of living.

But eventually Ginny became increasingly agitated and would not sit under the hairdrier. This behavior was disruptive to the normal business in the salon, so Marguerite made Ginny's appointment for after her shop had closed for the day, when she could give her full attention. This kind accommodation on Marguerite's part was maintained until Betty took over in our home.

In addition to Ginny's personal care, getting our noon meal (which she ate with us), and our supper, Betty did our laundry, as time allowed, and kept the house clean, except for my studio and the basement, which were my responsibility. I also cleared the supper table and washed the dishes.

When I first explained to Ginny that we were going to have someone come in to help (not mentioning, of course, that she was the reason), she was against the idea. She had never needed to have anyone help with her housework before—except the kids and me, sometimes—and she could not understand why it was necessary now. She indicated that she thought it would be an invasion of our privacy. However, when Betty had begun working for us, Ginny and she took to one another, and Ginny enjoyed having her in our home.

With Betty's help, the quality of our lives improved noticeably. I could spend time in my studio, concentrating on my work, not having to wonder at Ginny's whereabouts or what she was doing. I was also free to leave the house when the necessity arose, knowing that she was being cared for.

This arrangement with Betty worked well, but it took care of only two days a week. Though she could not spare more of her time, she suggested another woman with excellent recommendations to fill in the other days. As a result, Joan Moore came two other days. Joan, too, was a blessing in our house, as was Joy Buss, a third woman who filled in when Betty could not be there.

Ginny felt comfortable with and became fond of these "angels in our need," and they in turn loved Ginny and were saddened when she went to live at the Iowa Veterans Home, no longer needing their care.

CHANGES

As has been repeated to the point of becoming cliché, "Change is a part of life." We were finding out, close-up, that it was also a part of dying, as far as Alzheimer's is concerned.

As the weeks went by in the latter part of 1985 and early 1986, the process seemed to accelerate to the point at which I was looking back to just a short while before with nostalgia, to when Ginny had been more alive than she was presently. This decline made the extra help given us by our caregivers increasingly more appreciated. The hours they helped out made it possible for me to do my work, thus fulfilling my obligations to the *Globe,* and care for Ginny the rest of the time. I felt reasonably comfortable and secure in our situation.

But then came another change—the *Worthington Daily Globe* was sold. The new owners immediately took action to maximize their profits, which included cuts in personnel. On a winter afternoon in the middle of March 1986, my studio phone rang with a chilling message. I answered it and was informed that the caller was the new business manager at the *Globe.* He said he had been intending to come and see me, but because he did not have the time, he was phoning instead to say the paper would no longer need my services and my salary would stop on April 1.

Just like that—I was fired!

It happened that as I received the phone call, I had been visiting with an insurance representative who had dropped in to make a "cold call." Because the message I'd just taken meant that my company benefits, along with my salary, would shortly be terminated, that salesman had no trouble signing me up for a medical insurance policy to replace the group insurance we were losing along with my job.

That disturbing phone call also made it necessary for some hasty calculations to revise our budget. In the past Ginny and I had struggled over this balancing act together. But now I was on my own, sorely missing her help. In barely two weeks our income would drop considerably. We would be depending on our social security, a small income from my syndicated cartoons (which had nothing to do with the job I'd just lost at the *Globe*), and the modest once-a-year royalty check from my books. We would definitely need to cut back.

Rob came to our rescue. Together, he and I went over the situation resulting from the sudden financial crisis. Our savings were small, with most of what would have gone into savings going instead into our home.

We put our house up for sale and started looking for an apartment with rent considerably less than what we were paying for our house, besides the insurance and taxes. We put our names on a waiting list for a two-bedroom apartment in a subsidized senior citizen apartment building, formerly the old Lutheran hospital where our two oldest children had been born. While the prospects of apartment living, removed from contact with the good earth, did not appeal to me, I thought we could probably adjust.

Such a change in living style would mean that we would have to get rid of, or put into storage, many of the things with which we had become accustomed to living and which we thought necessary for a full life. And what would we do with Simon, the furry member of our family? (Kelly, our Irish setter, had been killed by a car the previous Thanksgiving, during one of his numerous escapes.)

Furthermore, living in the limited space of an apartment would mean crowding my studio into one of the two bedrooms, leaving no place for our family when they came to visit. The prospects were definitely *not* what Ginny and I had planned for our golden years, but then those dreams had evaporated some years before when we first learned of the nature of Ginny's illness.

Then a fortuitous change occurred. Basil and Ila Rowland, who had been living in Mom's house on the farm, asked if Ginny and

I would like to live there. A house they had been wanting to buy in town had become available. If we were to move into the house on the farm, they wouldn't feel bad about informing Dean and Reggie that they would be leaving.

This turn of events was another time in our life together when I felt we were being "looked after." Not only would this make it possible to live on our limited budget, because the rent and other expenses would be less than living in town, but we would have the space we desired. Furthermore, Ginny and I would be going *home!*

With Ginny's limited awareness, she could not fully savor the joy that the rest of the family shared in our prospective move. However, with the help of family and friends and borrowed vehicles, we celebrated the Fourth of July in 1986 by moving back to the farm—the place of my roots and Ginny's home, too, for many years.

Even in her restricted awareness, Ginny seemed happy to once again be within the walls of the old farmhouse that had been so much a part of both our lives through the years. We made the downstairs bedroom with the adjoining half-bath ours, with one door opening into the living room and the other (through the half-bath) into the kitchen—a comfortable, cozy arrangement.

The large upstairs southwest bedroom became my studio, in which I had Dan build bookshelves and cabinets along the west wall. Ginny's caregivers, Betty, Joan, and Joy, agreed to come the extra distance to the farm and continue to give their help. This made it possible for me to again spend time in my studio writing and doing the weekly cartoons for syndication.

Ginny seemed to be enjoying the extra space in which to wander about the house and farmyard. While she still had to be watched, there wasn't the constant concern of street traffic. However, there were some anxious times when she would take off walking down the road past the farm.

One evening I came home from being away most of the day to find Joan, who had been caring for Ginny that day, quite distraught. While she had been busy doing some work about the house, Ginny had gone outside. Joan was aware of this and could still watch her charge through the window from time to time, as she continued her housework. But suddenly, Ginny was out of sight, so Joan went out to see where she was. After searching about the houseyard and garden and farmyard without finding

Ginny, she spotted her small figure walking over the brow of the hill, about a quarter mile south down the road.

Joan hurried after Ginny until she overtook her. Walking by her side, she tried to persuade her to return home. But Ginny kept walking, not paying any attention to what Joan was saying. But then she did turn, much to Joan's relief, and started back toward home—but only for a short distance; turning again, she headed for the busy highway, less than a mile away.

This pattern continued for a long time, first one direction and then the other, back and forth on the dusty, hot, gravel road under a blazing summer sun. Joan thought they "must have walked like this for miles."

Eventually, with Joan pleading and cajoling at her side, and all but grabbing hold of her and physically dragging her (Ginny would not let Joan touch her), the two unwilling walking companions were headed up the farm lane and home. Ginny apparently was none the worse for the ordeal that had left poor Joan ready to call it a day.

Thankfully, there weren't many times when Ginny's freedom became a problem. She and I could go for our walks arm in arm, along the farm lanes and the gravel roads of the neighborhood. Once again we could enjoy the fragrances and sounds from fields and farmyard, where we could once again, as in years past, move in relative privacy under the open sky and feel the living earth yield to our footsteps. And how in these same fields we would hear the melodic song of the meadowlark, and Ginny, in her lilting voice beside me, would interpret its lyrics into our language. It would be a message, according to her, that was directed to and included the names of "Ginny" and "Bob." I'll never know, of course, the extent to which Ginny could share in all of this, because her communication ability had become less and less. But she *seemed* content, and I perceived her as being as happy as her limited awareness would permit.

The children seemed pleased to have us in the ancestral home where they could come to visit as of old. They and their children shared those summer days with us on the farm—even though there was the constant sad awareness of the mental decline of their mother/grandmother. The extended family also shared gatherings there. Sometimes we walked through the grove to the house Ginny and I had built years before, where Dean and Reggie now lived, to

have a meal with them. Under the circumstances, things once again seemed to be working reasonably well for us. We were comparatively happy during those summer days.

However, in mid-August, a chill wind, foretelling another greater change in our lives, blew across our warm, green and gold landscape. We received word from the Iowa Veterans Home in Marshalltown that they would be ready to take Ginny into the new Alzheimer's unit in early March of the next year, when it would be opened. This was supposed to be *good* news, but I did not receive it as such.

The previous winter the family had finally persuaded me that, in view of Ginny's steady decline, I should begin planning for her to enter a care facility. For economic reasons, as well as the need for specialized care for Alzheimer's victims, we decided to check out the Iowa Veterans Home in Marshalltown, which we had heard was an excellent care facility and also included a new Alzheimer's unit.

Leaving Ginny at home with one of the women caring for her that day, I rode to Marshalltown with Rob and Kris. There we were given a tour of the home, specifically the new Alzheimer's unit in the Loftus Building. This new, state-of-the-art facility was completed but could not be opened because of lack of funding for staff.

We met some of the officials, talked with people in the business office concerning necessary financial arrangements, and made formal application for Ginny's admission. I was secretly glad that the place was *not* likely to be open and ready to receive her for some time. And I longed mightily to hurry home to my Ginny.

As we drove toward home in the gathering darkness late that afternoon, I was glad to be in the back seat among the shadows. Rob and Kris tried valiantly to bolster my spirits by recounting the attractive features of the place and "how good it will be for Mom"; how it was designed to give the residents freedom to do their restless wandering without being in danger; how it was made so as to minimize those things in their environment that might aggravate their confusion; how the decorator had used calming, harmonious colors that were nevertheless cheerful; how the television was fixed so that only the staff would be able to operate it so that they could select programs that would not agitate.

They reminded me how, mounted on the walls along the hallway between the rooms, were knobs that could be turned or moved to various positions through slots by the Alzheimer's patients in their constant need to be doing something; and how, for their safety, the doors in and out of the unit were secured by making passage possible only by a key carried by staff members at all times; and how sensitivity to the patients' needs had been shown by the planners, in providing that one door opened onto a porch from which patients could walk along walkways through an attractive, fenced-in garden area that included a gazebo, where on mild days they could sit on benches and listen to piped-in music; how even the flowers, shrubs, and trees of this garden were selected for their nontoxicity, in case they would be ingested.

By reminding me of all these features designed for the welfare and comfort of the residents who would be living there once it was open, Rob and Kris were trying to make me glad for the action we had taken that day. But I could not be glad. My heart was heavy and full of dread.

Such had been my mood as we came home that winter evening, as it would be for much of the time from then on until Ginny was actually admitted. And now, with the disturbing (to me) message from Marshalltown giving a specific date, March 2, 1987, when they would be ready for Ginny, the timer had been set. Each day ticked off, relentlessly bringing closer that fateful day when Ginny would no longer be at home. There was a conspiracy, I felt, that Ginny, in her trusting, loving, nature, would never have suspected—and I, of all people, was a part of it!

There were times when I thought I would collapse under the burden, and I longed to be able to share it with her, the one who had been my strength and comfort in times past—in all the crises we had gone through together. But *this* one, our greatest ever, she would not even be able to comprehend. I thanked God for a loving, supportive family.

The autumn was full of activity: harvest, school resuming for the young people and teachers of the family, birds beginning their southern migrations, and family times spent together for birthdays, Thanksgiving, and Christmas celebrations.

In October Joni and Bob spent a few days with us on their way to Germany, where Bob, with a brand new doctorate in biology

from the University of Minnesota, would be taking a year's position in limnology at the Max Planck Institut in the town of Plön. It was wonderful having them home for even a short while. They enjoyed being on the farm and imbibed the farm atmosphere. They bought some bulbs for spring blooms and planted them for us beside the front porch, while Ginny looked on with apparent incomprehension.

The early morning they left on their long journey, Joni spent her last few moments standing quietly with her head leaning against the door frame of our bedroom, beholding the sleeping form of her mother. Then she bent down and kissed her before she quickly left, not knowing I was looking on.

Steve and Denise, with children Peter and Scotty, came down from Minneapolis several times to be with their mother/grandmother. Scotty had been born only the past August, and Ginny and I had driven to Minneapolis to see our newest grandson—it would be Ginny's last trip to Steve and Denise's home. She had been fascinated by the baby and seemed pleased when he was given to her to hold, but there was so much missing from the grandma/grandchild interaction.

Many Christmases had been celebrated in this old farmhouse. My first memories of Christmas had been of this place, where the love and magic and wonder had first become real to me, coloring all the subsequent Christmases through the years. That most wonderful of seasons had continued to be celebrated here in this home through various family situations. Many times through the years, when there was supposed to be "Joy to the World," our hearts had been heavy because of someone's absence because of illness, war, or death. But with the approach of that great season of light, during the darkest time of the year, the promise of hope and love seemed to transcend the darkness, drabness, meanness, hurt, and loneliness that is so much a part of the human experience.

As we planned for the first Christmas our family had experienced in this house for several years, we all knew it would also be Ginny's last there. This time we all would be trying desperately to make it a "season to be jolly," even though our hearts were breaking.

Of course, Joni and Bob, now in Germany, were not able to be

Ginny grandmothering her first two grandchildren—
Jennifer and Andy—in 1971. Fifteen years later, suffer-
ing from Alzheimer's, Ginny was no longer able to
experience the full pleasure of the grandma/grandchild
interaction when she met grandson Scotty.

with us; nor were Jeannie and Chris and their children able to come from Washington, D.C. However, both families had sent gifts, and their presence was felt in spirit.

My mother's condition had deteriorated to where she could no longer leave the nursing home as she had in the past when we had brought her out to be a part of family gatherings, but Steve and Denise and children and Rob and Kris and their family spent that Christmas day with us.

Our dinner was built around a large turkey I had bought and that Betty had prepared the previous day before she left, for us to put into the oven in the early morning of Christmas Day. She had also brought some Christmas goodies she had made for our family. In addition, Kris and Denise prepared all sorts of good food, making the old farmhouse once again fragrant with the festivities of Christmastime.

The old round oak table that had been the setting for so many family gatherings through the years was stretched out to accommodate all of us and once again was overloaded with its bounteous fare. As in the past, good-natured banter and laughter filled the air; though genuine, it nevertheless masked a deep sadness within, for those who were absent . . . and this time, for the one beside me who, although attempting to enter in, could only perceive that the mood, noise, and confusion were happy and loving. In this Ginny seemed happy. I'm sure I was not the only one around that table who had difficulty swallowing my food because of the lump in my throat.

Later, when we all gathered in a semicircle around the Christmas tree to exchange gifts, Ginny, who had always found childlike pleasure in this activity, seemed to not comprehend what was taking place. When the wrapped gifts were put in her lap, she just stared at them, not knowing what to do. The grandchildren had to unwrap them for her.

I don't recall any two months passing as quickly as January and February. Our time was active and full, with family and friends doing their utmost to help us in our helpless situation, but even though Ginny's condition continued to decline, she, as always, seemed pleased when folks came calling.

One time, when some friends were leaving after a pleasant afternoon visit, Ginny, who had sat quietly in our midst (a welcome change from her restless pacing) apparently enjoying the sound of voices around her, unexpectedly said with a warm smile as they were leaving, "You must come again." Even though this warm, gracious gesture, sincerely spoken directly from the heart and appropriately timed, was typical of Ginny, we were all startled, because for a long time most of her utterances, if there were any, had been unintelligible.

With the exception of a rare moment, now and then, the Ginny-that-had-been became further buried in the debris of a deteriorating mind. As the fateful day of her entrance into the Iowa Veterans Home drew ever closer, in spite of my dread, I was coming to realize (in my more rational moments) that she would no doubt be ready. Along with increasing confusion and other evidence of mental decline, there were beginning to be instances of incontinence. She was increasingly requiring constant supervision and more vigilance on the part of her caregivers, including me when those I'd hired went off duty.

In fairness to Ginny, I must point out that, even in her last few weeks at home when she was becoming less and less of the person she had been, never do I recall her ever spilling or breaking anything. Even in her illness, she was not the klutz her husband had *always* been. However, she was constantly busy: picking things up and putting them in strange places; opening doors and rummaging through drawers; flipping electric switches and turning knobs. We had to continually watch that she didn't turn on the kitchen stove.

The day we had moved to the farm, we had all just sat down to the table to eat our noon meal when we became aware that the hot day was becoming even hotter. A blast of torrid air was coming out of the furnace duct—Ginny had turned the thermostat up. To remove the threat of future heat waves of this kind was simple; I turned off the furnace switch in the basement.

We also had to make sure that she didn't try to drink or eat anything that might harm her, such as the juice in a pickle jar left out on the counter, or dishwater from a cup in the kitchen sink, or even worse, the solvents or cleaning fluids kept under the sink. She was harder to watch than a toddler.

One day I found a wet wad of Kleenex tissue she had dipped in the washbowl and plastered against the wall just inside our bedroom door. The little patch of water stain on the wallpaper remains there as a sad reminder to me of those last days when Ginny (but *not* Ginny) was still at home.

But even with all the accumulating evidence of Ginny's decline, I vacillated in my resolve to follow through with checking her into the Veterans Home on the fast-approaching date of March 2. I even asked if we could put it off for a while, but was told that she would lose her place and her name would then be put at the end of a long waiting list. I contemplated keeping her at home anyway, but I knew that, even if I could be lucky enough to find more caregivers of the quality we now had, we would not be able to afford it.

There were periodic visits by the county nurse. These calls were paid for on a sliding scale, according to one's ability to pay. But as kind and helpful as the county nurse was, Ginny would undoubtedly be needing nursing attention more often than the nurse could give on her occasional visits.

I would wake up at night with these thoughts rushing into my head, dreading the time, coming ever closer, when Ginny's sleeping form would no longer lie beside me. How could I stand her not being near me after all these years? And I was overwhelmed with a feeling of guilt for my part in the "conspiracy" to have her "put away." I would gently, so as not to disturb her, put my hand on her shoulder or her arm, seeking to gain some reassurance from the warmth of her sweet body, breathing quietly in deep sleep. My tears were hot on my pillow, and I prayed to God the equivalent of "Please remove this cup from me . . . from us," to no avail.

IOWA VETERANS HOME

There have been several wakeful nights in my life that have preceded a day full of dread for me: among them, the night before my first day of school, the night before the county exams required for those going from country school into high school, the one before I left for college, and the sleepless night I listened to the sound of katydids while dreading my induction into the Army. However, none of these lonely, gut-wrenching, sleepless nights measured up to that night in March of 1987 when I lay awake dreading the dawn—the day that Ginny would be taken from me to live out the rest of her life at the Iowa Veterans Home.

Steve had come down from Minneapolis by himself, the afternoon of March 1, so that he and Rob could accompany Ginny and me on our sad journey. Wanting to be as positive as possible about this trip, I had bought a new suitcase so that Ginny wouldn't have to arrive at her new home with one of our old beat-up ones—another futile attempt at trying to make things seem better than they were.

The people at the Veterans Home had encouraged us to bring along something that would be a familiar home object for Ginny to have near her bed. So when Rob came to the farm with his van, early on the morning of March 2, we loaded one of our companion easy chairs into the back along with the new suitcase filled with Ginny's things. She and I took our places in the seat behind Rob and Steve and sat close to one another, hand in hand.

The only thing that made that soul-wrenching trip endurable

was Ginny's incomprehension of what was taking place. Certainly, Ginny was not suffering like Rob and Steve and I were, for she was in the same blinding fog she had been in for weeks. Our sons tried to include us in improvised casual talk, but my heart was too heavy to participate.

No matter how many times I make the round-trip from our home to Marshalltown (well over four hundred, thus far), I shall never cease to experience twinges of the hopeless dread I experienced that day as we came over the hill on Highway 14, north of Marshalltown, and descended into the Iowa River valley with the wooded hills and a skyline dominated by the tower of the Marshall County Courthouse.

With Ginny's hand in mine, my thoughts went back to our first journey to separation, more than forty years before, when she and I sat side by side in the back seat of Grandma Artley's car, on our way to the farm where Ginny would have our first baby while I would be away in the Army.

Those responsible for setting up the new Alzheimer's unit at the Iowa Veterans Home had given careful thought to the project, considering the welfare of the people who would be living there. The same concern went into planning for the influx of those waiting to be admitted. To minimize the stress on new residents and their families, each one was to be admitted individually with plenty of cushion time between admissions so that full attention could be devoted to each incoming resident and his or her family members.

It happened that Ginny was the very first person admitted to this new facility. Soon after our arrival at the appointed hour at Loftus One (the name of the facility), Ann Cordes and her staff and Doug Freeman, the home's social worker with whom we had been in earlier contact, greeted us warmly and set about making Ginny feel welcome and at ease. While Rob, Steve, and I were directed to the admissions office to fill out the necessary papers and otherwise deal with the business of her admission, Ginny enjoyed the undivided attention of her newfound friends.

This type of individual attention and care has come to be expected throughout the care facility. The staff and caregivers become like family to the residents. They become involved with their charges. It must cost them much emotionally, but it greatly enhances the quality of care—imbuing it with human compassion.

This compassion and honest individual concern, a hallmark of the place, are things to which Ginny could relate. As the time came for us to leave without her, seeing her apparent contentment with her new friends made it a little easier for us to go. When I, with an extreme effort at nonchalance, kissed her good-bye and bid a jaunty "see you later," she barely paid any heed, so engrossed was she with one of the staff.

I'll never know if she ever realized that she had been left behind by those she had always loved and trusted. I'll never know if perhaps she awoke in the night, wondering where she was—wondering where is Bob? I could and did torture myself many lonely nights as these and other such thoughts kept creeping into my mind. But to my knowledge she did not suffer in this way. If it can be called a merciful aspect of this cruel disease, the very thing that had brought this heart-breaking situation about had also apparently dulled her perception of it.

Rob, Steve, and I had no such softening shield against the reality. As the three of us hurriedly left our wife and mother behind the secured doors of the Alzheimer's unit and made our way down the hall toward the nearest exit, we were silent, each with his own thoughts, struggling against the grief that was welling up within us. Then Steve, with his inimitable sense of humor, came to our rescue with, "Let's all go and get drunk." His off-the-wall remark broke the dam and our emotions poured forth in laughter instead of sobs. We were then able to proceed on our lonely trip home with a modicum of emotional stability.

When negotiating with the Iowa Veterans Home about Ginny's admittance there, I had dickered with them as if I were making some large financial deal. I told them (and my family) that I would consent to her admittance if I could be assured that I could bring her home often. I was told this would indeed be possible as long as Ginny's condition allowed. They said it would be best, however, if I didn't take her out of the facility for about three weeks so that she could become used to her new surroundings. Of course, I could visit her as often as I wanted in the meantime. There were guest cottages on the grounds in which I could stay overnight, if I so desired.

Subsequently, I have stayed many times in nearly every one of those ten clean, comfortable, and reasonably priced nearby accommodations. But, those first few weeks, I mostly made visits, a day at a time, two or three times a week.

It was even arranged, if I was there at mealtime, for me to buy a meal ticket and have a tray delivered along with Ginny's so the two of us could eat together at a table in her room. But this didn't turn out as cozy as I'd envisioned. Even though Ginny was still feeding herself at that time, she was restless and agitated and the meal was not a time for quiet conversation—Ginny's speech being very limited and her attention span almost nonexistent.

As spring came and the weather allowed, I would take her out of the unit for long walks outside around the beautiful grounds. Or we would go arm in arm through the corridors of the home and sit together in one of the lounges, until Ginny, in her restlessness, wanted to move on.

When Ginny's "quarantine" was ended and I was able to bring her home for the first time, I was as ecstatic as when I had gotten my first pass home from the Army. And speaking of passes, it was required that Ginny have a pass to leave the home, the same as when we were back in Ft. Wood. We left the Veterans Home with pass in hand on Friday afternoon, knowing we had to return on Monday. It was a wonderfully warm feeling, having Ginny again beside me as we drove toward home. I could reach over and take her hand—like old times. Well, not quite like old times; Ginny no longer responded with a squeeze of her hand, we could not visit as of old, and she paid scant attention to the passing landscape. She seemed not to be sharing my happiness about her homecoming.

Most of our trip was silent, as I found contentment in the prospects of again having her at home—and in the warmth of simply holding her hand. Thus, I was startled, upon reaching the farm (about an hour and a quarter's drive), as we drove up our lane and turned into the farmyard, when Ginny, in her soft voice, said, *"This is what I have been wanting."*

That one sentence, the most I had heard her speak in several weeks, burned itself into my consciousness for all time. Suddenly, I felt less sure of how well I perceived Ginny's awareness of her situation. Had she been homesick the past few weeks, actually longing to be here? My heart was heavy and ached at the thought. She obviously recognized these surroundings that had been such a part of our lives together for so many years—it was where I had brought her home from Ft. Wood to meet my family for the first time, more than forty years ago, a week before our wedding; where she had lived with my family for several months at the time of Jeannie's birth; where we had lived and worked at farming for four years after the war; where we had come home to visit with a carload of kids and a dog many times in the following years; and finally, where just the two of us had been living the past few months.

In spite of the temporary nature of this visit and my unsettling questions about the extent of her awareness, I was glad to have the place warmed again with her presence. When I put her to bed that first night, there was great satisfaction in knowing that she was in our bed in the next room, where I could see her from my chair in the living room—and knowing that I could go in and take her into my arms. Our home felt whole again with her presence, however impaired that presence might be.

When it was time to take her back to the Veterans Home, I tried not to make a fuss about it. As casually as possible, I said, "Well, it's time we go," gathered up her things, got her into the car, and left. This never seemed to be a problem for her, and when we got back, she wasn't reluctant to go through the doors into Loftus One—not nearly as reluctant as I was to take her into her "compassionate prison."

Each time I took her back, whether from a visit at home or from a stroll around the grounds, I found it hard to leave and dreaded the return trip alone. The car seemed so very empty, as did the familiar route, without her presence, and of course, the house . . . the whole farm echoed her absence anew upon each return.

My family was sensitive to my loneliness and did all they could to ease it, just as they had been doing year after tedious year for us, through this long dying process. I have become more and more aware of the importance of family and friends and a feeling of closeness with God—what a hell on earth this would be without them!

Through that spring and into early summer of 1987, my life was made bearable by the times spent with Ginny, either at the Veterans Home, where we would walk the pleasant tree-shaded grounds arm in arm, or on the farm when I'd bring her home on pass. I brought her home often during those weeks. We would spend some time with family, but mostly the two of us just enjoyed being together.

One weekend in the latter part of July, when I had Ginny at

home, I sadly realized it was to be the last. She seemed suddenly harder to manage. She wouldn't sit down at the table to eat; she balked at everything and would not stay put, becoming more agitated than ever.

From then on our times together were limited to my visits (at least once a week) to the Veterans Home. Sometimes I would stay in one of the guest cottages overnight so that I could spend most of two days with her. There were twenty-one Alzheimer's victims who were residents in Loftus One, Ginny and her roommate, Hilda DeFrance, another veteran, being the only women among nineteen men. They were all ambulatory but in various stages of the disease. Most of them moved about with the familiar, slightly forward-leaning posture and shuffling gait. Each of them more or less was in a world of his or her own. Some futilely tried to open the secured doors leading out of the unit. Some fiddled with the wall gadgets put there for that very purpose. Some carried an article of clothing—a shoe, a sock, a shirt—their own or someone else's. One of Ginny's shoes disappeared and never was found.

Though there is a similar pattern in patients' behavior, those of the staff working with them emphasize that no two are totally alike in their symptoms and actions. They still seem to have the stamp of their individualities and need to be dealt with accordingly. Apparently, the kind of person each one formerly was is still somewhere within.

Ginny, for instance, had always been gentle and compassionate, reaching out to others. Even as the disease, in its latter stages, continued to smother her vitality and means of expression or communication, at times those lifelong traits still shone through, however briefly. Four years after her entrance into the Iowa Veterans Home, this compassionate spirit came through, even though by this time Ginny was bedridden, requiring constant care. Barb Peters, one of her caregivers, told me about how Ginny had helped *her*.

It was during the Middle East war, Desert Storm, in the winter of 1991. Barb's soldier son was in the midst of the action, and she had come to work distraught with worry about his safety. When she came in to care for Ginny, needing to talk to someone about her deep concern, through tears she unburdened on Ginny. Barb told me, with deep feeling, how, even in Ginny's disabled condition and in her silence, she had managed to convey comfort and reassurance to Barb, a suffering mother. As Barb said, "Here I was, the one who was supposed to give care and comfort to Ginny, and *she*, by the look in her eyes and a crippled smile, had helped *me*, the caregiver."

Our children have, of course, gone to see their mother when possible. While it is not evident that she knows them, they want to visit her, remembering who she *was* and the love between them.

There was an amusing, and touching, incident when Jeannie came to see her mother one time not long after she had entered the Veterans Home. It was a pleasant spring day so Jeannie and I, after greetings at Loftus One, brought Ginny outside for a leisurely stroll about the grounds. We walked three abreast with Ginny in the middle. Jeannie and I were, of course, carrying the conversation. Presently, Ginny, who had been watching Jeannie as we talked, turned to me and in a confidential tone said, "Aren't they cute at this age?" Jeannie, who was forty-two at the time, delighted in her mother's prideful remark.

Ever since the onset of Ginny's affliction, the family and I have constantly needed to make adjustments to the changes in her personality. Some of those adjustments have been harder to make than others. Though they kept me constantly off balance, I managed, I thought, to keep some semblance of equilibrium. However, there was one incident on one of my visits to Loftus One that gave me quite a jolt, partly because it was so unexpected. As Dad would have said, using one of his earthy expressions, it made me "weak in the poop."

Upon arriving at the Alzheimer's unit, I entered the dayroom as usual, first scanning the place to see if Ginny was there before going to her room. There were several residents in the room, some milling about and some sitting in chairs. Suddenly, I spotted Ginny sitting on a couch next to one of the men residents. They were holding hands.

Ann Cordes, seeing my confusion, took me aside for a hurried consultation. She explained that this type of attraction between patients sometimes occurred and that I should not be upset by it because it meant nothing. She said that the two sometimes walked around hand in hand.

I must confess, I was bothered by this discovery more than I wanted to admit. I wanted to punch the guy in the nose—the cad!

I knew I should never have brought Ginny to this place. Now she had fallen for someone else! Of course, these were not my conscious thoughts—just my gut feelings, and I was embarrassed by my primeval reaction, only hoping I had kept it well concealed. Ginny and I spent our usual time together the rest of that day and countless visits since with no further such problems, and we're *still married.*

Early on the morning of August 31, 1987, I answered the phone to hear Joni's husband, Bob, as clear as if calling from nearby Hampton rather than Germany, say that Kathryn Virginia Sterner had been born in the hospital at Kiel, Germany, that morning. Both mother and daughter were doing fine. I, of course, spread the word on this side of the Atlantic. Even though I wasn't sure of how much Ginny could comprehend, I delighted in telling her that our youngest daughter had given birth to a "Kraut."

Later that fall, a movement, starting in Plön, Germany, and spreading to the people around me, eventually resulted in my flying over to inspect our newest grandchild. Even though I wanted desperately to go, I was reluctant to leave Ginny. My heart ached with the thought that she could not share in this adventure. My family, and the folks at Iowa Veterans Home as well, assured me Ginny would be fine. So in November, I went, for the both of us, and spent three weeks in Germany with Joni and Bob and their baby.

On January 20, 1988, Ginny was moved from Loftus One to Two East, where again Hilda DeFrance was one of her room-mates, with two others making it a room of four. Hilda had been moved there first, leaving Ginny the only woman on Loftus. That also left an empty bed in her room, while the list of those waiting for admission included only men. In addition, Ginny had become more unstable on her feet and had fallen a couple of times, fortunately without injury. Moving her to Two East, where she could have more individual care, seemed the prudent thing to do.

When nurse Ann Cordes phoned me about their plans for Ginny, to see how I felt about it, I was reluctant. To me, it meant yet another period of adjustment for Ginny, to add to all the others she had been subjected to over the past two years. Sadly, Ginny's life has been one of moves and adjustments, beginning at the age of eight months with the death of her mother. Besides, I asked, wasn't the facility at Loftus One supposed to be the latest in the state-of-the-art Alzheimer's care? Would Ginny get the same concerned care in the new place that she had received in Loftus?

Ann assured me that her care at Two East would indeed be every bit as good as in Loftus. Furthermore, knowing Ginny and the staff there, she knew they would love her. She felt confident that the move was in Ginny's best interest and that I would be glad in the long run.

Ann was absolutely right on all counts. It *was* a good move for Ginny, and we couldn't have asked for better, more compassionate care. Like family members, the staff, nurses, and caregivers become emotionally attached to their charges. On Two East, as in Loftus One, Ginny was much loved—and with such love shown, she was in a place she could understand.

When Ginny had become bedridden, Kim Schryver, the home's dietician and one who had befriended Ginny since her early days there, took her by wheelchair, from where she was then living on Two East, to Loftus One, for a farewell gathering for Ann Cordes, Ginny's first nurse and friend at Iowa Veterans Home. Ann was leaving to follow her husband, who was being transferred to Texas. Ginny's caregivers at Two East had "prettied her up" for the occasion and, as luck would have it, she was comparatively alert and responsive that day.

I would like to share some notes from Ann Cordes's initial nursing assessment of Ginny on Loftus One, of which I was not aware at the time but which now put additional light on those early days of Ginny's adjustment to her new home. It confirms much of my perception of that period. However, there doesn't seem to be evidence of undue anguish and suffering related to the changes of surroundings, as I had feared there might be. The comparative ease of Ginny's assimilation into her new home at the Iowa Veterans Home was no doubt largely due to the sensitivity of the staff. Ann referred to Ginny as a "very gentle lady. In fact she is considered to be our most vulnerable resident here because she is so gentle and cautious about things." Then Ann notes:

A few days after Ginny's admission, we admitted a resident named Bob and she immediately identified with this name. We were quite concerned about this because she would go up to this resident and stand there, trying to figure out what was going on, and he is one who has a potential for being abusive. However, fortunately, Ginny was able to simply read signals and understand that he was not responding to her in the same way one bearing that name had previously, and therefore we have really not had any problems with them.

Ann went on to say that there are others who were friendly and that Ginny seemed to "read" them and respond accordingly. She told about one resident who was quite social, who talked to everyone and held out his hand to those who came near him. Ann related that he and Ginny immediately became good friends and would be seen "walking hand in hand down the hall. . . . So she again seems to sense the people that are safe for her."

These notes tell of how the staff did their best to "at all times keep Ginny as low-key as possible." They would not hurry her but would give her freedom to wander in the secure environment of the facility. "But essentially," Ann wrote, "the biggest thing we are doing for her safety is to reinforce her cautious, gentle nature, and allow her to use her own intuitions about things that feel right or don't feel right to her."

Nurse Ann told of Ginny's being a very private person, "and it was difficult for her to undress in front of strangers and persons that she did not sense were people that she knew." She also said, "Sometimes, if we are trying to toilet her or do other care activities, she may say Bob's name, and this is pretty much a clue to us that she is looking for Bob and that we don't feel right to her." However, as Ann reported, these incidents decreased in frequency as she came to know her caregivers and feel more at home. "She is a very tidy lady," Ann wrote, "and when you work with her, you use, again, a very gentle approach. Her husband used the approach of trying to massage her face gently as he washed it so that it would be a relaxing activity, and our staff finds this quite effective."

During Ginny's early weeks in Loftus One, therefore, the staff worked at following basically the same pattern as we had at home so that there would be a minimal adjustment for her. To meet her constant need to be doing things, they gave her paper to tear into strips and washcloths to fold. She also stayed busy dusting things and carrying things from one room to the next. After awhile, she felt comfortable enough to enter any of the rooms and, if tired, lie down on any vacant bed for a nap.

Ginny seemed to enjoy all of the group activities, as Ann related:

> She is one of our better participants in things like balloon
> volleyball and any singing that we do. I am very pleased with
> the fact that during the time Ginny has been here, she has
> become more animated, and where she used to watch you very
> carefully with large eyes, as though she was somewhat fright-
> ened, now you see Ginny much of the time wearing a bright
> grin that literally goes from ear to ear. Again, she seems to
> sense those residents who are safe and friendly toward her,
> and with those residents, she warms up very quickly.
>
> Ginny was a well-rounded individual who took some
> courses at the University of Iowa in history after she was
> married, and enjoyed the subjects of math and literature, as
> well. She also liked to study the Bible . . . Right now, she very
> much enjoys the music that we have on the unit and she will
> take part in pretty much any type of singing that we have,
> whether it is hymns or a faster "golden oldie" type of song.
> She played softball at one time and tosses a ball with more
> skill than most of our residents. She enjoys things like classical
> music, ballroom dancing, and movies like *Dr. Zhivago* and
> *Fiddler on the Roof.* It is interesting to watch Ginny with a pad
> of manila paper because she is right at home with it. If we
> have a pad out on the unit and set it down, Ginny will always
> pick it up. Bob keeps one for her in her room, and she draws
> figures on it a lot of times, like a cross or other things, but
> again tries to look very purposeful with it. Bob is a cartoonist
> by trade, so again, writing and drawing has been a part of this
> family for many years. Ginny was also very domestic in her
> interests and at home would work at "doing the dishes" for a
> long period of time. On at least one occasion, we have found
> the water running in her bathroom sink, which I am sure was
> a replication of her trying to do this.

Access to these notes by Ann Cordes has given me additional insight into Ginny's early days at Loftus One and her adjustment to it. Mostly, it reinforces my own perceptions of the process. However, I can read into it the fact that she did indeed miss the unique security she knew, however limited was her awareness, in the love we shared in our own home. This knowledge does nothing to alleviate the ache in my heart.

When I wrote to Ann Cordes to ask her permission to use

material from her notes in this book, she replied that she would be pleased to have them thus used. Then she added, "Ginny was like a gift to our unit [it must be remembered that Ginny was the first patient admitted to the new Alzheimer's unit at the Iowa Veterans Home] in that her personality and needs were so crucial in shaping Loftus One into a sensitive, caring place. We truly needed her."

Those words are but another example of how Ginny, simply because of the person she is, even in her infirmity, has been able to exert a positive influence on those about her. Most of us, certainly myself included, would do well to be such an influence in our *wholeness*.

At first after Ginny was moved to Two East, she was still ambulatory, as she had been at Loftus. Each morning she was given her breakfast, her "cares" (meaning she was washed, her teeth and mouth cleaned, her hair combed, etc.), and then dressed to be up and about. For her own safety she was sometimes put in the dayroom, with the bottom half of the "Dutch"-style door closed so that she might do her restless pacing in safety. She was also given something to do; she seemed to enjoy using a feather duster on the furniture and window sills. However, as in Loftus, there was still concern over her falling, so she had to be watched closely. She and I would still take our walks, outside when the weather permitted, often making a stop at the canteen for ice cream.

As time passed and Ginny's condition deteriorated, she was put more often in the wheelchair customized to fit her needs. (There is a shop in the basement where this customizing is done—where patient and wheelchair are "fitted" by specialists.) She had entered a stage where her restless motion was expressed in kicking out her feet when riding in her chair, and she didn't keep them on standard foot rests. A platform was fitted to the front for her feet to rest on, allowing more movement.

In some ways, pushing Ginny in her wheelchair was easier and less stressful than walking with her had been. With her in the chair, I didn't have the concern of her stumbling and falling nor the worry about her getting overly tired on our strolls around the grounds of the Veterans Home.

Joni, Bob, and baby Kathryn Virginia came back from Germany in December of 1987, not long after my visit there. They went directly to Arlington, Texas, where Bob had been hired as professor of biology at the university, but the following spring they made a trip to Iowa to introduce their baby girl to the family. It was a happy experience for everyone as little Katie and her proud parents were warmly embraced by all. It was an especially joyful occasion for me, seeing Joni now with her little family, basking in the admiring attention of the family that had always meant so much to her.

With mixed feelings I anticipated our trip to Marshalltown, for grandmother and granddaughter to meet. Although Joni and Bob knew the extent of Ginny's condition when they had last seen her before leaving for Germany eighteen months before, and even though I had filled them in on how much she had deteriorated since then, Joni wanted desperately to show her mother the beautiful granddaughter she had produced—like when she brought home some little thing she'd made in kindergarten or Bible school, saying, "Look, Mom, what I did."

The reunion was bound to be a disappointing one. Ginny barely responded to the greetings and paid practically no attention when the little one who bore her grandmother's first name as her middle one was placed in her lap. My heart ached for both Joni and Ginny. It was another cruel twist of this miserable disease that caused Joni's beautiful eyes to moisten.

After some desultory conversation around Ginny's bed in that room with three other occupied beds, she was put into her wheelchair, and we all went for a walk around the grounds, showing our kids her new home. We ended our tour at the canteen for some ice cream treats, sitting at one of the large round tables. While we visited, Ginny, in her wheelchair, sat looking across the table at the baby on Bob's lap. Suddenly, she spoke as if to herself, "Isn't she *something!*"

Those three words, typical of those spoken from the heart of a proud grandma, heard by all of us, were not a lot, but it was a small keepsake that Joni could carry away with her, tucked close to her heart—her mother *had* shown appreciation of her baby!

I keep saying that Ginny doesn't seem to be suffering. Maybe some of this is based on hope or wishful thinking, but there are times when I'm not so sure, anymore, that she isn't. Once when I was visiting her, I saw her lower lip tremble, as one who is about to cry. But nothing came of it, and I held her in my arms.

I do know that there was a period in the earlier stages of the disease when Ginny *did* suffer. When first she realized what was happening to her, she suffered greatly, but not for long. She soon forgot. And there were, in the first years of Ginny's affliction, times when she was depressed. I don't know if this was due to her knowledge of what was happening or was just another manifestation of the disease. One time while we were living in Hampton, I came up from my basement studio to find her lying on the floor. She hadn't fallen (I would have heard that). She simply seemed depressed and had lain down in resignation.

During that same time, we received word from Pennsylvania that Ginny's sister Meriam had suffered a heart attack and died. Meriam and Ginny had been close, and when the news of Meriam's death came, Ginny broke down and cried in quiet sobs, as one might expect. But her grief lasted only for a short while, and then it was apparently forgotten and never brought up again.

Around the same time, her older sister, Laura, died after a long illness following a series of strokes. Ginny, in her failing mental condition, was not able to grieve as one might have expected her to, because she had loved and respected Laura like a mother, having lived in her home in her latter teen years until she enlisted and left for Ft. Des Moines for training in the WAAC.

Later, when Ginny's condition had deteriorated even more, we didn't even tell her of her brother Art's death, for by then her comprehension was even less.

In May of 1989, Mom died at the age of ninety-seven, after ten years of declining health. Her passing was something we had been expecting and even wishing for, for her own blessing, toward the last. Ginny, who dearly loved Mom and who, even in her declining mental awareness, had been solicitous of her when we'd visit her in the nursing facility during our years in Hampton, was in no condition now, we felt, to deal with her death, so we didn't tell her of it.

We also spared her the news of the deaths of her brother Bill, of her brother George's wife, Margaret, and (even later) Art's wife, Laura, all of whom she loved. The same was true when her beloved brother Ed passed away. While I sometimes feel that there *might* be "windows" or brief periods of awareness, I feel it is important to tell her, at such times, only that which will bring her joy and not cause more hurt. I tell her of my deep love for her, and the wonderful difference she has made in my life, and how much I thank God for bringing us together. While I have expressed these feelings to her many times during our years together, I hope the message gets through to her now especially, and that it might bring her some joy.

Have I been right or wrong in this? I don't know. I guess this is but another aspect of dealing with this cruel disease—so much uncertainty. I've had only my love for Ginny to guide me.

Late in the fall of 1990, while I was visiting Joni and her family in Texas, I received a call from Ginny's nurse, Becky, saying that a private room had become available and that, if I agreed, they would move Ginny in it. Her condition had deteriorated to the point where she was having difficulty swallowing and was choking more; the room of which Becky spoke was near the nurses' station, where they could keep a close watch on her.

Of course, I was in favor of the move, and when I returned a few days later, I found Ginny in this private room with a magnolia tree outside the second-story, southern windows. It was bright and cheerful . . . and private.

I was encouraged to make it *our* room by bringing some pictures for the walls and other items from home. I bought a radio/tapeplayer for Ginny's birthday and later brought in a recliner chair and a small television. The staff even moved in a small desk for me, where I have done much of my writing with Ginny at my side. In effect, this is the last home Ginny and I will share. It's the next best thing to being in our home at the farm.

One of the pictures from home is a group photo of our family. I'm moved to marvel at how the people in it were all brought to that place at that particular time in late summer of 1984 by so many diverse, seemingly random forces. My mind goes back through the train of events that eventually brought a lonely, young GI and a lovely, young WAC together during World War II, making this photo possible—the capture of an instant in the ongoing lives of those depicted.

As with all records, this photo, because it is of a particular moment in time, is now obsolete. Mom, there in her wheelchair, is no longer with us. And Ginny, pictured in the early years of her affliction, has since been brought low by the inevitable progression

Our family group in Hampton, Iowa, summer 1984. This photo hung on the wall of our "home" on Two East at the Iowa Veterans Home. Left to right, front row: Tauna and Todd Szymanski, Heidi Artley, Grandma Elsie Artley (in wheelchair); second row, seated: Chris Szymanski, Jeannie (Artley) Szymanski, Jennifer Scheel, Rebecca Artley, Kris Artley, Rob Artley; back row, standing: Steven Artley, Peter Artley, Denise Artley, Bob and Ginny Artley, Andy Artley, Joni (Artley) Sterner, Bob Sterner (Burmester Photography, Hampton, Iowa).

of this cursed disease. The grandchildren have grown, some beyond recognition from the way they were depicted then. And most noticeable of all, four more grandchildren (Scotty, Katie, Sharon, and Nicky) have since joined the family, bringing the count to eleven. How my heart aches to think that she'll not know and experience them and that they will not have the blessings of Ginny's grandmothering that our older ones were fortunate enough to have had.

Are we happy? What is happiness? Within the perimeters of our circumstances, I guess we are happy. I say "we," speaking for Ginny, in her silence, in whatever awareness she has. The folks at Iowa Veterans Home are kind and loving to her. She's kept clean, fed, and comfortable, and doesn't seem to be suffering.

When I'm sitting beside her bed, holding her hand and am able to lean over and whisper my love to her and give her a kiss now and then, I guess that, within the reality of our situation, this is happiness. At this time and in this place, I know of no greater contentment than simply being at Ginny's side, holding her hand.

But there are times when I feel somewhat resentful as I see couples of our age dining in restaurants, shopping, going out for a drive, or walking arm in arm. At such times I feel, Why do *they* get to be together to enjoy one another and their family as a couple, and *we* can't?" I think how nice it would be to have our grandchildren come to visit Grandpa *and* Grandma! Why do our gray-headed peers get to do these things when *we* cannot? Why did this miserable thing have to happen to *us?* What have *we* done to deserve this long passage through the shadows in this dark valley? I suppose there are blessings that have come our way, in spite of, or even because of this horrible affliction—of those people we've come to know and love as a result; of being made aware that there are a great many good souls, of all shapes, sizes, and colors, in this world, who are loving and caring individuals capable of making this a better world in which to live . . . and die. And that even dying, because of these caring ones, is made easier.

I suppose this then can be looked upon as a furthering of our education, as we travel together, helping us to grow into what God has in mind for us. And if this is true, I'm just sorry that Ginny had to be the one to bear the burden of this awful disease—but on second thought, I'd not want her to suffer as I have. Perhaps it *is* better this way . . . if it has to be.

Seeing her lying in her bed, in her silence, I remember what a positive force she has been in our life together. It was at her gentle urging that we left the farm and went to the University of Iowa to finish my schooling. It was Ginny's idea that launched the *Waukee Journal,* and again her prompting that moved us to Minnesota and a whole new life. Two of those steps that she initiated were painful for all of us. She often expressed her sense of guilt for having taken me "away from the farm," knowing my love for it. But each of the actions she initiated proved to have been in the right direction. How dull my life would likely have been without her!

It is thought that hearing is the last of the senses to remain with Alzheimer's patients—hearing and touch. Thus, we use music to try to help Ginny. She seems to enjoy it, as tapes of familiar old tunes are played quietly in her radio/tapeplayer. But loud music or noise of any kind seems to distress her.

When God designed the human race, He used humor as a very important ingredient. It is as essential to the total makeup of healthy human beings as are the other basic elements. Thankfully, the people here understand and use humor as therapy, not only for their charges, but also for keeping their own sanity in dealing with situations in their work that are anything but funny.

One hot summer day, when I came to see Ginny, I was surprised to see one of the staff carrying a large Uzi-type water gun at the ready against one shoulder. She explained, in answer to my perplexed look, that it was for self-defense. Someone had slipped a loaded water pistol to Richard, who, while bedridden, is delightfully high-spirited. He had "shot" the unsuspecting Leann, so she had armed herself for defense.

There are times when this very professional, caring place reminds me of the MASH unit in that popular, long-running television series. Those characters, too, were trying to keep their sanity in stressful situations.

In our attempts to make Ginny more comfortable, I brought her eyeglasses from home. She had not worn them since her arrival at the Veterans Home. A few months before she came, when still in our home during her restless, wandering-and-carrying-things stage, I had put them away so they would not get lost or broken.

(She was no longer reading and would not keep them on.) When she's awake and propped up in bed, we put them on her so that she can better see her surroundings. I show her family photos, and she seems to look at them more intently through her glasses, as she does at greeting cards she receives, when they are shown to her.

Usually her glasses are put on her at mealtime so she might better see the face and expressions of the one feeding her. This, hopefully, makes that one-to-one process a more sociable experience for Ginny.

Alzheimer's is a debilitating process in which hard decisions constantly have to be made as the disease progresses. As early as 1982, when Ginny was diagnosed as having Alzheimer's, and periodically ever since, there have been confrontations with the reality of this insidious disease that have forced us all to make decisions with which we would so much rather not have been burdened.

Until a breakthrough is made when, hopefully, the medical profession will be able to cure or prevent this devastating brain disease, there is no possible chance for a victim of Alzheimer's to get better. In fact, the only prospect is a worsening and further wasting away of the mental processes and the personality, until finally death occurs. Thus, at every stage of decline along the way, decisions have to be made in adjusting to these realities.

Each decision is difficult. However, what I hope to be the final choice for Ginny was probably the hardest—what to do about the type of care to be given to our loved one as she progresses toward the final transition. Should we fight off the inevitable for as long as possible, for as long as our resources, physical and emotional, hold out, regardless of the quality of the life we're trying to hold onto, or should we cooperate with the natural process of dying and make it as dignified, humane, and comfortable as possible for our Ginny as she passes through the opaque curtain we call death?

The great technical strides made in medicine in the past several years force us, as family members and caregivers, to make these agonizing decisions. "Miracle" technology and drugs available to the medical profession make it possible to keep one "alive" far beyond the point of living. Because of their ethical standards, medical professionals have no choice but to use this life-sustaining technology to the fullest, regardless of how they may feel individually. So it falls to us, the patients or responsible loved ones, to determine whether or not these life-prolonging measures are employed. What an awful burden of responsibility to have to bear! Perhaps it is a case in which knowledge is a burden. If we didn't have this possibility of prolonging life, we wouldn't have to make these decisions that should be God's.

Is it possible that this is why, in the story of the Garden of Eden, Adam and Eve were forbidden to eat of the fruit from the Tree of the *Knowledge* of Good and Evil?

When the awful realization that Ginny's condition would only get worse soaked in and I was finally able to accept it, only then was I able to come to the difficult decision that I wanted no extraordinary means used in prolonging her life—prolonging her dying. I didn't want her hooked up to tubes and wires or stuck with intravenous needles for medication or whatever. And I certainly didn't want her to suffer the traumatic indignity of a stomach-feeding tube. I had seen this method of feeding in use and felt then, and still do, that it is inhuman.

Even after Ginny could no longer feed herself and had to be fed by someone else, there was still the social aspect of eating that is an integral part of being human. Even as the disease progressed and it became increasingly difficult for her to swallow and each spoonful of pureed food had to be slowly and carefully fed to her, there was a social, one-to-one intercourse between her and the one feeding her. This would not be the case with a feeding tube, in which the "meal" is in a bottle hung from a stand, and the feeding is done by gravity, the same as in intravenous feeding of glucose or saline.

In the final stages of Alzheimer's, when the brain can no longer send the messages for the swallowing process, there is continuous difficulty. This can lead to choking, which in turn can cause food to enter the lungs, causing pneumonia. This failure of the swallowing process can therefore lead to the lack of sufficient nutrition and starvation, choking to death, or pneumonia, which in itself is most generally fatal. Some of the hazards, of course, can be avoided with the use of the dehumanizing stomach tube. But in the case of those in the final stages of Alzheimer's, to what purpose?

Ginny has always lived with dignity, and even in the extremities of her final illness, she has maintained a certain grace that is an integral part of her being. I was determined that nothing would take this from her . . . even in her dying. That is what I would want for myself, and I want nothing less for my beloved wife.

My family was in agreement with this so, with the sensitive assistance of Yvonne Fry, Ginny's social worker, we prepared a statement, signed and notarized to that end, and gave it to the appropriate people at Iowa Veterans Home. Then Becky Conard, Ginny's primary nurse, drew up a specific program of hospice care, and with my approval, put it into force for Ginny's care.

One of the conditions agreed upon in Ginny's hospice care, in addition to allowing no intravenous or other "invasive" procedures, was that she was not to be moved from her room, even in her final hours. She would be able to remain in her private room, surrounded by family pictures, furniture, and other familiar objects (however much she may be aware of them) that have made it her home for all these final months of her affliction. This room is Ginny's home because she is here, and because I have spent so much time with her here, it has become my home, too—another of *our* homes, places that we have shared through the years. Most important, by her remaining here, she will continue to be cared for by those familiar, gentle, loving people who have ministered to her for so long and have become her family.

Those dealing with hospice care suggest the importance of letting the dying loved one know that it is all right to let go and die, in case she is hanging on for the sake of the ones she's leaving behind.

I must say, this is not an easy thing to say to the one I love, but because of my love, I want what's best for her, regardless of the hurt. So, just like all the other big moves through our years together, I am content to leave the initiative to Ginny and God.

The day I told her specifically that it was all right for her to leave when she was ready, she looked me right in the eyes for a long moment as if she understood what I was saying. And then I said, as always when we're saying good-bye, "I'll see you later."

EPILOGUE: *The Dream*

I've had many dreams of Ginny since her illness, but this one was the most wonderful yet.

It was very involved, as many of my dreams are, and try as I might, I cannot reach back and untangle the intricacies that led to the most vivid and beautiful part of the dream. But there was a presence who emerged as a lovely young woman.

In the confusion, as I try to unravel the tangled skein and make some sense of it all, it seems that there was an inspection of the electrical wiring of an old dilapidated building. The lovely young woman seemed to be the chief inspector.

I had gone ahead up the crumbling corridors, inspecting some old electrical outlets on my own. Presently, the young woman and a man who vaguely seemed like my brother Dean caught up with me. Then the man said he would go back and let us go on alone. I was glad for this. As the young woman, whom I recognized as Ginny, and I proceeded through the crumbling passageway, I put my arm around her waist and was pleased with the warmth of the experience.

We came to a side door in the passageway that was ajar, open slightly to the outside. I tried to close it, but the double doors were so much out of line that they would not close. Then I said, "Well, I guess we don't have to worry about this anymore," meaning that the old building, which seemed to be the old bank building in which Ginny and I had formerly had our Print Shop, was no longer ours.

As we moved on, we walked through leaves in a beautiful

autumn forest. Presently, a woman who seemed to be a nurse came up behind us and told us she and the doctors thought we were making a mistake by leaving. But we were adamant—Ginny and I were in agreement that we were going to go on together.

As she and I continued to walk up this side hill through the colorful leaves of this autumn forest, Ginny said, "Things couldn't be any better with our family and all." And I turned and looked at her beside me, seeing Ginny's fine-featured profile so young and fresh and happy. And I broke into sobs of happiness.

Ginny Artley died in the early morning hours of February 25, 1993, at the Iowa Veterans Home; Bob and their son, Steven, were at her bedside. She had been at the Veterans Home for almost six years, the last three under hospice care. As son, Rob, said at her funeral in Hampton, "We never really knew when to say good-bye."

The simple lack of her is more to me than others' presence.

EDWARD THOMAS (1878–1917)